Computer Graphics
Environments

COMPUTER GRAPHICS
ENVIRONMENTS

John L. Bradberry

SAMS
PUBLISHING

A Division of Prentice Hall Computer Publishing
11711 North College, Carmel, IN 46032 USA

This book is dedicated
to my wife, Judith, and my daughter, Adriane,
for their patience and support.

Copyright © 1993 by Sams Publishing

International Standard Book Number: 0-672-30305-1

Library of Congress Catalog Card Number: 92-82104

96   95   94   93   4   3   2   1

Interpretation of the printing code: the rightmost double-digit number is the year of the book's printing; the rightmost single-digit, the number of the book's printing. For example, a printing code of 93-1 shows that the first printing of the book occurred in 1993.

Composed in AGaramond and MCPdigital by Prentice Hall Computer Publishing

Printed in the United States of America

Trademarks

OVERVIEW

CONTENTS

ACKNOWLEDGMENTS

Thanks to the editors and technical support staff at Sams Publishing for their assistance in all phases of this book.

Special thanks to Charlie Hudgins for his continued technical support and encouragement.

ABOUT THE AUTHOR

John L. Bradberry has a B.S. in Electrical Engineering from the Massachusetts Institute of Technology. Since 1977, John has been involved in a wide range of scientific and industrial applications at both senior management and design levels. John has also written and sold graphics application software for his own company (SCI) and is involved in academic research at the Georgia Tech Research Institute. He is pursuing an M.S. in Computer Science (degree expected in June 1993). John has written several technical articles and manuals; his book on software portability was released in January 1993.

INTRODUCTION

As computer architectures and languages have evolved over the years, the way in which users communicate with an application also has altered dramatically. The user interface has changed from simple text-based question and answer prompts to sophisticated 3-D button selections made popular by the Windows environment. Multicolor, ultrahigh-resolution workstation displays have replaced single-color, low-resolution terminals. Computer processing power and speed have increased, costs have stayed modest, and the expectations of end users have risen. Users demand more realistic and detailed visualization of data. The ability to create, control, and present high-resolution graphics has become an essential part of *any* computer programmer's toolkit.

In the past, expertise in writing algorithms for the user interface and for graphics was considered to be a skill different from the skills needed to handle applications. The field of computer graphics was small and highly specialized. More recently, desktop publishing and computer-aided design (CAD) applications began to push the envelope to graphical realism through the use of graphics interaction techniques. The quality of performance that users demand of traditional analytical applications continues to grow. It is no longer practical to consider the graphics and user interface as entirely separate problems to be addressed.

In today's market, the ability to visualize data by means of simulating and constructing pictures and graphs is indispensable. The corresponding ability to create and to customize the presentation of information is equally indispensable.

Computer Graphics Environments covers:

- The techniques of graphics device interfacing at both the hardware and software levels

- Many levels of graphics interfacing—from vector primitives to complex higher-level polygon transformations

- Menu interfaces, including text and graphics menu interfacing design

- Examples in pseudocode that are applicable to *any* modern computer language, with complete application software in disk form for C compilers

Graphics Standards

There are many existing graphics libraries and graphics standards to choose from. Compiler vendor or third-party graphics libraries provide many good graphics operations for the application developer. There is little chance that any one graphics library will suffice, however, because there are usually three major problems:

■ You are locked in to a specific version of a compiler, an operating system, a limited set of graphics operations, or a combination of all three.

■ The graphics device you are most interested in or a future device that you may be required to support is not supported by the library.

■ The library can be extended only by the supplier, and there usually is no source code that you can modify yourself.

Graphics standards such as GKS (the Graphics Kernel System) and PHIGS (Programmer's Hierarchial Interactive Graphics System) attempt to solve these problems by requiring a certain syntax and grouping of graphics primitives. There are indeed implementations of libraries using these standards, but there are two major drawbacks:

■ Standards (by definition) tend to address issues of what must be done with little or no regard as to *how*. It is necessary to ensure language and system independence in implementing the standard. Therefore, implementations of the standard differ.

■ In order to satisfy large and diverse interest groups, standards must often compromise to the least common denominator. For example, backward compatibility with older technologies or design limitations of supported devices often have an impact on how well an implementation of a standard can perform.

The DIGL library concept presented in *Computer Graphics Environments* attempts to solve these problems by adhering to three basic principles:

■ All source code and application code is supplied with the DIGL, along with explanations of what, how, and why. Design and debug information is supplied, and there is even an appendix dedicated to troubleshooting.

■ Expansion of graphics device support and capability should be expected, so DIGL is presented with the expectation that additional device drivers will be required and written. By presenting the DIGL system in library form, you are provided with several libraries and support tools to assist you in defining your own graphics operations.

■ No one should have to reinvent the wheel, so DIGL is presented with recognition of the fact that the easiest way to learn is by example. By providing complete working and practical examples throughout the text, the chances are very good that you will find at least a large portion of what you need to do already in working source code form.

What You Need

No prior knowledge of graphics techniques is assumed. However, you should be familiar with implementation of computer solutions at a programming level. There are a few theoretical discussions involving matrix operations and transformations for polygon control. A background in basic algebra and analytic geometry is required if you intend to modify the algorithms discussed or the source code provided for these operations. However, in most cases, the algorithms can be used as is.

Some knowledge of the C programming language is recommended but not essential. The complete code samples may be compiled with your favorite C compiler. *Computer Graphics Environments* provides working examples using two of the most popular computer architectures: MS-DOS and UNIX. Appendixes C and D provide system-dependent hints and suggestions for both of the configurations. There is configuration information provided in Appendix G on the details of working with other computer architectures.

As is the case with many large C applications, you may need to modify some of the low-level drivers to accommodate compiler differences. Explanations as to when and how to do this are provided as the code is introduced throughout this book.

Conventions Used in This Book

Computer Graphics Environments uses the following typographic conventions:

- Code lines, commands, statements, variables, and any text you see on the screen appears in a computer typeface.

- *Italics* highlight technical terms when they first appear in the text.

DIGL represents a small subset of what can be done in graphics using today's technology. However, the beauty of the DIGL system is that you have complete control over how it is modified. It is up to you to expand or redirect the scope as desired.

My approach is to share significant information on graphics and menu generation techniques. By studying source code examples, you should be well on your way toward designing any level of customization that you require.

CHAPTER

1

ARCHITECTURES, LANGUAGE, AND APPLICATIONS

Almost as soon as computers were created, there emerged the need and desire to control individual *pixels*—picture elements or dots within a letter cell. Applications that required pictorials and the rendering of graphics images began to dominate research and development labs. Throughout the last two decades, many different architectures have been used to develop graphics solutions, with varying degrees of success. These architectures have an impact on software requirements and application performance.

Graphics Architectures and Techniques

Many different graphics architectures are useful for a wide range of graphics applications. Each has advantages and disadvantages. In this chapter, I concentrate on two of the most common: the *distributed graphics architecture* (the CPU host with peripheral node) and the *integrated graphics engine architecture* (sometimes known as the dedicated graphics engine).

Distributed Graphics Architecture

Figure 1.1 illustrates one of the most popular forms of graphics architectures. In this case, one or more graphics applications are connected indirectly to a remote graphics peripheral. Although hundreds of different graphics terminals or plotting devices could be connected to a minicomputer or workstation, usually only a few at any one time are connected. However, this type of architecture poses many design problems for the graphics application programmer.

Graphics Protocol

Graphics protocol refers to the character sequence required to perform graphics operations, such as drawing a line segment from point A to point B. As you might suspect, these operations are different for almost every type of graphics device available. Terminals typically require a nonprintable ASCII preamble, such as <ESC x,y>. Devices such as Hewlett-Packard digital plotters require simple ASCII commands, for example, PA 1234,4567;. Often, the decision of which device protocol to use is made by a *graphics library*. (Imagine trying to hard code each option into one application!) The graphics library may be part of the graphics application or a third-party solution provided by the vendor of the CPU.

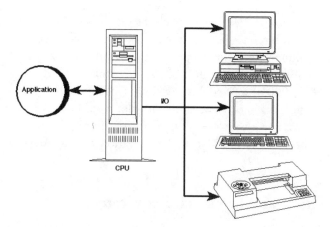

Figure 1.1. Distributed graphics architecture.

It is worth noting that this type of interface tends to be independent of language and the operating system. Any language capable of performing unformatted I/O operations can be used to control this peripheral. The decoding process is discussed in more detail later in this book.

I/O Interface

The input/output mechanism has to do with the physical and logical connections among the graphics device, the computer, and ultimately the application program. The physical channel may be a serial connection (terminals), an IEEE—Institute of Electrical and Electronic Engineers—connection (digital plotters), or a special high-speed direct connection to the CPU backplane.

The graphics library deals with the difference in graphics protocols. It also has to do with with the logical connection —computer address map or runtime, for example—to each device.

In the case of serial communications, the options are much simpler—for example, *baud rate* (serial transmission in bits per second or bps) and "handshake" (Xon/Xoff). The graphics library does not handle the low-level details of this interface, but it must ensure the proper connection to the device before characters are transmitted.

In the case of more complex connections, such as an IEEE 488 GPIB bus interface or direct bus interfaces, the driver interfaces are more challenging.

The *bandwidth*, or speed with which the graphics image is drawn, is affected by the type of I/O interface used. In the case of simple vector graphics operations, it is not uncommon for a single operation to require as many as 20 characters. This might not sound like much, but consider small 3-D plotting applications consisting of 50,000 or more points. At 9600 baud, a serial interface is transmitting only 1,200 characters per second. The plot would take 13.89 minutes on a serial link! With more complex plots requiring more plot points by orders of magnitude, there is little wonder why workstation graphics devices continue to be so popular.

Initialization and Feedback Requirements

Not surprisingly, different graphics devices require different initialization sequences. Two categories characterize the differences—*automatic initialization* and *manual initialization*. Video devices, such as terminals, can be considered automatic; one or more commands can be issued to erase the current screen and to place the device in graphics mode. Once these commands are issued, you can assume that the graphics mode is set and continue on with image rendering.

In the case of some digital plotters, the initialization sequence requires a human or robot to manually load a sheet of paper before the graphics mode is safely established. Plotters such as the Hewlett-Packard 7550A recognize page eject commands, but some issues, such as pen selection (for example, transparency or ink), must be resolved manually. These operations may also require feedback or two-way communications with the applications program or driver. There are also other types of manual initialization. For example, many types of videographic display adapters require a user to select a new driver to be loaded, which selects a new display resolution and sync mode on a multisync monitor.

Integrated Graphics Engine Architecture

Figure 1.2 illustrates another popular form of graphics architecture. In this case, there is no external graphics peripheral. The graphics area is connected to the computing engine by means of memory-mapped I/O. This architecture performs significantly faster than the distributed graphics architecture. However, there are tradeoffs.

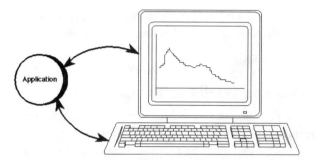

Figure 1.2. Integrated graphics engine architecture.

Graphics Protocol

Important graphics protocol issues are related to this type of architecture. In this case, usually a much more complex layer of graphics driver software must be used as a layer of interface. Unlike with an external peripheral, the link between the graphics application and this graphics device is strictly logical or by means of the software.

Instead of sending character streams of graphics commands and data, the application program must communicate directly with the driver routine(s). The most important consequence of this is that these types of protocol interfaces are typically language-specific. Unlike the distributed graphics architecture, the drivers supplied are based on one or at most two languages—C, Fortran, or even assembly. Unless your language of choice is included in this driver package, you must rely on a mixed language interface to a supported language.

I/O Interface

Because this interface is highly specialized, the input/output mechanism is also a specialized sequence of operations that you might not have control over. In the case of memory-mapped I/O to which you are able to write and read directly, you might be able to customize some of the graphics operations.

The bandwidth is determined by the speed of both the memory access and the CPU. This means that this model supports significantly more numbers and types of vector or raster operations than the distributed graphics architecture model does. Instead of dealing with hundreds of characters per second, this architecture deals with several hundred thousand per second. Ten-minute plots become one-second plots.

Initialization and Feedback Requirements

As with external peripherals, this architecture has special requirements for initialization. Automatic initialization applies as well. Once again, drivers are used to handle all sorts of issues relating to special requirements of the initialization sequence.

Graphics and Language Standards

Many graphics language and protocol standards have been adopted over the years. During the late 1970s, several efforts were underway to create and adopt graphics standards to

■ Reduce duplication of effort and the complexity of graphics code

■ Reduce the cost of implementing graphics solutions

■ Promote graphics application portability

In *Computer Graphics—Principles and Practice* (Foley et al., 1990), the authors present a detailed discussion of graphics standards from a historical perspective. The following is a summary of this discussion.

The Special Interest Group on Graphics (SIGGRAPH) of the Association of Computing Machinery (ACM) produced a 3D Core Graphics System in 1977; the specification was refined in 1979. It was in widespread use and acknowledged by the American National Standards Institute (ANSI). In 1985, however, the Graphics Kernel System (GKS) became the first graphics standard officially standardized. In 1988, an advanced form of GKS—along with yet another graphics standard, Programmer's Hierarchial Interactive Graphics System (PHIGS)—became official standards.

Not only were these standards complex, but they also placed severe restrictions on how graphics operations were performed. In the case of PHIGS, this often required special hardware support.

Unfortunately, it is the nature of standards that not all types of graphics operations are supported. In addition, not all graphics devices are capable of implementing an operation in the same manner. Many issues must be considered to create a standard powerful enough to address a wide variety of graphics operations.

For example, what does a screen clear operation mean to a digital hard copy device such as a pen plotter? What do you do when you have a device that doesn't support a graphics operation that a standard supports? How do you extend a standard to cover a graphics innovation? Are performance limitations worth the compromise in adopting the standard? As you can see, creating and adopting a graphics standard that addresses a large superset of graphics operations is not a trivial task by any means.

Graphics Application Models

Many programmers write code for a specific architecture or library and simply don't worry about supporting other graphics devices. With the examples and methods in this book, I intend to demonstrate a different approach. By designing a layered graphics library based on a flexible model, you can indeed write graphics applications between compilers and machine architectures that are general, portable, and device-independent.

The DIGL Graphics Model

The structure of a device-independent graphics library (DIGL) supports a wider variety of architectures. The DIGL diagram in Figure 1.3 shows that it is somewhat similar to the distributed graphics architecture discussed earlier. However, the DIGL implementation assumes that a built-in driver exists for each graphics device. Interface hooks to the graphics device are handled at the lowest levels of the DIGL. Additional graphics devices can be supported by adding a driver template for the new device.

The structure of the library is based on programming practices discussed throughout this book. A structured design approach is essential as preventative maintenance for software support of extensions or bug fixes. The term *top down* software design has become a cliché. The top down programming approach is usually complemented with *bottom up* implementation. This layering of software ultimately results in the form of an inverted pyramid (see Figure 1.4).

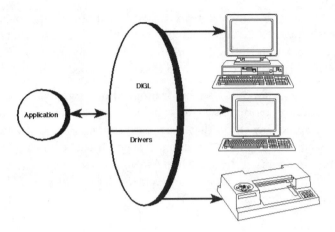

Figure 1.3. DIGL architecture model.

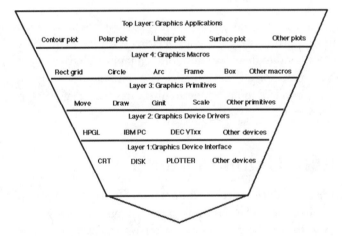

Figure 1.4. Structure of the DIGL model.

Lower layers represent the device- and CPU-specific implementations of key functions. At the graphics device driver level (layer 2), other third-party vendor software can be merged for completeness. The following three features of this structure readily support the portability process:

■ As the tree is implemented, the top two levels maintain a fairly generic high-level code—in this case, C. All code at these levels exists in a form that is application- and CPU-independent.

■ Each layer provides unlimited expansion of capability by the easy addition of plot algorithms or graphics devices, with little impact on existing code.

■ As the inverted pyramid structure suggests, the software most affected by changes in the CPU or graphics devices represent the smallest amounts of code in the entire system. For source code that could grow to as many as 100,000 lines, typically less than one percent—the bottom of the pyramid—is device- or CPU-dependent.

Summary

This chapter introduces you to many of the design issues that you must consider when you write graphics application code for the two basic graphics system architectures: distributed graphics architecture and integrated graphics engine architecture.

Although graphics standards are lacking, you can write graphics applications that are general, portable, and device-independent if you design a layered graphics library based on a flexible and general model. The DIGL (device-independent graphics library) is such a model.

Chapter 3, "The Graphics Application Environment," Chapter 4, "Graphics Visualization," and Chapter 5, "A Design Prototype for DIGL," focus on the technical details of specific graphics operations with emphasis on the step-by-step development of a DIGL model.

FUNDAMENTAL
GRAPHICS ISSUES

Chapter 1, "Architectures, Language, and Applications," introduces you to two basic graphics system architectures under which graphics operations are performed. Specific computer manufacturers—such as IBM, Apple, and Digital Equipment Corporation (DEC)—are not included because I want to present a generic overview of capabilities.

In this chapter, I refine the DIGL model and introduce the graphics operations required to support the graphics applications presented in Chapter 5, "A Design Prototype for DIGL."

Questions and Answers

This chapter provides additional background information on graphics terms and operations. At this point, let me answer a few basic questions that you might be asking.

All I need to do is write a simple plot routine. Do I really need this much information?

This question is asked typically by those who want to get to the heart of the matter without much additional effort. The fact is that many times a graphics requirement—just as other software requirements—starts as a simple request. Unfortunately, it rarely remains such. Days, weeks, or even months later, additional requests usually are made, such as "Because it worked for the IBM, how much trouble would it be to get it working for the Mac?"

What I attempt to do here is present a wide range of issues in sufficient detail so that you are prepared for modifications and changes in scope. If you feel that your particular requirement is simple and restricted, feel free to use the DIGL without understanding the details of implementing it.

Which computer platform is best for graphics applications?

The term *computer platform* refers to the integration of software tools and hardware architectures to assist a programmer in developing or running an application. The best one for you depends on what your requirements are, how much money you have to spend, how much time you have to solve the problem, and how much expertise you have with the architecture of your choice.

To choose the best computer platform for your needs, you must understand the limitations of the programming language you are using and the graphics architecture you intend to use. Once you do, you can begin developing and using a graphics library that enables you to solve a graphics application problem in as straightforward a manner as possible.

There is no such thing as the perfect graphics language or specification, because the number and type of graphics applications are infinite, just like the number and type of pictures that can be reproduced.

Any computer language or graphics specification that attempts to be all things to all people is doomed to fail. Likely, its syntax is overly complex, or its implementation is poor and inefficient. This is a harsh statement, but developments in computer science in the last three decades support my opinion.

What does device independence really mean?

Device independence represents the capability of creating a graphics program that can be drawn on more than one graphics device with the same outcome and without changing the program. In the case of the DIGL model, the DIGL translates the program into a set of commands compatible with the various graphics devices it supports.

Don't portability and device independence result in slow graphics?

This question reflects concern about using higher-level macro instructions or calls in place of more direct inline instructions. Generally, high-level portability and device independence imply additional instructions for accomplishing an objective.

The trend toward faster CPUs and more efficient hardware supports an effort toward simplifying and planning for more general application support. By today's standards, a CPU running at 4 to 8 MHz is slow compared to CPUs running at 33 or 40 MHz or faster—and the latter are readily available.

The third-party graphics library I'm using supports device independence. Why should I redevelop code?

It is difficult to resist the temptation to develop code that is already supported in a given library. In many cases, it is not necessary; the graphics libraries available with each compiler for a computer make claims about the number and types of devices that they support. The DIGL model in this book provides you with the logic, algorithms, and code to develop and maintain your own version of a DIGL. Third-party libraries rarely supply source code with documentation sufficient for you to accomplish this.

Isn't GUI just another word for Windows?

The term *GUI (graphical user interface)* is used interchangeably with Windows. The GUI concept, however, is much more diverse than that. Windows may exist in a form that is text with the help of extended graphics characters such as the IBM PC character set. In the case of bit-mapped window interfaces, design requirements involve manipulation of individual pixels at high rates of speed. Both text-based and bit-mapped window interfaces are discussed in detail in Chapter 6, "A Design Prototype for Text-Based Pop-Up Windows," and Chapter 7, "High-Resolution Graphics Windows."

Doesn't an object-oriented technique address all these problems?

Object-oriented programming (OOP) refers to the ordered structuring of data and access techniques that make it easier to apply many of the principles discussed so far in this book. Chapter 8, "The Object-Oriented Approach," discusses OOP in more detail, but it is worth noting that applying OOP techniques to graphics operations can greatly enhance your product.

Computer Platforms

Computer platforms pose interesting options when you attempt to establish a uniform graphics development environment. Each architecture has distinct advantages and disadvantages. Issues related to operating system constraints and development environment support are worth noting because of the varying impact on the development of applications and software libraries.

Large-Scale and Minicomputer Platforms

As a rule, larger computers—from minicomputers to supercomputers—distribute graphics and other driver duties to smaller nodes, or centralized CPUs. The displays are either remote low-resolution terminals or special high-performance video displays with special driver requirements. Operating systems are proprietary; development support from the manufacturer is critical. Software libraries are larger and more complex, and the process of compiling, linking, and executing a program might require several extra steps. The advantage, of course, is the fast speed of the main CPU element(s).

Low-Cost/High-Performance Workstations

The workstation has introduced an intermediate-level computer platform. Popular workstations—such as Sun's SPARC series—provide processing power comparable to low-end minicomputers with the personal feel of PCs. Workstations provide special graphics hardware for much higher-resolution video for ultrahigh-resolution and high-performance graphics.

Using UNIX as the primary operating system ensures a wide variety of utilities and development environment support. Some programmers are at a disadvantage here. There is not support for languages other than C and C++ because of the typical UNIX operating systems provided on workstations. Languages such as Fortran 77 take a back seat to native C.

In the case of graphics programming, the Windows interface also must be dealt with. A Windows environment—such as Xlib—and a vendor-specific environment—such as DEC or HP—might create additional problems when you are developing general-purpose graphics libraries. I address many of these issues in Chapters 6 and 7 and Appendix D.

PCs—The Ultimate Low-Cost Solution

Smaller computers on the PC end of the spectrum provide more direct access to the display features that you need for graphics control. As in the case of workstations, the popular PC configurations provide a wide range of third-party and utility support for development. The main disadvantage of this platform is that compilers and programmers rely too much on system-specific features for performance. This affects the portability of the application and software libraries even when you are merely changing compilers.

Programming Language Support

Computer software languages provide a list of issues for the applications programmer to consider. Graphics requirements can be generalized to one basic subset of capabilities or low-level operations. Unfortunately, computer languages, as a rule, have not been developed to address graphics operations.

Performance Limitations and Requirements

Generally, the concept of a graphics device type is not considered standard to any of the modern computer languages. Fortran, C, C++, Ada, Pascal, Prolog, Lisp, Forth, FP, and so on, were developed for various purposes—scientific programming, logic programming, artificial intelligence. Most of these languages have some form of built-in simple I/O for devices such as files and a terminal/teletype (TTY).

In fourth- and fifth-generation languages, where object-oriented approaches become standard, the I/O device-type model must be expanded to provide for more graphics support. Unfortunately, a general-purpose graphics device that supports a basic set of graphics operations is not part of the I/O packages. Part of the reason for this is the wide variety of graphics devices being built. An interesting point worth noting is that Windows standards—such as Xlib and Motif—have been created that have greater demands on graphics operations than the DIGL proposed in this book.

This lack of standards means that application programmers must develop their own graphics device types. Usually, the result is slightly lower-performance graphics that cover a limited range of graphics operations.

Assembler or Dedicated Hardware?

To achieve the ultimate in performance for a specific graphics architecture, there are alternatives that are less attractive. Writing in assembly language or using custom or dedicated hardware almost always guarantees performance advantages over higher-level languages. However, the overall cost in development and debugging time and the resulting lack of portability hardly balance the increased performance edge.

Graphics Primitives

General-purpose computer languages in use today have not been designed to handle the demands of graphics applications using any built-in language constructs. The general-purpose graphics device type must be built into the software. Therefore, the next best option is to establish a set of low-level, general-purpose graphics operations that are used to develop a graphics library.

Level 3 of the DIGL model presented in Chapter 1 (refer to Figure 1.4) consists of a middle layer called *graphics primitives*. Graphics primitives can be thought of as low-level instructions—such as move and draw—that can be used to construct higher-level macro operations—such as rectangle and circle.

Table 2.1 illustrates a set of basic graphics primitives. Notice that not all graphics primitives may apply to a particular graphics device. This becomes evident as the primitives are used with other graphics protocols introduced later in this chapter.

Table 2.1. Basic graphics primitives.

Primitive	*Description*
Initialize	Initializes graphics device for drawing
Draw	Draws by using current pen from current point to point specified
Move	Moves from current point to point specified
Select Pen	Selects pen number specified (used for color control)
Line Width	Sets width of current line in terms of preset number of pixels
Line Style	Selects one of *n* predefined line styles as current drawing (stroke) format
Foreground Color	Sets foreground color to one of *n* preset colors
Background Color	Sets background color to one of *n* preset colors
Erase Screen	Erases screen for video (ejects page for hardcopy units)
Color Mix	Selects one of *n* preset color mixes based on IBM RGB color standard
Bell	Sounds audible tone at graphics device

The Color Mix primitive is based on the RGB (Red Green Blue) color model. Table 2.2 illustrates the IBM IRGB (Industry Red Green Blue) color standard using four bits, one each for intensity, red, green, and blue. As with many devices, the first eight standard colors (0 to 7) are formed by mixes of the three basic primary colors. An additional eight (8 to 15) are produced by mixing in the intensity bit, that is, turning the bit on, which produces the same effect as adding more white ink.

Table 2.2. IBM IRGB color standard.

Color Mix Number	I R G B	Color Mix Name
0	0 0 0 0	Black
1	0 0 0 1	Blue
2	0 0 1 0	Green
3	0 0 1 1	Cyan
4	0 1 0 0	Red
5	0 1 0 1	Magenta
6	0 1 1 0	Brown
7	0 1 1 1	White (Light gray)
8	1 0 0 0	Dark gray
9	1 0 0 1	Light blue
10	1 0 1 0	Light green
11	1 0 1 1	Light cyan
12	1 1 0 0	Light red
13	1 1 0 1	Light magenta
14	1 1 1 0	Yellow
15	1 1 1 1	Intense white

Direct Graphics Device Support

A rather large set of graphics languages and protocols currently exists for what should be the same general purpose—to make it easier to describe a graphics figure that you want to represent. Unfortunately, the form and capability of the different languages and graphics protocols is so varied that it is difficult to establish a nucleus of similar commands and capabilities. Establishing such a command set is a formidable task, but it can be done—although with some limitations.

Hewlett-Packard Graphics Language (HPGL)

The HPGL protocol represents a generation of ASCII-based commands used for controlling a wide range of digital plotters. The digital plotters range in size from small desktop models to larger floor-standing models. These plotters can support paper sizes, including 8 ½ by 11, 11 by 17, and large blueprint-size drawings. These devices represent generations of electromechanical development, and they require sophisticated electronics for the precise positioning of ink pens. These devices are capable of moving pens at speeds up to 31.5 inches per second, with an accuracy of .00098 inch per single plot point (depending on the plotter).

In general, the HPGL protocol is based on the *Cartesian coordinate system.* The Cartesian coordinate system is based on the grid system invented by the French mathematician René Descartes. The *grid,* or plotting area, is represented much like the drawing area of a sheet of graph paper. From a starting point, called the *origin*—typically (0,0)—the pen, pencil, or drawing stylus is moved across the paper and connects long or short line segments. The collection of line segments represents a graphics figure, as Figure 2.1 shows.

HPGL, as in other forms of computerized Cartesian representations, relies on *numeric units* for horizontal (*x* position) or vertical (*y* position) movements. As the DIGL model is developed later on in this chapter and throughout this book, you can recognize this as a standard form of vector representation. Aside from the specific mnemonics required by the HPGL syntax, these units must also be established. Examine the HPGL mnemonics shown in Figure 2.1. Notice the use of rather large numbers in the numeric portion of mnemonics, such as PA5062,3934. In this case, the mnemonic PA represents the Plot Absolute instruction, and 5062,3934 represents the Cartesian vector. This vector seems reasonable if you recall that plotter units are on the order of 0.025mm (0.00098 inch).

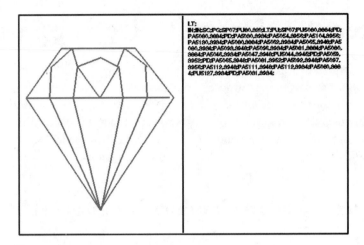

Figure 2.1. Example of the HPGL protocol.

HPGL supports a wide range of operations—pen control, labeling, digitizing operations, polygon operations, and so on. In addition, many software programs provide direct interpretive support for the protocol, such as the WordPerfect word processor. Unfortunately, there are two significant problems in handling HPGL protocol:

- Not all HPGL implementations are the same.

- Few software interpreters for HPGL support more than a simple subset of line drawing operations.

HPGL has been around in one form or another for more than two decades. As different generations of plotters were designed, more commands were added to the protocol. Some HPGL commands—such as Page Feed (PG) for the model HP7550A plotter—may not be recognized by HPGL emulators.

If a graphics program issues a large set of HPGL commands, many HPGL plotters or software interpreters cannot render the drawing properly.

Syntax Examples

Figure 2.1 illustrates an example of HPGL protocol for drawing a diamond. The left side of the figure is the sketch represented by the HPGL instructions, which are shown on the right side of the figure. HPGL instructions are simple ASCII character codes used to access the graphics functions of the plotter. Each HPGL instruction consists of a two-letter mnemonic that identifies the function. For example, PD represents the Pen Down command, and PU represents the Pen Up command.

Obviously, there is much more to the protocol than these two simple commands. This book deals primarily with constructing software drivers to produce a small subset of valid HPGL commands. Table 2.3 shows the HPGL syntax applied to the base set of primitives that were introduced in Table 2.1. A complete description of the HPGL syntax can be found in any number of HPGL reference manuals.

Table 2.3. HPGL implementation of basic graphics primitives.

Primitive	HPGL Syntax	Comments
Initialize	PG;IN;	May require other options depending on device
Draw	PA X,Y (,...);	Plots to point in absolute units (one or more vectors may be used if followed by a comma separator)
Move	PU;PA X,Y;	Moves first because pen is raised
Select Pen	SP num;	Selects physical pen from carousel (graphics driver could ensure that pen number is not greater than number of pens available)
Line Width	NOP	Not valid for this device (the width is set by type of pen used; otherwise, software must simulate by using Redraw)
Line Style	LP pattern number	Driver uses single (, pattern length); integer and sets up instruction based on preset line styles

continues

21

Table 2.3. continued

Primitive	HPGL Syntax	Comments
Foreground Color	SP *pen number*;	Driver maps colors of RGB model to standard pen configuration
Background Color	NOP	Not valid for this device
Erase Screen	PG;	Page eject command (for some plotters this must be a manual operation)
Color Mix	NOP	Not valid for this device
Bell	NOP	Not valid for this device

ANSI and Vendor-Specific Protocol

Because languages such as C do not provide built-in features for support of graphics operations, it is left up to the compiler writers and hardware vendors to provide solutions. This opens the door for a wide variety of vendor-specific hardware devices, such as video cards and custom graphics libraries, that are developed with no regard for standardization between compilers. This section examines some of the popular alternatives available. There is an ANSI standard escape sequence for cursor control at the video level, but it has not been extended to cover graphics operations.

Graphics Terminals and Displays

There are many different vendors for graphics terminals and displays. Unfortunately, there are many different graphics protocols as well. In the case of the typical graphics terminal, the lack of standards for graphics operations means that vendors have been free to reinvent protocols and graphics features at will. For serial interface terminals, this takes the form of sequences of ASCII characters for each graphics operation, such as Move and Draw. For example, a DEC VTxx terminal has a graphics command set completely different from what a Tektronix 42xx terminal has.

Character Fonts

In addition to drawing an image on the graphics device, the use of text annotation is a major obstacle to be overcome. There are three classes of character generation techniques: *bit-mapped, stroked,* and *algorithmic.*

Bit-mapped character sets are dot matrix cells that are fixed for a graphics device. Almost always, the device that supports this is video whose lower-resolution display permits fast hardware-generated implementation of character sets. On the IBM PC, for example, the character sets are stored in memory that can be rewritten to alter slightly the appearance of the characters.

Bit-mapped character sets have several disadvantages:

■ Bit-mapped characters are fixed in size and cannot be scaled or rotated easily.

■ High-resolution devices expose the grainy nature of the dot-matrix appearance.

■ Some graphics devices, such as pen plotters, are extremely inefficient. Imagine the time required—and the noise generated—to move the pen to draw each dot for each character in an 80-character string.

Stroked character sets offer many advantages over bit-mapped character sets. A table of values exists in memory—typically at the driver level—that tells the graphics device how to draw each character. Different tables can be used to implement a different font. Unlike bit-mapped characters, stroked characters can be scaled and rotated. In addition, stroked characters can be implemented easily by each graphics device. The disadvantages of stroked characters are

■ The memory requirements for the stroke table can be very large.

■ For ultra-high-resolution devices, stroked character sets produce narrow characters, which are not as pleasing as publication-quality character sets.

With algorithmic (or outline) character sets, algorithms or equations of outlines are used to draw each character. Unlike for a stroked character set, the operations for an algorithmic character set can include polygon operations, such as Fill. This produces characters with a better, publication-quality appearance.

The PostScript language standard uses the algorithmic method almost exclusively. However, there are disadvantages:

- The operations are complex and time consuming, depending on the graphics device.

- Although scaling these character strings is relatively easy, the exact placing of a string on a graphics display is not always a simple process.

Direct Printer Support

Similar to direct pixel control of a 2-D grid, each printer provides a set of controls based on a row of dots for each grid. A device-independent approach to control printers is impractical because printers vary too much.

The PostScript Format

The PostScript format represents a complete language specification that was designed as a standard for electronic printing. Compared to the HPGL language discussed earlier, PostScript is much more powerful and—as you will observe later—more difficult to program. PostScript is designed to support the properties of devices generally classified as *raster output devices*—for example, raster-scan displays and printers.

Raster Representation

In the raster system, the grid is a collection of dots that can be addressed individually. Controlling the color of large or small groups of pixels permits line art—vector operations—or images of text and graphical shapes. The resolution of the raster device determines the visual quality of the rendered image and the number of dots per unit area—typically, per inch, as in 300 *dpi* (dots per inch). Table 2.4 shows the typical resolutions of raster devices.

Table 2.4 refers to display resolution, which should not be confused with the *addressable resolution* of a device. The addressable resolution of a device might be considerably higher than the corresponding display resolution. Typically, addressable resolution must be compared with dot or pixel size for a true representation of the visual quality of an image.

Table 2.4. Typical resolutions of raster devices.

Device Type	Resolution (dpi)	Comments
Camera or photographic technology	1000	A trade-off—higher resolution for higher cost
Laser scanners	300 to 600	Desktop scanners implementing xerographic technology
Laser printers	300 to 600	Desktop models might be equipped with built-in PostScript interpreters
Dot-matrix printers	100 to 360	Resolution ranges from 9- to 24-pin
CRT (computer terminals)	50 to 100	Low-resolution display terminals

Scan Conversion

The Cartesian coordinate system was discussed earlier in terms of x,y-coordinates and vector operations that connect x,y pairs. In the case of raster representations, however, the grid is much more restricted. For graphics representation, the Cartesian coordinate system is implemented by using integer coordinates. However, this creates a problem for representing simple graphical entities such as lines and circles.

Figure 2.2 illustrates the typical problem encountered. On the left side of the figure, a line segment is represented with the Cartesian system of x,y pairs. The segment extends from point $(0,1)$ to point $(3,3)$. In drawing the line segment, hundreds or thousands of individual pixels are connected along the way. The fact that the segment is not jagged means that the equivalent raster representation requires a resolution of at least 300 dpi.

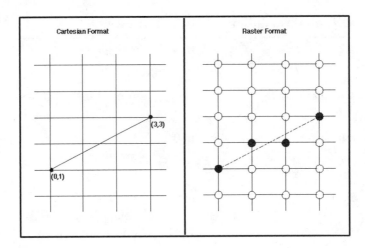

Figure 2.2. Scan conversion of line segments.

The problem of converting a smooth analog representation of a line segment to a digital representation involves a process of discrete sampling—a limited number of bits are available in the digital case to represent a waveform such as a curve or line segment. The next best solution is to approximate the curve based on the best fit of the number of bits available. In graphics, this is called the *scan conversion process.* Algorithms to accomplish this have been around for several decades. A classic algorithm for line scan conversion was created by J. E. Bresenham in 1965. Figure 2.2 illustrates why outputting some graphics to low-resolution devices such as dot-matrix printers results in coarse approximations. A complete discussion of the scan conversion techniques for most geometric shapes is beyond the scope of this book.

Page Description Properties

In the PostScript format, a page to be printed or displayed is a 2-D grid of pixel values. The grid is represented by higher-level abstract commands. The graphics device—typically, a laser printer—converts these commands to patterns of ones and zeros in memory, where complex scan conversions and other Postscript commands are used to alter the grid until the page is finally printed.

Generally, page description languages leave the complex and time-consuming requirements of scan conversion to the particular graphics device. This presents several advantages over transmitting the grid directly to the device:

- As Table 2.4 illustrates, different devices have different resolutions. Modularity requires that a new grid be constructed for each different device.

- The 2-D grid can be large, requiring much computer memory and many instructions. This is an excessive burden for a graphics application program.

- Support for new devices and graphics operations can be handled at the individual device level. The graphics application program does not need to be modified to support a new device.

Syntax Examples

A complete description of the PostScript syntax can be found in any number of PostScript reference manuals. Table 2.5 shows the PostScript syntax as it is applied to the set of basic primitives that were listed in Table 2.1.

Table 2.5. PostScript implementation of basic graphics primitives.

Primitive	Postscript Syntax	Comments
Initialize		No simple command—many operations such as defining macros to be used, orientation of page, and headers, are required
Draw	X Y lineto	Appends line segment to current path
Move	X Y moveto	Starts new subpath in current graphics state
Select Pen	NOP	Not applicable without using predefined macros
Line Width	num setlinewidth	Sets line width in pixels to be used when the stroke command is activated
Line Style	array offset setdash	Line style consists of array used to control pattern

continues

27

Table 2.5. continued

Primitive	Postscript Syntax	Comments
Foreground Color	red green blue	Driver maps colors of setrgbcolor model to standard pen configuration
Background Color	NOP	Not valid for this device
Erase Screen	erasepage	Erases entire page by setting gray level to 1— typically, white
Color Mix		Uses internal data storage of RGB model for combined use with Foreground color operation
Bell	NOP	Not valid for this device

Summary

This chapter compares computer platforms and provides advantages and disadvantages of each. Large-scale processors tend to distribute tasks among several peripherals or CPUs in a "divide and conquer" strategy. This allows for faster program execution by concurrent processing of portions of its task requirements. However, one of the costs of this overall performance improvement is more complex development.

There are several options on graphics protocols. Some protocols—such as HPGL and PostScript—require a conversion process using a set of basic graphics primitives.

The information that you have learned so far is used to develop the layers of graphics operations in the DIGL and in a few sample applications in the next three chapters.

THE GRAPHICS APPLICATION ENVIRONMENT

This chapter presents a more detailed look at graphics hardware, software, and some of the common peripherals. It addresses a few issues about Human Computer Interface (HCI). An overview of the variety of techniques required for efficient and creative use of graphics devices is also presented.

Chapter 1, "Architectures, Language, and Applications," presents two abstract representations of the DIGL model. This chapter presents a more comprehensive view of the DIGL model structure, especially the lower two layers (refer to Chapter 1, Figure 1.4). Now the emphasis is how various application commands are routed through the model to the proper graphics device, and how the model is implemented in software.

Recall that applications are often designed from the top down and implemented from the bottom up. The lowest layer of the DIGL configuration model is concerned with the graphics device interface requirements and performance.

Interactive Graphics

An important distinction should be made between the DIGL model developed in this book and other graphics models that rely heavily on concepts such as interactive graphics. In supporting interactive graphics, a graphics application program must be able to set up events that enable the user to control the output. The user control is based on events caused by input devices, such as a mouse, graphics tablet, or light pen. In the initial implementation of the DIGL, no user interaction is allowed other than a keyboard signal for aborting a program or signaling the end of a video display. The graphics application is modeled as a series of sequential commands that are routed through an interface to the DIGL and, subsequently, to the graphics device currently selected. This procedure is described in more detail later in this chapter.

The DIGL model can be expanded to include many other forms of real-time interactions. The initial model developed, however, is limited in scope and complexity. Adding the device driver commands necessary to handle mouse interrupts or other forms of buffered I/O adds significantly to the level of complexity of the model.

Programming Considerations

The first two chapters introduce you to the protocol required for commonly used graphics devices. This section presents additional device characteristics and issues that have a significant impact on other programming considerations.

Video Displays

Improvements in display technology and demands for faster and higher resolution displays have produced a range of video devices for interface and control. The fact that a CRT display can be rapidly changed to permit high-resolution animation sequences makes it by far the most commonly used graphics display device.

Display capabilities range from low-resolution black and white to high-resolution color with millions of color variations to choose from. Depending on the computer used or the video device selected to display the graphics outputs, a variety of issues must be considered when you write video display drivers.

Vector versus Bit-Mapped

Video displays can perform vector operations and bit-mapped operations rather easily. Because the pixels are controlled at so fast a rate, there is little or no need for individual pixel control, regardless of the graphic instruction to be performed.

Speed

Each pixel is controlled by an electron gun being turned on and off. There is a relationship between bandwidth, pixel resolution, refresh rates, and the overall performance of a given monitor. The speed of pixel control is typically hundreds or thousands of times faster than your ability to observe the transformations.

Device Dependence

The one major drawback to virtually all video displays is that there is essentially no standardization of control mechanisms among manufacturers. Interfacing and cost are often sacrificed for the sake of significant gains in performance and speed. It is not uncommon for a graphics display to require custom hardware accelerators and elaborate proprietary graphics software. This is true with the high-end video used in some computer aided design (CAD) applications.

File Storage Overhead

File storage overhead deals with the ability to store and retrieve graphics images from a device. Depending on the resolution of the video display, this can require only a few thousand bytes or as many as several megabytes per image. Reading and writing the latter to any disk medium may take from a few seconds to a minute.

Complexity of Control and Interfacing

Video display technologies represent, perhaps, the most diverse group of graphics devices to be controlled. Not only are the characteristics of each video device different, but also the software interface mechanisms range from direct access to memory maps to the use of third-party library calls for controls.

In the case of the IBM PC, there are several graphics adapters to choose from. Each adapter has more than one mode setting that offers variations on colors available and pixel resolution. The set of software commands includes instructions as diverse as selecting one of the graphics modes (described in Table 3.1) to clearing the graphics screen. Your choice of software language, compiler, and selection options determines how many of these modes are available to you.

Table 3.1. Graphics modes available for the IBM PC.

Display Mode	Resolution x,y	Comments
CGA	320x200	Black and white—low resolution
CGA	640x200	2 colors—medium-high resolution
CGA	320x200	4 colors—low resolution
VGA/MCGA	320x200	256 colors used most often for image processing—low resolution
HGC	720x348	2 colors, Hercules Graphics Adapter required—high resolution
EGA	320x200	16 colors—low resolution
EGA	620x350	4 or 16 colors

Display Mode	Resolution x,y	Comments
VGA	640x400	1 of 16 colors—Olivetti
SVGA	640x400	256 colors
SVGA	640x480	256 colors
SVGA	800x600	16 colors
SVGA	800x600	256 colors
SVGA	1024x768	16 colors
SVGA	1024x768	256 colors
SVGA	1280x1024	16 colors
SVGA	1280x1024	256 colors

The DIGL video interface for the IBM PC relies heavily on a few interface calls provided by the compiler library chosen. The graphics functions supplied by the compiler of choice will not work with a different compiler. However, it can be used as a template to make another version compatible with another compiler. Appendix C discusses these design tradeoffs in more detail.

In the case of other video devices—such as the X Window library interface workstation displays or dedicated graphics terminals—the corresponding drivers handle the necessary translation of these commands. Often, the workstation provides a window that allows interface with a graphics command subset as well as general purpose menu development. The UNIX version of interfacing to X Window libraries is introduced in Chapter 7, "High-Resolution Graphics Windows," with a sample menu application provided as an example. DIGL also provides a video graphics driver for X Windows. See Appendix D for a detailed discussion of how this works.

Libraries such as Xlib or other X Windows toolkits solve this complexity problem somewhat, but at the expense of adding yet another layer of complex and language-dependent interface calls. This problem can have an impact on the choice of programming languages used. In the case of memory-mapped interfaces where direct read-write instructions to memory addresses are used, a language such as Fortran must be augmented with mixed language assembly or C calls to accomplish this.

Digital Plotters

Pen plotters range from small desktop units to larger floor-standing models. All software commands are translated to control pens to draw lines from one point on the paper to another. There are pen plotter protocols other than HPGL syntax. However, efficiency and control are similar in virtually all cases.

Vector versus Bit-Mapped

The simple move and draw vector operations are handled easily by all models of plotters. Usually, a microprocessor is used to handle higher-level commands, such as polygon fills and edging.

Bit-mapped operations are not considered practical or relevant for these devices. The drawing grid can be addressed down to thousandths of an inch. However, because of the mechanical nature of the controls and operation of digital plotters, bit-mapped operations may require several seconds or minutes to implement—and you run the risk of making a hole through the paper.

Speed

Speed varies considerably for pen plotters for a number of reasons. Using transparency pens requires a slower drawing speed to prevent uneven drawing lines. Unlike with video CRTs, the larger the plotter and the larger the area traced by the vector, the longer a single operation can take. For example, larger floor-standing or flatbed plotters can handle paper sizes larger than four feet by four feet. To draw or move from one corner to the next can take as long as two to ten seconds, depending on the type of pen used.

Device Dependence

Unlike for video devices, much of the interface protocol for digital plotters is standardized for formats such as HPGL. Even plotters that have different protocols frequently emulate HPGL as a secondary mode. For this reason, the DIGL plotter driver is based on HPGL.

File Storage Overhead

In order to reproduce an image, the plotter commands must be captured and stored. So, file storage considerations are based on buffering commands representing the graphics image that will be rendered. It is not possible to read a plotter in order to retrieve information about an image that has already been drawn. Therefore, reproducing an image depends on file capture of the plotter commands issued.

Because digital plotter formats are usually in ASCII format and often verbose, compressing plotting instructions to reduce file size is valid. Consider, for example, the two sequences of graphics instructions shown in Table 3.2. Move commands the device to move the graphics cursor or drawing instrument to a new location. No vector is drawn. Draw also commands the device to move the drawing instrument, but a vector is drawn from the first draw command to the last. Line segments are connected to produce the line art.

Table 3.2. Graphics sequence comparisons.

Generic Sequence 1	*Generic Sequence 2*
1. Move(X1,Y1)	1. Move(X1,Y3)
2. Move(X2,Y2)	2. Draw(X4,Y4)
3. Move(X3,Y1)	
4. Move(X1,Y3)	
5. Draw(X4,Y4)	

Both sequences produce identical results—a vector drawn from (X1,Y3) to (X4,Y4). Examine the sequence more closely, and you notice that the first four are successive move instructions. The actual result of the instruction sequence is the same, regardless of whether the first three are executed. However, the number of bytes represented by instructions that have no effect on the result should be considered significant.

On average, the length of a single HPGL instruction is 12 bytes. Applying this statistic to Sequence 1 of the graphics instructions in Table 3.2 yields an average total byte count of 5×12, or 60, bytes. Applying the same statistic to Sequence 2 of the graphics instructions yields an average total byte count of 2×12, or 24, bytes. This means that Sequence 1 contains an excess of (60 - 24)/60 bytes, or 60 percent. This is even more significant for file sizes of several hundred thousand bytes.

Complexity of Control and Interfacing

Most of the interfacing for the digital plotters is either serial or by means of IEEE-488. With serial interfaces, the control is fairly simple. The driver simply must output ASCII strings consistent with a protocol such as HPGL.

With IEEE-488 interfacing, the driver must issue ASCII strings to another device driver compatible with a handshake protocol for the IEEE bus. An IEEE device protocol is an instrument bus protocol with an effective data transfer rate much faster than a typical 9600-baud serial interface. More important, the IEEE instrument bus permits multiple device communication with a single controller that is soft-configurable. If you interface with a digital plotter in this fashion, you are likely using dedicated hardware and software to support the IEEE protocol directly. It is not something you would want to build into a graphics driver.

Impact Printers and Other Hard Copy Devices

The increased resolution of impact printers makes many graphics programs consider them a special case. Printers present a different set of problems for graphics applications because of the complexities of producing printer graphics.

Vector versus Bit-Mapped

Dot-matrix printers have 7 to 24 pins, and each pin can be individually controlled. Inkjet printers are part of this class. Laser printers are high-resolution devices in which a rotating drum coated with selenium is written on with a laser beam. Both types share characteristics in principle with video CRTs and digital plotters.

Only a bit-mapped operation, in effect, is available. Printers are similar to video in that the printing area is considered one large grid of addressable dots used to render a graphical image. Unlike CRTs, however, the speed and agility with which these dots are addressed is very limited. The print head must be physically over the area to be written on. Unlike with digital plotters, the paper typically moves in only one fixed direction. Therefore, as each line is drawn on a printer, all the dots on a line must be set before the print head moves to the next line.

Speed

Printers tend to be the slowest of the graphics devices, with the exception of some digital plotters. The effective speed depends on the type of graphics being rendered. It is interesting to note that a printer takes the same amount of time to produce a graphics image composed of stroke vectors as it takes to produce a scan-converted polygon. The reason is simple: for most printers, it takes the same amount of time to print a short line segment as it does a long one.

Device Dependence

Unfortunately, among printers there is virtually no standardization of the software control of individual pixels or pins on the print head. There are hundreds of printers of varying capabilities with an equal amount of software reference manuals for interfacing at this level. There are two possible ways to avoid this interfacing nightmare:

- Design your graphics application so that you can export a file which a popular software application (a word processor, for example) can import. Use word processors or other software with extensive printer support to import a supported graphics protocol, such as HPGL or PostScript.

- Use a third-party printer support library, and build it into your graphics driver package.

    In either case, you avoid the duplication of effort.

File Storage Overhead

It is usually impossible or very impractical to store the printer control commands that represent graphical images. The space requirement is not prohibitively large, but usually a modest amount of two-way I/O is required for proper handshaking. If you need to store these images, use a file format that is not specific to the printer (for example, TIFF, GIF, TGA, etc.).

Complexity of Control and Interfacing

A significant number of printer interfaces are parallel—the Centronix protocol. They are supported by some form of operating system services—BIOS services, for example, in the case of the PC. The control protocol is not significantly complex, and a large number of different printers and formats are available. Even if you support only a few popular printers, you undoubtedly suffer the headache of adding or modifying drivers to accommodate the changes to versions and model numbers.

Graphics Input Devices

Image scanners, graphics tablets, light pens, and mice—two- or three-button— are the more commonly used input devices. Unlike the devices previously discussed in this chapter, these are primarily interactive. They represent input in the form of high-resolution bit-mapped scanned picture data or x,y-coordinates transmitted in real-time to a graphics application program.

The initial implementation of DIGL does not include provisions for direct support of these devices. However, it is worthwhile to look at some of their features in relation to graphics driver support.

Vector versus Bit-Mapped

Image scanners are considered bit-mapped devices, because their primary mode of operation involves transmitting entire grids of pixel data that represent the scanned image area. On the other hand, the mouse and light pens involve small amounts of data based on vectors of Cartesian space. Ideally, the numbers that are transmitted represent scaled coordinates based on the text mode or graphics mode your application program is using (see Table 3.1).

Besides menu operation, mouse and light pen operations can be used interactively in the graphics editing mode to cut and paste portions of an image. These operations are outside the scope of the DIGL introduced in this book.

Speed

Image scanners are typically slow devices because of the time required to scan an area—usually a few seconds for an 8 ½ by 11 inch scan area. In addition, there may be several steps to complete the scan process, such as image editing, dithering, and final file format conversion. Mouse and light pen options typically transmit data by means of serial interfaces or a direct connection to a special interface card at a rate of 30 to 80 Hz.

Device Dependence

All these devices require some type of custom software or operating system services support to be useful in a graphics application process. The level of customization required for these devices presents some difficulties in permitting multiple platform support. These difficulties include the cost and time required to debug interfacing with these types of devices. In addition, the level at which the software must interface often requires low-level assembler code or nonportable machine addressing.

File Storage Overhead

Image scanners present the largest amount of file storage overhead. Tagged Image File Format (TIFF), for example, requires as many as 5M for each image, depending on the filtering or dithering process that is selected. File storage overhead for mice, light pens, joysticks, trackballs, and graphics tablets is typically very small, except for macrorecording of user actions (for example, recording mouse movements).

Complexity of Control and Interfacing

Each of these devices presents a unique interfacing problem to the support I/O software and hardware. Although most mice have both serial and direct bus interface options, writing a serial interface routine usually requires a combination of either mixed language calls to BIOS services—for the PC—or calls to a third-party support library. Image scanners provide some programming information for direct I/O support, but generally they rely on the use of vendor-supplied software packages to scan pictures and produce files for later use by an application program.

Operator Interface

An important part of any application program is the operator interface. Over the years, there have been three major advances in the design and presentation of user interfaces:

- Simple text-based question/answer interfaces
- Pop-up windows based on function keys and text
- High-resolution GUIs

The term *text-based* means that the high-resolution graphics plane is not used for individual pixel control. Simple text-based question/answer interfaces were the first and simplest form of user interface in which a TTY interface was the primary form of I/O considered.

Video terminals were more advanced, allowing the graphics- and text-mode capabilities of pop-up windows. Using advanced graphics characters to draw boxes grouping parameters became the standard approach.

PCs and workstations eliminated the bandwidth problem of using high-resolution graphics with serial interfaces. Now, there are questions about *icons*—pictures that represent actions to be performed. Window standards provide a common look and feel across computer platforms.

By design, the DIGL model introduced so far does not assume any particular interface. In fact, the DIGL concept effectively disconnects the operator interface from the graphics library.

Many of the issues associated with user interfaces are addressed in Chapter 6, "A Design Prototype for Text-Based Pop-Up Windows," and Chapter 7 "High-Resolution Graphics Windows." In the next section, however, I introduce some of the programming concerns and tasks necessary to connect the user with an application.

Operating Systems and GUIs

DOS and UNIX are two of the most popular operating systems available in today's market place. Both present a variety of challenges to systems and application programmers.

GUI implementations on UNIX tend to be based heavily on C and a popular version of Windows standards, such as Motif. DOS GUIs tend to be based on a version of Microsoft Windows or a close approximation of it. In both cases, some form of library toolkit is available to provide portability between the two systems.

Dialogue Design

Before you implement a GUI interface, it might be necessary for you to change how you structure your program to handle parameter modifications. A properly designed GUI should never force the user into a number of question/answer sequences. Instead, a menu-based implementation should *minimize* the amount of questions asked by the user. In addition, user mistakes or errors should be trapped and serviced by error handling routines prior to further processing.

Windows programming is more event driven than procedural. You can take a few basic steps to make the program conversion process a little easier:

1. Centralize your application parameters as much as possible.

2. Group parameters based on association.

3. Utilize defaults and automatic variable initialization when possible.

In a menu system, parameters or variables are displayed in related groupings so that a user can see the current value at a glance and make changes by exception. If you centralize the routines for setting and displaying these global variables, functions or subroutines can be used as entry points to respond to user input for modifications. In X Window programming, for example, the user defines the buttons or other predefined input areas and the routines that are notified when the user makes a selection. The centralization process in this case is built into the program development process. Chapter 8, "The Object-Oriented Approach," provides additional insight into design issues related to X Window programming.

As an extension of the centralization process, related variables can be placed in subroutines representing one or more submenus. When the user clicks an icon or widget to make a selection, the location of a pointing device or cursor position identifies a variable from the list.

At program startup or on demand, every variable of any consequence should be given a meaningful initial value, a value that is consistent with both the range allowed by the data type and with your graphics application. This approach should be used for all user selectable values in any application. A good design prevents the user of the program from assigning meaningless values to any parameter. These techniques are explored in Chapters 6 and 7.

Parameter File Usage

Implementing the DIGL involves using a parameter file, a disk file that contains ASCII representations of all or most data values that are used to control an application program. Parameter files are used to disconnect applications from any sort of direct user interaction. Figure 3.1 shows how the user application is structured and organized around parameter files.

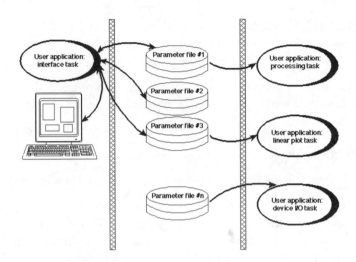

Figure 3.1. Parameter file structure.

The user application is divided functionally into modular areas of activity, or tasks, such as user interface, processing, linear plot, and device I/O.

Any number of parameter files may exist at any time for a variety of purposes, and they may be created by a user interface task, by a text editor, or by any application that can read and write the structure.

The task or routine that performs an action that is based on the contents of the file usually has read-only access. It is possible for more than one task at a time to read the same parameter file in concurrent applications.

The actual structure and contents of a parameter file vary depending on application requirements. Figure 3.2 illustrates a portion of a parameter file format that is used for the DIGL implementation. This particular implementation of the parameter file permits comments that begin with a semicolon (;). Because the file is in ASCII format, string handling and conversion between data types is necessary. For example, the value of the parameter USERXMIN in Figure 3.2 is represented by the portion of the string -180.00. However, the entire line from the file that contains this value is

```
USERXMIN   //-180.000                 ;x axis minimum range
```

```
GRAPDEV        #VGACOLOR                      ;graphics mode selected
VIEWPORT       #.00,100.00,00,100.00          ;plotting area
OUTTOFIL       #FALSE                         ;plot to file?
DIRECT         #                              ;file directory
DATAFI         #LINETEST.DAT                  ;user data file
POLYFI         #TERMINALPOG                   ;user polygon file
PLOTFI         #LINEARPLT                     ;plot output file
USERXMIN       #-180.000                      ;x axis miminum range
USERXMAX       #180.000                       ;x axis maximum range
USERYMIN       #-10.000                       ;y axis miminum range
```

Figure 3.2. Sample parameter file for the DIGL model.

If a floating point value represents the parameter USERXMIN, the string that contains its value must be parsed. In other words, the comment and the characters leading the delimiter string // must be removed. Once this is done, the ASCII string -180.000 is converted to the floating point value -180.000. The string handling portion of the DIGL support library provides routines for this conversion (see Appendix A). The support library contains parameter file read and write routines.

This approach to task control has several advantages:

■ The application routines are less cluttered with I/O and editing features.

■ Several different types of menu interface may be designed to drive the same application.

■ Parameter files are completely device-independent, although the format is somewhat arbitrary.

■ Parameter files make it possible to port an application and test it on another platform without a menu interface. For example, a parameter-driven DOS application can be ported to UNIX. The ASCII-based parameter files can be copied to the UNIX platform and used to test the port immediately, and a UNIX-based menu interface can be designed at a later date.

Window Design and Management

The basic window structure is a box in which text data is displayed. A box consists of a rectangular area of graphics characters that are required to draw a single or double line frame around an area of text. When you make calls to your window library, you specify what the information is, where you want it displayed, what color you want for borders, and so on.

Once the information is displayed, you must decide what action needs to be taken. A keypress or mouse click tells your window library what has happened in relation to the data that are displayed. Usually, this means scroll bars for visualization of user interaction. In the DOS model, you can handle this by waiting for and processing a keyboard or mouse event. At the highest level of interface with the GUI library, you need only to supply information about the window elements, location, and event processing.

Text-Based versus Bit-Mapped Windows

Text-based pop-up windows are the fastest techniques for providing real-time interaction with the user. Recall that text-based means that the high-resolution graphics plane is not used for individual pixel control. Instead, the video pages reside at locations that start at a fixed memory location—for example, segment address B0000h through B0F9Fh in DOS. A *text video page* is a section of memory reserved for the display of 24 lines by 80 columns of information. A *graphics video page* requires more memory for higher resolution displays. Cascaded submenus can be formed by reading and writing to more than one video page and then displaying the results to simulate pop-up submenus. Figure 3.3 shows a text-based menu system display.

The user selects choices that are highlighted by horizontal or vertical bars. The input and pointing devices that are recognized can be mice, keyboards, digitizer pads, or light pens. A *digitizer pad* or *tablet* is a flat or slightly raised surface used to detect the position of a pointer device such as a mouse or light pen. An imbedded wire grid is used to provide *x,y* position data at high resolutions. It can be used to trace or digitize portions of a simple drawing or line segment for data entry into an applications program.

In the case of a more sophisticated GUI interface—such as Microsoft Windows or UNIX-based X Windows—the required support functions grow in number and complexity. Instead of text-based video memory being used, the high-resolution graphics plane is used. Each pixel on the screen is individually controllable. I/O becomes more complicated as event handling requirements are distributed across machines. Controlling and responding to events in a multi-tasking environment requires higher levels of sophistication in programming because events that cause interrupts at runtime may come from a variety of input devices— including those external to the local application or machine configuration. Figure 3.4 illustrates a typical bit-mapped GUI menu.

```
P │Selections        │   Miscellaneous and Advanced Plot Control Features  │E
D │                                                                         │E
D │n│2D Modifications  │eral -    - 2D Specific -   - 3D Specific -          │E
P │h│                  │e ?: FALSE│XandY?      : FALSE│Undersurf: FALSE      │E
O │l│n) XandY ?        │f ?: FALSE│Plot Top    : 0.00 │Azimuth  : 0.00       │E
G │f│p) Plot Top       │e  : 1    │Bar Width   : 0.90 │Elevation: 0.00       │E
  │p│b) Bar Width      │   : 1    │Poly X Scale: 1.00 │Cont. Ivl: 60.00      │
  │b│x) Poly X Scale   │b.?: FALSE│Poly Y Scale: 1.00 │Rotate?  : FALSE      │
  │v│y) Poly Y Scale   │          │Poly Angle  : 0.00 │                      │
U │e│a) Poly Angle     │                                                    │
U │s│                  │e:                                                  │
U │c│R) Return         │s:                                                  │
  │o│                  │  : 0.00,100.00,0.00,100.00                         │
D │2)      2D Specs    │Penorder : 0707050402030106060606060606060606060606060
D │3)      3D Specs    │Setcolors: CYA,GRE,BRO,LI,RED,DAR,LIGHTBL,LIGHTGREEN,LIG
D │R)      RETURN      │Con. LnSt:                                          │
```

Figure 3.3. Text-based pop-up menu with cascaded submenus.

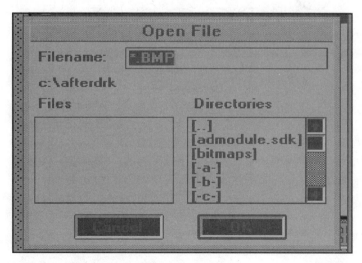

Figure 3.4. High-resolution bit-mapped menu.

45

Fast Display Techniques

If the software language that you choose enables you to write and read directly from memory locations, you can readily exploit the advantages of high speed and simplicity. The effect of real-time window popping is achieved through careful attention to the speed of low-level graphics primitives.

In the case of bit-mapped window libraries, the graphics plane is controlled at the pixel level. This permits the detailed icons and button images that are popular in today's window-oriented operating systems. The price of this improvement in visualization is low-level primitives that are much more complex.

Implementing the DIGL Model

You have examined the development and support of graphics applications. In Chapter 1, an abstract model of the DIGL environment is presented. Figure 3.5 shows a more detailed representation of that model. Several concepts and features of the model require explanation before you begin to implement it.

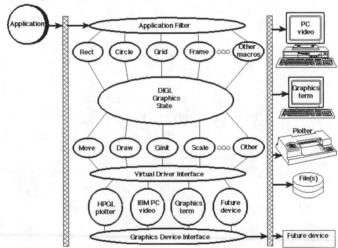

Figure 3.5. Detailed representation of the DIGL model.

Data Flow Sequence

The DIGL model presented in Figure 3.5 establishes a data flow that is noninteractive. The assumption here is that a graphics application has all the information that it needs at runtime to produce a plot or graphical image. The parameter file forms the basis of this assumption. Figure 3.6 uses a data flow graph to illustrate the typical sequence of events that lead to controlled data flow through the DIGL model. The DIGL data flow pertains to those tasks in the right column of Figure 3.1.

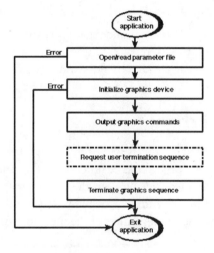

Figure 3.6. Data flow through the DIGL model.

The figure shows the first step taken by the application as it attempts to open a specified parameter file. If the file cannot be found or some fatal error is encountered, the error path to the application exit is taken.

The next step is to initialize the graphics device. Depending on the type of graphics device, this step might be immediate—for CRTs, for example—or it might require user intervention, such as loading a sheet of paper into a plotter. As in the previous step, a fatal error encountered results in taking an error path to the application exit.

Once the parameter file is read and the graphics device is initialized, the application can output a sequence of graphics commands to the graphics device specified. This step also begins the process of initializing the graphics state of the model.

47

The optional step, indicated by the dotted box, depends on the type of graphics device. A video device, such as a PC screen, generally requires that the application pause before it terminates. Otherwise, the graphics mode is terminated before returning to the text mode without giving the user sufficient time to examine it.

The final step restores the graphics device to what its state was before the application program started. Some video displays, such as the IBM PC, share the same video surface for both text and graphics operations, although there are separate memory regions reserved for text and graphics (see Chapter 7). When an application exits the graphics mode on a PC, the text mode is restored, erasing what was left of the graphics image.

Workstations using the X Window mode allow the user to create multiple windows that can be opened, closed, resized, or relocated without requiring that the image partially or completely covered by the window be destroyed.

Application Interface

The application interface—or filter—refers to the functional interface implemented in software. All calls to graphics procedures or functions follow the same structure regardless of whether the parameter file requests the specific graphics application or the graphics device. Graphics commands such as Move and Draw have the same appearance and parameter structure regardless of the specific graphics application requirements.

Initialization of the DIGL Model

Initializing graphics devices requires that you manage two different control states of software. These states are *hard initialization* and *soft initialization*.

Hard Initialization

Hard initialization is analogous to a cold boot in the initialization of hardware—in other words, a startup from a completely unknown initial state. With video CRTs, hard initialization assumes that no information is already displayed on the screen and that the screen is to be erased completely before the first graphics command is executed. With graphics hardware such as a digital plotter, hard initialization assumes that the user needs to replace the current page—sheet of paper.

Soft Initialization

Soft initialization is analogous to a warm boot in the initialization of hardware. In this case, the assumption is that there may be information on a display or sheet of paper that is to be added to by the current series of graphics commands. The sheet of paper is not ejected, and the screen is not erased; instead, the internal graphics state of the DIGL model is modified.

Figure 3.7 illustrates the output of a graphics illustration where a soft initialization is required to perform *multiquadrant plotting*—the display output of two entirely different graphics algorithms using the same display or page. The left side of the figure is the output of a standard linear plot application. The right side is the result of two different contour plots of different data files. Without soft initialization, the screen display or hard copy plot produced consists of the last plot—a contour in the case of video—or three separate sheets of paper in the case of digital hard copy plots.

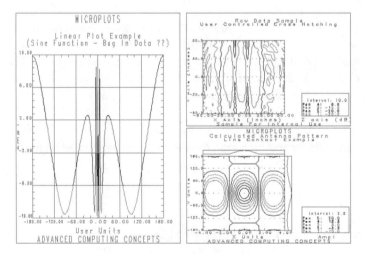

Figure 3.7. Multiquadrant plot featuring soft initialization.

DIGL Graphics State

After a specific graphics device is initialized, the DIGL model requires an internal graphics state to be set up and controlled. As Figure 3.5 shows, the DIGL Graphics State is the soft connection between higher-level graphics macros—such as Rect and Grid—and lower-level primitives—such as Move and Draw. This soft connection is represented in software terms by globally visible data areas. Many graphics commands create side effects that must be maintained for interaction with other commands. For example, in DIGL, the Draw command is represented by the endpoint vector—as in Draw(X2,Y2). The starting point is assumed to be the current position in coordinate space, which must be maintained by the graphics state. In other words, Draw(X2,Y2) means "draw a vector from where the graphics cursor currently is to the point X2,Y2."

Based on the contents of the current parameter file contents, a file of constants and variables is used to initialize the graphics state. This concept is discussed further in Chapter 4, "Graphics Visualization," and Chapter 5, "A Design Prototype for Device-Independent Plotting."

Device Driver Interface

At the upper level of the DIGL graphics model, all graphics application commands are interpreted and executed in data units that are consistent with the application. For example, a graphics plot based on income (x-axis) versus age (y-axis) expects data in terms of dollars for income and years for age. However, before a graphics device can properly execute commands based on these units, the data must be scaled consistent with the physical limits of the plotting surface. In Figure 3.5, the Virtual Driver Interface is responsible for this conversion; it uses the data visible in the current graphics state. As you might suspect, based on its own unique requirements and capabilities, each graphics device performs a different set of data conversions.

Graphics Device Interface

The Graphics Device Interface portion of Figure 3.5 is the final interface to the graphics device. At this lowest level of the DIGL model, the commands are translated to raw signals and data necessary to control the graphics drawing stylus.

File Capture of Output

For some graphics devices, such as digital plotters and PostScript drivers, the ASCII nature of the commands permits output to a sequential file instead of directly to the device. The advantage of this is that the file can be imported to other graphics programs. The multiquadrant plot of Figure 3.7, for example, was output from a graphics application to a file and imported to a word processor for use in this book. To permit this option, the DIGL graphics drivers contain an optional file output flag that can be set as a parameter.

Summary

This chapter focuses on the characteristics of graphics devices from a system programmer's point of view.

Improvements in display technology and demands for faster and higher resolution displays have produced quite a range of video devices for interface and control. Each should be evaluated according to operations, speed, device dependence, file storage, and complexity. Digital plotters, printers, and graphics input devices can be evaluated by the same criteria.

Operator interface requirements in relation to the DIGL model may require adjustments. The parameter file structure can be used as a mechanism for separating the user interface portion of an application from its corresponding tasks or processes. This method provides a useful means of streamlining the various portions of the application.

In Chapter 4 you begin to develop the next layers of the DIGL, using software engineering techniques to assist you in developing and extending the DIGL routines.

CHAPTER

4

GRAPHICS
VISUALIZATION AND
TRANSFORMATIONS

This chapter introduces you to some of the intermediate algorithms needed to design a DIGL. Pseudocode and code fragments are used to explain the algorithms of existing systems. Techniques for software engineering, including the software coding conventions that are used, are presented, along with a quick review of basic C language constructs. If you are interested in converting some of the algorithms presented in this book to a programming language other than C, this chapter is very useful as a template for the conversion procedure. A detailed presentation of the theory of graphics operations is supplemented by detailed, practical examples.

Software Engineering

The DIGL consists of several source files. Each contains more than one function. You must have some basic software engineering skills to develop the functional DIGL hierarchy properly. This book reviews the more important aspects of software engineering and the many development conventions that are used.

Pseudocode Conventions

To help you use algorithms in the code of specific programming languages, I use pseudocode extensively to describe graphics algorithms. The pseudocode presents constructs that are common to most programming languages without added confusion from the syntax of a particular language. However, without conventions and explanation, a pseudocode fragment can be open to different interpretations.

Consider, for example, an algorithm that gets two numbers from the user, adds them, and conditionally prints the results. Here is the corresponding pseudocode fragment:

1   *Get first number and store in variable* `FirstNum`
2   *Get second number and store in variable* `SecondNum`
3   *Result* = `FirstNum` + `SecondNum`

4   *If Result > 10 then*
5   *Print Result*
6   *End if*

Now consider that two programmers read this pseudocode specification. One writes in C, and the other writes in Fortran. The first programmer, who implements the pseudocode algorithm in C, might produce the following code:

```
int FirstNum, SecondNum, Result;
printf("Input first number: ");
scanf("%d", &FirstNum);
printf("Input second number: ");
scanf("%d", &SecondNum);
Result = FirstNum + SecondNum;
if (Result > 10)
  {
     printf("\nThe sum of %d and %d is %d.\n", FirstNum, SecondNum,
Result);
  }
```

The second programmer, who implements the same pseudocode algorithm in Fortran, might produce the following code:

```
    WRITE(lu,*)'Input first number: '
    READ *,FirstNum
    WRITE(lu,*)'Input second number: '
    READ *,SecondNum
    Result = FirstNum + SecondNum
C
    IF (Result.GT.10) THEN
      WRITE(LU,'(1X,A11,F6.2,A5,F6.2,A4,F6.2)')'The sum of ',
    +        FirstNum,' and ',SecondNum, ' is ',Result
    END IF
```

Programmers who implement the same algorithm in other languages might produce other syntactically different sentence structures.

Not only is pseudocode shorter and easier to understand than actual code, but also the details of implementation do not interfere with the basic premise of the algorithm. There are differences between the two implementations. The C implementation assumes that the numbers are integers (%d in the printf statement). The Fortran implementation assumes that the numbers are floating point (F6.2 in the write statement). You could argue that both programs are correct, because the pseudocode does not define what type of numbers should be used. For this simple case, whatever result is obtained is not important.

You can reduce the ambiguity of your pseudecode if you adopt the following conventions:

1. If data types are important to the pseudocode algorithms, they are identified accordingly.

2. Indentation is used to indicate block structure. (The `if-then` block contained in lines four through six of the previous pseudocode illustrates this.) In general, indented blocks are used—instead of `begin` and `end`—for better readability.

3. Unless stated otherwise, all variables are assumed to be local to the routine. If a routine requires formal parameters, the routine name, followed by a parameter list, precedes the statement lists. Variables with global visibility are identified as such.

4. If special initialization of variables is required, the initialization sequence is described as part of the pseudocode.

5. No assumption about the runtime initialization of variables is made.

6. Unless stated otherwise, parameters are passed to routines by `value`. This means that a copy of the data is used for the parameter that is local to the routine. If you intend the routine to modify the parameter, the parameter should appear on the left side of an assignment statement.

7. The name of an array and its index are identified with square brackets, as in A[x]. The array name is followed by an index. In this case, the *x*th element of array A is accessed.

8. Functions and procedures are denoted by the keywords `Begin` and `End`. If the procedure requires input parameters, they are enclosed in parentheses followed by a colon and a data type specification. Here is an example of a pseudecode procedure declaration:

```
Begin Transform(InputMatrix :POLYGON, OutputMatrix
                :POLYGON)
End Transform
```

Common C Language Constructs

All code fragments in this book are analyzed with the C programming language. In this section, I review some common C traps. I explain several of the design and programming style decisions that affect the structure and performance of the DIGL, and I help you to know which decisions to avoid.

General Programming Style

C provides an increment operator (++) and a decrement operator (- -), which are used in various statements. Here are examples of the increment operator. Statements 1 and 2 are equivalent, and statements 3 and 4 are equivalent.

```
(1)    i++;
(2)    i = i + 1;

(3)    a += 11;
(4)    a = a + 11;
```

Here are examples of the decrement operator. Statements 5 and 6 are equivalent, and statements 7 and 8 are equivalent.

```
(5)    i—;
(6)    i = i - 1;

(7)    a -= 11;
(8)    a = a - 11;
```

With all the C code developed here, the emphasis is on readability. Unless it is absolutely necessary to use C syntax, I use conventional language constructs. Therefore, in most cases, I use statement 2 instead of statement 1.

Program headers are used for all functions and include both programmer comments and comments on the usage of the function. Program headers make it much easier to locate functions and to tell where one function ends and the next one begins.

Here is an example of a program header. This header contains the function return type, a brief description of the argument list, and copyright information:

```
/*+================================================================
== void fixtabs(): replace each tab with 8 spaces...            ==
==                                                             ==
== Argument list:    char =t        target string pointer      ==
==                   char =s        source string              ==
==                                                             ==
== Return value:     void                                      ==
==                                                             ==
== Author: Scientific Concepts, Inc.                           ==
== Copyright (c) 1990-1993. All rights reserved worldwide.     ==
================================================================*/
```

Block Structure

All *block-structured* statements—such as do and while—use the format of indented and aligned braces:

```
while (Count < 10)
  {
    block of statements here
  }
```

This format more closely follows the block structure of other programming languages.

Side-Effect Programming

For *side-effect programming*, C language control statements such as while or for loops can be used to modify variables or to call functions directly. Consider the following code fragment:

```
while (--lim > 0 && (c=getchar()) != EOF && c!= '\n')
  s[i++] = c;
```

The character input (c=getchar()) is embedded in the control part of the while statement. This is a simple example of side-effect programming. It makes for compact code, but more complicated versions of this technique can make debugging code a nightmare. Only limited side-effect programming techniques are used in the code for the DIGL.

Array Indexing and the Option Base

One of the most common errors in writing in C code or converting C code to other programming languages involves *array indexing* and the option base. The option base refers to the lower addressable bound of an array index. In many languages—Fortran, for example—an array declared with 10 items is indexed for 1 to 10. In C, however, the lower bound is 0. This means that in order to declare an array Ax in which element 10 is indexed, use this statement:

```
int  Ax[11]                 ;/* An 11 element array */
```

This array has 11 elements, but it must be indexed as Ax[0], Ax[1], and so on through Ax[10]. With many array-based algorithms—polygon transformations, for example—you must index and declare the for loops to avoid indexing the nth element. In many C implementations, the compiler does not prevent this. This type of mistake causes the program to behave differently depending on the platform that you use. For example, in the UNIX implementation, in which the memory allocated to a program is more strictly monitored by the operating system, your program likely will halt with segmentation fault or bus error. In DOS environments, your program might execute correctly until you attempt to access the area overwritten.

Include Files

Include files are files external to a source code module that are required or referenced during compile time using a compiler or preprocessor directive. In languages such as Fortran, often an include file is denoted by an .inc file extension. In C, however, the include preprocessor directive begins with #, followed by include and a filename. Include files are also called *header files* in which the .h extension, which stands for header file, is most commonly used. Consider the following code fragment:

```
    .
    .
    .
#include <stdio.h>
#include <stdlib.h>

#include "diglstr.h"
#include "diglfile.h"

    .
    .
    .
```

In this code fragment, the brackets (< and >) indicate that the include file is one that is usually supplied by the compiler vendor in a reserved directory on the disk. Files enclosed in double quotes are usually local to applications such as the DIGL. Note that the .h extension is used.

Function Prototypes

Function prototypes are used primarily to solve forward referencing problems and to provide for function interface checking at compile time. Before the ANSI version of C, an older form of function prototypes was used. Most modern C compilers permit either the older or the ANSI version of function prototypes and definition structures. Consider the function prototypes for the function getline:

Before the ANSI version:
```
int getline();

int getline(s,lim)
char s[];
int lim;
{
    function body here
}
```
The ANSI version:
```
int getline(char s[], int lim);

int getline(char s[],int lim)
{
        function body here
}
```

The earlier format for the function header and prototype is used to increase compatibility with older UNIX compilers such as cc and with support utilities. If you are concerned about your source code being correct, you can use the UNIX lint utility—a C program verifier—to ensure function interface correctness.

In UNIX System V, cc is the standard C compiler. It translates programs written in the C language into executable load modules. In many versions of UNIX System V, however, cc does not support ANSI function prototypes. Many of the GNU tools, such as gcc and g++ (the GNU project C and C++ compiler, respectively), do support ANSI function prototypes. Unfortunately, many C utilities and options do not.

For DOS or other PC-based development environments, the most recent versions of Turbo C from Microsoft, Borland, and other companies can handle either function format.

Representation of Data Types

A few basic data types are needed to support the DIGL. Because you want the DIGL to be portable and adaptable to other languages, you should be aware of a few potential problems.

Strings

C makes some allowances for string manipulation, but it does not have a string data type. In C, *strings* are simply character arrays that the user must manage to ensure the proper operation of the few built-in string functions. The character array *must* be NULL terminated (\0)to prevent functions from reading beyond the end of a character array, which is a very common problem in C. Strings are used extensively in the DIGL for data files and graphics parameter files. The DIGL includes a supplemental string support library (see Appendix A, "DIGL Support Libraries").

Integers

The default integer size in C implementations varies, depending on which environment you use. On small machines, such as PCs, the default integer might be only two bytes. On larger machines, such as UNIX workstations, the default integer is four bytes. With the DIGL, any time there is a chance that an integer value may exceed two bytes (32,767—the two-byte integer upper bound) the long data type is used.

Floating-Point Numbers

C provides for both *single precision*—often four bytes—and *double precision*—often eight bytes—for floating-point data types. In the DIGL, all floating-point values are treated and declared as double precision—the double data type.

Parameters or Constants

In the DIGL, the #define construct of C is used as the mechanism for defining constants and parameters. *Constants* such as DEGTORAD (degrees to radians) are defined at the beginning of header files in all capital letters for the sake of readability when they are used throughout the code.

Logical or Boolean Representation

The DIGL follows the convention common to many applications in which the Boolean states TRUE and FALSE are represented by 1 and 0, respectively. This corresponds to ON and OFF, which are also represented by 1 and 0. For example, in a parameter file, if a value is TRUE or ON, by definition it is greater than zero.

61

Complex Data Structures

Some data structures—for example, matrix representations—require more complex data structures. *Structures* are used to aggregate collections of data items that may or may not be of the same type. In the case of a 2-D matrix, a special data structure template has this form:

```
typedef struct 2dmatrix_st        /* structure for 2-D matrix row,col*/
  {
    int    mrows;                  /* Number of rows in matrix      */
    int    mcols;                  /* Number of columns in matrix   */
    double melem[3][3];            /* First line table item         */
  } 2DMATRIX;
```

To declare and initialize a 2-D array named IdMatrix, the following code fragment is used:

```
static 2DMATRIX IdMatrix =    { 3,3,
                                1.0, 0.0, 0.0,
                                0.0, 1.0, 0.0,
                                0.0, 0.0, 1.0
                              };
```

In these cases, a DIGL header file is used to define the data type template.

Global Variables

Software engineering purists often argue against global variables because of the problem of data visibility. However, in a large system with many parameters, global variables are the most convenient method of sharing information and maintaining states, such as the DIGL graphics state. The DIGL implements and controls its graphics state by using a few header files included with the DIGL disk. The global data space helps to limit the number of formal parameters that are needed for the various graphics functions.

File and Data Formats

File and data formats can vary from binary to ASCII and from direct record access to sequential. In addition, applications can impose special fields and record layouts for data. All these options can make data exchange and platform portability very difficult.

The DIGL uses a simple ASCII sequential file and data format. A floating-point data value is an ASCII string that represents a number followed by an optional decimal point and an optional fractional part. An optional exponent is also allowed. Floating-point values are separated by one or more white-space characters—Space, Tab, or EOL. Here is a sample data file fragment:

```
1.7     1.7     1.6     1.5     1.3     1.1     0.9     0.6     0.3
0.0    -0.3    -0.6    -0.9    -1.1    -1.3    -1.5    -1.6    -1.7
3.4     3.3     3.2     2.9     2.6     2.2     1.7     1.1     0.6
```

Compilers

Many issues arise because of the specific compiler or computer platform that you use. This section explains some of the choices you might face, and offers a few useful design guidelines.

Compiler Language Extensions

Most programming languages fall short of supplying all the operating system services and I/O necessary for larger applications such as graphics libraries. In cases in which the main video interface differs from machine to machine, the programming language usually is augmented with compiler-specific features to enable full-featured programming.

In C, the problem of language extensions is further illustrated by the increasing number of compiler-specific include files. For example, DOS C compilers often rely on compiler-specific definitions for dynamic memory allocation and BIOS services, which vary from vendor to vendor. On UNIX systems, depending on the version and the machine, some header files that are fairly common—for example, #include <string.h>—do not exist. In the interest of portability, it is not desirable to use compiler-specific files. At the least, they should be restricted and isolated as much as possible.

Compiler Directives

In earlier sections, I mentioned the include compiler directive. Other directives, which vary from machine to machine, might be needed especially for video services. In the DIGL, the conditional compilation control lines are used, but not extensively. The three most common types that are permitted in C are

```
#if          constant expression
#ifdef       identifier
#ifndef      identifier
```

Each of these control blocks is terminated with #endif. The corresponding #define statement is used to set the value of the identifier—TRUE or > 0—to enable the code enclosed within the control block to be compiled.

Automated Program Development

For each C compiler environment, the manner in which source files are compiled and linked with compiler and user libraries differs. The manner in which libraries are built also differs from system to system and from compiler to compiler. In medium to large systems, simply trying to find out which files are used in a library or application can be a difficult task, depending on the level of documentation. In DOS environments, C compilers offer choices of memory models—small, medium, large, and huge for Microsoft. The memory model must be consistent with each source file that is compiled.

Automated development—using batch files, command files, script files, or whatever your operating system can support in order to automate command-line sequences—simplifies this process considerably.

Batch, Command, Script, and Make File Usage

Depending on the operating system that you use, *batch, command,* and *script files* are similar. By permitting simple string substitutions, these mechanisms enable the user to automate slightly sequences that are to be repeated. The following command-line sequence is used for compiling and linking a source file called showpoly.c; it uses the Microsoft C compiler:

```
CL /c /AL /Gt /Fs showpoly.c
link showpoly /E /STACK:12000,showpoly,, @pcc.lnk
```

In this case, Microsoft compiler syntax and the large memory model are used, and many optimized switch settings are selected. This sequence is contained in a batch file in which only the names of the batch file and the source file are required on the command line. This eliminates the need for remembering the options.It also makes it easier for someone else to figure out how to compile the code.

Make files are more sophisticated ways of accomplishing the same objective. In make files, file dependence is automatically checked to enable incremental compilation. Both these options are discussed in Appendixes B and C, which provide examples for building the DIGL and applications.

Graphics Visualization

You can produce the various forms of graphics displays by using intermediate algorithms—from the simplest forms of vector manipulation to the more complex polygon treatments, which are the basis for 2-D object manipulations. Then you can expand and generalize on the 2-D concepts to form the basis for 3-D wireframe analysis.

Logical versus Physical Device Coordinates

The terms *logical* and *physical* are used to describe the process of projecting a set of objects from an abstract unit-based coordinate system to the limited resolution and unitless coordinate system of a specific graphics device. Figure 4.1 illustrates this concept.

The graphics engine—DIGL software—is used to transform and project an object from abstract space to a physical portion on the graphics plane—in this case, a video display. Notice that some portions of the object in the world coordinate system are not included in the rectangular area. The process of excluding the object area that is not contained within the rectangle is commonly referred to as *clipping*. The size and orientation of the object in the device coordinate system are determined by one or more transformations performed by the graphics engine. Most of the transformations required for the graphics engine are described in this section.

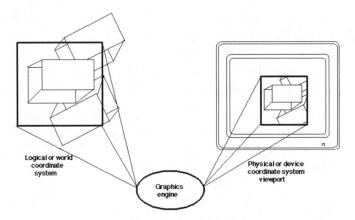

Figure 4.1. Device coordinate transformations.

Window-to-Viewport Transformations

Each vector or coordinate in the world coordinate system must be transformed to a corresponding coordinate in the device coordinate system. You can designate an arbitrary point in the world coordinate system as (Wx,Wy) and the minimum and maximum values in the world coordinate system as (Wxmin,Wxmax) and (Wymin,Wymax). You can also designate an arbitrary point in the device coordinate system as (Dx,Dy) and the minimum and maximum values in the device coordinate system as (Dxmin,Dxmax) and Dymin,Dymax). Equation 4.1 is the general-purpose *scaling* equation used to transform any point (Px,Py) from the world to the device coordinate system:

$$DX_{scaled} = D_{xmin} + \left[\frac{(P_x - W_{xmin})\ (D_{xmax} - D_{xmin})}{W_{xmax} - W_{xmin}} \right]$$

$$DY_{scaled} = D_{ymin} + \left[\frac{(P_y - W_{ymin})\ (D_{ymax} - D_{ymin})}{W_{ymax} - W_{ymin}} \right]$$

Given any point (Px,Py), you can solve for its corresponding device coordinates (DX_{scaled}, DY_{scaled}) accordingly. As this equation implies, points outside of the minimum and maximum range of the device coordinate system are not drawn.

Table 4.1 summarizes the parameter values that are defined for the scaling equation (Equation 4.1).

Table 4.1. Summary of variables for the scaling equation (Equation 4.1).

Variable	Description
DXscaled	*x*-axis device coordinate to be calculated
DYscaled	*y*-axis device coordinate to be calculated
Px	*x*-coordinate of point in world coordinates
Py	*y*-coordinate of point in world coordinates
Dxmin	*x*-axis coordinate of minimum value in device coordinates
Dxmax	*x*-axis coordinate of maximum value in device coordinates
Dymin	*y*-axis coordinate of minimum value in device coordinates
Dymax	*y*-axis coordinate of maximum value in device coordinates
Wxmin	*x*-axis coordinate of minimum value in world coordinates
Wxmax	*x*-axis coordinate of maximum value in world coordinates
Wymin	*y*-axis coordinate of minimum value in world coordinates
Wymax	*y*-axis coordinate of maximum value in world coordinates

The smaller the range of the device coordinate system is, the more likely it is for several points from the world coordinate system to map to the same point in the device coordinate system.

Because Equation 4.1 is a rather simple math formula, I don't present the corresponding pseudocode or C code here. If you're interested in the implementation, see the scale function in the DIGL graphics primitive library.

Polygon Representations in 2-D Space

A polygon is the natural extension of a line segment drawing in graphics. By connecting the endpoints of several line segments, a 2-D or 3-D polygon can be formed. Before I introduce additional mathematical concepts for 2-D transformations, let's examine a simple method for representing 2-D polygons in data files. The file structure that I will explain is used in all the polygon examples supplied with your DIGL disk. Figure 4.2 contains both the data—on the right side—and the graphical representation—on the left side—of a house.

The data shown are consistent with the data format described earlier for the DIGL. However, for polygon representations, the meaning of the data is based on three element values—X, Y, and P. X and Y represent *x,y-*Cartesian data points, and P represents a graphics pen control value. The pen control value is used to determine whether the corresponding X,Y pair represents a move or a draw command to be executed by the graphics engine. A value of 1 represents a draw instruction, and a value of –1 represents a move instruction.

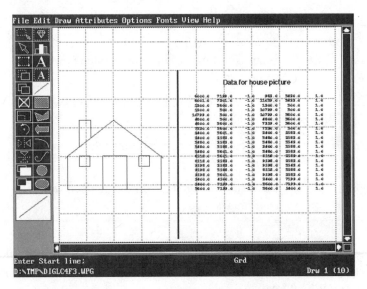

Figure 4.2. 2-D graphic of a house with absolute coordinates.

Absolute Polygon Data Representation

The data that represent the house in Figure 4.2 are in *absolute data coordinates.* The word *absolute* means that the data are scaled based on the minimum and maximum values for *x*- and *y*- coordinates of a device coordinate system. The origin and the range of values vary from device to device. There are two problems with polygon data represented in this manner:

- Many mathematical transformations require data in a relative format.

- The physical distances between vectors or vertices are not apparent.

Relative Polygon Data Representation

All polygon data used in DIGL is in what is called *relative format,* also known as *incremental format.* In relative format, the data for the polygon are assumed to begin at the origin (0,0) in Cartesian space of the device coordinates. Each pen control value that represents a successive move or draw operation is assumed to be relative to the last data point. Therefore, a move or draw operation to point (X,Y) is interpreted as an operation that is horizontally displaced *x* units from the previous *x*-axis value, and vertically displaced *y* units from the previous *y*-axis value. In the relative data format, negative values are common; they represent movement to the left or down. Figure 4.3 is a graphic of the same house as in Figure 4.2 but with the data converted to relative data values.

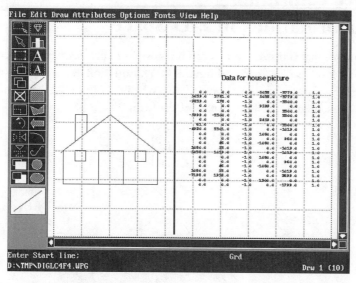

Figure 4.3. 2-D graphic of a house with relative coordinates.

With the data in the relative format, operations on the polygon can be described in general terms by the following relationship:

```
New Polygon = K * (Old Polygon)
```

In other words, you can visualize a constant K that you can use to scale a polygon up or down in size when you have data in relative format. For example, a square with K=1 is represented by the following graphics operations:

```
draw one unit to the right
draw one unit up
draw one unit to the left
draw one unit down
```

To scale the same square three times larger (K=3), the operations become

```
draw three units to the right
draw three units up
draw three units to the left
draw three units down
```

It follows that any polygon in the relative data format can be scaled by a constant when you use this simple technique. However, a few other transformations are not so simple as a scaling operation.

Device Coordinate Transformations in 2-D Space

Two-dimensional transformations can be more formally described by representing a point P by its Cartesian coordinates (X,Y). Equation 4.2 represents the general form of a transformation of point P to a new point P'. A 2-D transformation can be represented as a 2-D matrix T of the form:

$$T = \begin{bmatrix} A & B \\ C & D \end{bmatrix}$$

Equation 4.3 represents the general form of the equation for the transformation of point P to P':

$$P' = TP = \begin{bmatrix} A & B \\ C & D \end{bmatrix} * \begin{bmatrix} X \\ Y \end{bmatrix} = [(A*x + C*y), (B*x + D*y)]$$

Identity Matrix

The identity matrix is defined for any size matrix as a square matrix—the number of rows and columns is equal. In addition, except for the numbers in the main diagonal, all other values are 0. Therefore, the identity matrix for a 2-D transform has the following form (Equation 4.4):

$$I = \begin{bmatrix} 1 & 0 \\ 0 & 1 \end{bmatrix}$$

If you substitute the identity matrix I for the transformation in Equation 4.3, A=D=1 and B=C=0. Equation 4.5 shows the new equation for P':

$$P' = PI = (x, y) \begin{bmatrix} 1 & 0 \\ 0 & 1 \end{bmatrix} = [(1*x+0*y), (0*x+1y)]$$

$$P' = [(x, y)]$$

As you can see from the result, the identity matrix has the unique property of leaving the coordinate value unchanged. In the next series of transformations, the identity matrix is altered to produce other interesting effects on point P.

Scaling

Consider what happens if you use the values A and D along the main diagonal of an identity matrix. You have a new matrix S_c for the transform in Equation 4.3. In this case, A and D are along the diagonal, and B=C=0. Equation 4.6 shows the new equation for P':

$$P' = PS_C = (x, y) \begin{bmatrix} A & 0 \\ 0 & D \end{bmatrix} = [(A*x+0*y), (0*x+B*y)]$$

$$P' = [(Ax, By)]$$

If A and D are identical values, the vector result is uniformly enlarged. If A and D are different values, the result is stretched differently along the *x*-axis and the *y*-axis.

Shearing

If you use a value of B as the second element of the first row of an identity matrix, you have a new matrix S_{hy} for the transform in Equation 4.3. In this case, A=D=1 along the diagonal, and C=0. Equation 4.7 shows the new equation for P':

$$P' = PS_{hy} = (x, y) \begin{bmatrix} 1 & B \\ 0 & 1 \end{bmatrix} = [(1*x+0*y), (B*x+1*y)]$$

$$P' = [(x, Bx+y)]$$

Note that the transformation causes the *y*-coordinate to become a linear function of the *x*-coordinate; the *x*-coordinate is unchanged. The result of this type of operation is called *shearing* in the *y* direction.

If you use a value of C as the second element of the first row of an identity matrix, you have a new matrix S_{hx} for the transform in Equation 4.3. In this case, A=D=1 along the diagonal, and B=0. Equation 4.8 shows the new equation for P':

$$P' = PS_{hx} = (x, y) \begin{bmatrix} 1 & 0 \\ C & 1 \end{bmatrix} = [(1*x+C*y), (0*x+1*y)]$$

$$P' = [(x+Cy, y)]$$

In a manner similar to the previous example, the transformation causes the *x*-coordinate to become a linear function of the *y*-coordinate; the *y*-coordinate is unchanged. The result of this type of operation is called shearing in the *x* direction.

Reflection

Reflection is the process of flipping the point P around the *x*- or *y*-axis, or both. If −1 is used for the values along the main diagonal of an identity matrix, and you substitute this new matrix R_f for the transform in Equation 4.3, you have a new equation for P' (Equation 4.9):

$$P' = PR_f = (x, y) \begin{bmatrix} -1 & 0 \\ 0 & -1 \end{bmatrix} = [(-1*x+0*y), (0*x+-1*y)]$$

$$P' = [(-x, -y)]$$

The result of this operation is a reflection about the origin. If you use −1 for only one of the values along the main diagonal, the result is a reflection about a single axis.

Rotation

Rotation is, perhaps, the most common and interesting of the point transformations. In general, a vector can be rotated about some arbitrary point by some angle θ. To implement rotation in matrix transformations, sine and cosine functions are used.

By substituting these functions with the proper sign used for each value, you can define a new matrix R_o for the transform in Equation 4.3. Equation 4.10 shows the new equation for P':

$$P' = PR_0 = (x, y) \begin{bmatrix} \cos(\theta) & -\sin(\theta) \\ \sin(\theta) & \cos(\theta) \end{bmatrix} =$$

$$P' = [(x*\cos(\theta) +y*\sin(\theta)), (-x*\sin(\theta) +y*\cos(\theta))]$$

The result of this operation is a rotation counterclockwise through a positive angle θ. Changing the location of the -sin θ term to the second element of the first row produces a rotation counterclockwise around θ.

Translation

A natural 2-D point transformation is the translation operation. Translation shifts or slides points in a plane. Equation 4.11 is the general form of a translation on point P by the translation matrix T_{xy} to produce P' (where T is a scalar value, a real number):

$$P' = PT_{xy} = [(x+Tx), (y+Ty)]$$

To produce additive instead of multiplicative operations, this particular matrix has a form different from all the other matrices that I have introduced so far. Therefore, a slightly different coordinate system is needed to provide more uniformity among the transformation matrices. You want to represent all 2-D point transformations in a uniform manner. Hence you use the mathematical technique of homogeneous coordinates.

Homogeneous Coordinate Transformations in 2-D Space

To expand the functionality of the 2x2 matrix transformations that I have discussed so far, you can use a homogeneous 3x3 matrix. Instead of representing the data points as (x,y) pairs, you can represent them as (x,y,H), in which H represents a scale factor that must be nonzero. To simplify things, you can set H=1 which maps homogeneous point (x,y,1) to (x,y). The general-purpose transformation matrix now can be expressed with the following mapping (Equation 4.12):

$$\begin{bmatrix} A & B \\ C & D \end{bmatrix} \longrightarrow \begin{bmatrix} A & B & 0 \\ C & D & 0 \\ 0 & 0 & 1 \end{bmatrix}$$

Adding the third column vector has a significant impact on the mathematics of the transformations. In many graphics operations, it is desirable to combine transformations into one composite matrix. This simplifies the algorithms. In addition, the use of the homogeneous coordinate system enables the same matrix form to be used for translation. Therefore, all transformations now can be implemented as a series of one or more matrix multiplications.

It is also interesting to note that the structure of the new 3x3 form of the homogeneous transformations is similar to the data format for the 2-D polygons. This is no coincidence.

Revised 2-D Scaling Transformation

Equation 4.13 shows the new homogeneous scaling matrix S_c:

$$S_c = \begin{bmatrix} S_{cx} & 0 & 0 \\ 0 & S_{cy} & 0 \\ 0 & 0 & 1 \end{bmatrix}$$

Successive scaling operations can be combined into one composite scaling matrix, and the result can be applied to the points or polygon to be scaled. Figure 4.4 illustrates the result of the scaling operation on the figure of the house polygon from Figure 4.3.

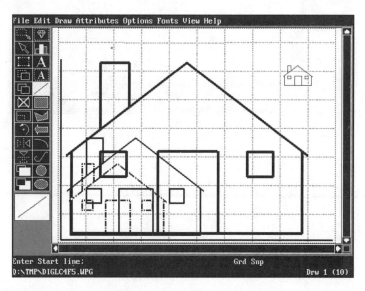

Figure 4.4. Result of the scaling operation applied to the house.

Revised 2-D Shearing Transformation

Equation 4.14 shows the new homogeneous shearing matrix S_h:

$$S_h = \begin{bmatrix} 1 & S_{hx} & 0 \\ S_{hy} & 1 & 0 \\ 0 & 0 & 1 \end{bmatrix}$$

Figure 4.5 illustrates the result of the shearing operation on the figure of the house polygon.

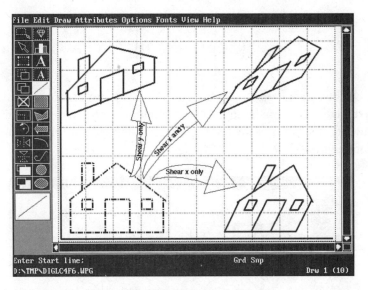

Figure 4.5. Result of the shearing operation applied to the house.

Revised 2-D Reflection Transformation

Equation 4.15 shows the new homogeneous reflection matrix R_f for reflection about the origin:

$$R_f = \begin{bmatrix} -1 & 0 & 0 \\ 0 & -1 & 0 \\ 0 & 0 & -1 \end{bmatrix}$$

Figure 4.6 illustrates the result of the reflection operation on the figure of the house polygon.

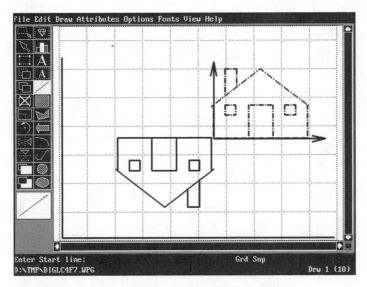

Figure 4.6. Result of the reflection peration applied to the house.

Revised 2-D Rotation Transformation

Equation 4.16 shows the new homogeneous rotation matrix R_o for counterclockwise rotation about a point:

$$R_O = \begin{bmatrix} \cos(\theta) & -\sin(\theta) & 0 \\ \sin(\theta) & \cos(\theta) & 0 \\ 0 & 0 & 1 \end{bmatrix}$$

Figure 4.7 illustrates the result of the reflection operation on the figure of the house polygon.

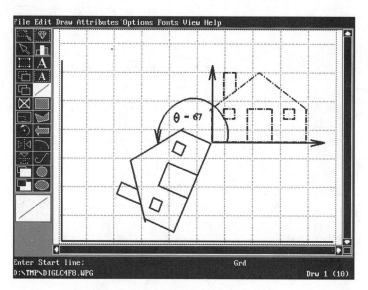

Figure 4.7. Result of the rotation operation applied to the house.

Revised 2-D Translation Transformation

Equation 4.17 shows the new homogeneous translation matrix T_{xy}:

$$T_{xy} = \begin{bmatrix} 1 & 0 & 0 \\ 0 & 1 & 0 \\ T_x & T_y & 1 \end{bmatrix}$$

Figure 4.8 illustrates the result of the translation operation on the figure of the house polygon.

Extending Device Coordinate Transformations to 3-D Space

Many of the mathematical concepts derived for 2-D transformations can be applied to 3-D transformations. However, the mapping from 3-D coordinates to a 2-D viewing surface requires additional algorithms.

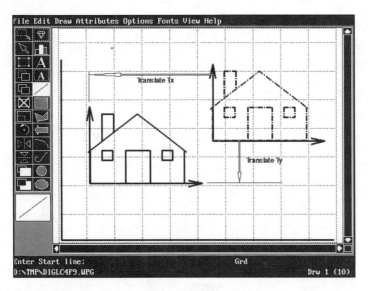

Figure 4.8. Result of the translation operation applied to the house.

You can represent the 3-D coordinate system as three orthogonal—that is, perpendicular—planes. Concepts such as perspective viewing and right-handed and left-handed orientations are based on long-established mathematical conventions. Applying the same concepts of homogeneous coordinates in 2-D space to 3-D space introduces a fourth row and column to the transformation matrix. The arbitrary point P(x,y) in 2-D space becomes P(x,y,z) in 3-D space. Now, the general-purpose 3-D transformation matrix becomes a 4x4 matrix that is expressed by the following mapping (Equation 4.18):

$$\begin{bmatrix} A & B & C \\ D & E & F \\ G & H & I \end{bmatrix} \longrightarrow \begin{bmatrix} A & B & C & 0 \\ D & E & F & 0 \\ G & H & I & 0 \\ L & M & N & 1 \end{bmatrix}$$

Although a complete implementation of 3-D viewing transformations is beyond the scope of the DIGL model presented in this book, the 3-D transformation matrices are included for reference. The 3-D applications presented in Chapter 5, "A Design Prototype for Device-Independent Plotting Libraries," are based loosely on the material in this section.

Scaling

To scale the point P(x,y,z) to a new point P'(x',y',z'), use the following 4x4 scaling transformation matrix (Equation 4.19):

$$[x', y', z', 1] = [x, y, z, 1] \begin{bmatrix} A & 0 & 0 & 0 \\ 0 & E & 0 & 0 \\ 0 & 0 & I & 0 \\ 0 & 0 & 0 & 1 \end{bmatrix}$$

As in 2-D, proportional scaling is accomplished by setting A, E, and I to the same value.

Rotation

The point P(x,y,z) can be rotated to a new point P'(x',y',z') around either the *x*-, *y*-, or *z*-axis. The three 4x4 rotation transformation matrices that are required are shown in Equation 4.20:

$$R_x(\theta) = \begin{bmatrix} 1 & 0 & 0 & 0 \\ 0 & \cos(\theta) & -\sin(\theta) & 0 \\ 0 & \sin(\theta) & \cos(\theta) & 0 \\ 0 & 0 & 0 & 1 \end{bmatrix}$$

$$R_y(\theta) = \begin{bmatrix} \cos(\theta) & 0 & \sin(\theta) & 0 \\ 0 & 1 & 0 & 0 \\ -\sin(\theta) & 0 & \cos(\theta) & 0 \\ 0 & 0 & 0 & 1 \end{bmatrix}$$

$$R_z(\theta) = \begin{bmatrix} \cos(\theta) & -\sin(\theta) & 0 & 0 \\ \sin(\theta) & \cos(\theta) & 0 & 0 \\ 0 & 0 & 1 & 0 \\ 0 & 0 & 0 & 1 \end{bmatrix}$$

To develop a planar composite matrix for rotation is not so straightforward as you might think. This is because, unlike the 2-D rotations, 3-D rotations are not commutative.

Shearing

To shear the point P(x,y,z) to a new point P'(x',y',z'), use the following 4x4 shearing transformation matrix (Equation 4.21):

$$[x', y', z', 1] = [x, y, z, 1] \begin{bmatrix} 1 & B & C & 0 \\ D & 1 & F & 0 \\ G & H & 1 & 0 \\ 0 & 0 & 0 & 1 \end{bmatrix}$$

The off-diagonal terms are used to produce the shearing effect.

Translation

To translate the point P(x,y,z) to a new point P'(x',y',z'), use the following 4x4 translation transformation matrix (Equation 4.22):

$$[x', y', z', 1] = [x, y, z, 1] \begin{bmatrix} 1 & 0 & 0 & 0 \\ 0 & 1 & 0 & 0 \\ 0 & 0 & 1 & 0 \\ L & M & N & 1 \end{bmatrix}$$

Translation is accomplished through (L,M,N).

Reflection

To reflect the point P(x,y,z) to a new point P'(x',y',z'), use the following 4x4 reflection transformation matrix (Equation 4.23):

$$[x', y', z', 1] = [x, y, z, 1] \begin{bmatrix} R_x & 0 & 0 & 0 \\ 0 & R_y & 0 & 0 \\ 0 & 0 & R_z & 1 \\ 0 & 0 & 0 & 1 \end{bmatrix}$$

As with 2-D reflection, setting values Rx, Ry, or Rz to −1 reflects the point through the YZ, XZ, and XY planes, respectively.

Implementing Polygon Transformations

The following steps describe the general procedure for implementing any of the transformation processes that I have discussed so far:

1. Set the values in the corresponding transformation matrix.

2. Multiply the input matrix by the transformation matrix.

3. Return the modified matrix.

Generalized Matrix Multiplication Formula

Recall from algebra or analytic geometry that, if matrix A is a 2x2 matrix, and matrix B is a 1x2 matrix, the multiplication BA is defined, but AB is not. Matrix multiplication, in general, is not commutative. For example, if A is an mxn matrix and B is an nxk matrix as in Equation 4.24:

$$
A = \begin{bmatrix}
a_{11} & a_{12} & \ldots & a_1n \\
a_{21} & a_{22} & \ldots & a_2n \\
\ldots & \ldots & \ldots & \ldots \\
a_{m1} & a_{m2} & \ldots & a_{mn}
\end{bmatrix}
$$

$$
B = \begin{bmatrix}
b_{11} & b_{12} & \ldots & b_1k \\
b_{21} & b_{22} & \ldots & b_2k \\
\ldots & \ldots & \ldots & \ldots \\
b_{n1} & b_{n2} & \ldots & b_{nk}
\end{bmatrix}
$$

the multiplication of AB results in a new mxk matrix R. The following is a genreal definition of the matrix multiplication procedure (Equation 4.25):

$$
AB = R = \begin{bmatrix}
\sum_{i=1}^{n} a_{1i}*b_{i1} & \sum_{i=1}^{n} a_{1i}*b_{i2} & \ldots & \sum_{i=1}^{n} a_{1i}*b_{ik} \\
\sum_{i=1}^{n} a_{2i}*b_{i1} & \sum_{i=1}^{n} a_{2i}*b_{i2} & \ldots & \sum_{i=1}^{n} a_{2i}*b_{ik} \\
\ldots & \ldots & \ldots & \ldots \\
\sum_{i=1}^{n} a_{mi}*b_{i1} & \sum_{i=1}^{n} a_{mi}*b_{i2} & \ldots & \sum_{i=1}^{n} a_{mi}*b_{ik}
\end{bmatrix}
$$

Transform Implementation in C

The following C code fragment analysis illustrates some of the fundamentals for the 2-D scale transformation:

```
#define MAXRSIZE          40        /* Maximum row size of polygons    */

typedef struct twodmatrix_st       /* Structure for 2-D matrix row,col*/
  {
    int    MatRows;                 /* Number of rows in matrix        */
    int    MatCols;                 /* Number of columns in matrix     */
    double melem[MAXRSIZE][3];      /* First line table item           */
  } TWODMATRIX;
```

The first portion of this code defines a template for a 2-D matrix data type. It is arbitrarily set for a maximum number of 40 rows (#define MAXRSIZE 40). From this point, all functions that require matrix operations use this typedef.

```
void MatrixScale(Mata,Smat,Mres,Xscale,Yscale)
TWODMATRIX *Mata;
TWODMATRIX *Smat;
TWODMATRIX *Mres;
double Xscale;
double Yscale;
{
  int RowIdx;
  int ColIdx;
  for (RowIdx=0;RowIdx<(*Smat).MatRows;RowIdx++
    {
     for(ColIdx=0;ColIdx<(*Smat).MatCols;ColdIdx++
       {
        (*Smat).melem[RowIdx][ColIdx]=0;
       }
    }
      (*Smat).melem[0][0]=Xscale;
      (*Smat).melem[1][1]=Yscale;

      MatrixMul2D(Mata,Smat,Mres);

}/* End of MatrixScale */
```

83

The matrix scale (MatrixScale) routine performs these two basic functions:

■ It initializes the values of Sx and Sy—elements 0,0 and 1,1—in the scaling transformation matrix (Smat) to the values passed in as Xscale and Yscale.

■ It calls the matrix multiply routine to multiply the input matrix (Mata) by the scaling transformation matrix (Smat), and returns the scaled result (Mres) to the caller.

```
void MatrixMul2D(MatA,MatB,Mres)
TWODMATRIX *MatA;
TWODMATRIX *MatB;
TWODMATRIX *Mres;
{
      int           ColIdx        ;/* Column index counter           */
      int           RowIdxA       ;/* Row index counter matrix A      */
      int           RowIdxB       ;/* Row index counter matrix B      */

      double        Summation     ;/* Intermediate column summation  */


      for (RowIdxA=0;RowIdxA<(*MatA).MatRows;RowIdxA++)
        {
          for (ColIdx=0;ColIdx<(*MatB).MatCols;ColIdx++)
            {
              Summation=0;
              for (RowIdxB=0;RowIdxB<(*MatB).MatRows;RowIdxB++)
                {
                  Summation =
Summation+((*MatA).melem[RowIdxA][RowIdxB])*
                            ((*MatB).melem[RowIdxB][ColIdx]);
                }
              (*Mres).melem[RowIdxA][ColIdx] = Summation;
            }
        }

      (*Mres).MatRows = (*MatA).MatRows;
      (*Mres).MatCols = (*MatB).MatCols;

}/* End of MatrixMul2D */
```

The matrix multiply (`MatrixMul2D`) routine performs the matrix multiplication described in Equation 4.25. It uses the row index variables—`RowIdxA` and `RowIdxB`—to form summation loops according to the algorithm.

Summary

This chapter explains software engineering techniques in enough detail to enable you to understand the algorithms in the next chapter.

Pseudocode presents constructs common to most programming languages. Pseudocode conventions reduce ambiguous translations.

Differences among compilers and operating systems play a large role in the level of difficulty in adapting large programs for more than one platform. In C, the problem of language extensions is further illustrated by the increasing number of compiler-specific include files.

Various forms of graphics displays are produced by using intermediate algorithms. The basis of 2-D object manipulations ranges from simple vector manipulations to more complex polygon treatments. Then the 2-D concepts are expanded and generalized to form the basis of 3-D wireframe analysis. These algorithms also represent higher-level routines that are built on top of the DIGL.

Now that you understand graphics fundamentals, graphics devices, library structures, and data formats, you can follow the development of most of the DIGL in Chapter 5. A subset of the source code that is required to create a DIGL is developed and used to examine a wide variety of graphics applications, such as numerical data patterns and 2-D and 3-D polygons.

A DESIGN PROTOTYPE FOR DIGL

This chapter implements the device-independent graphics library, presenting many general-purpose algorithms that you need for plotting complex 2- and 3-D data files. The specialized graphics language protocols that are required by various graphics devices are analyzed, with examples of popular language specifications.

The focus here is on developing algorithms for a type of virtual display that is mapped to one of many different types of physical displays. These physical displays vary in their capabilities.

Once the graphics state has been defined, you create a series of low-level graphics primitives to manipulate and control it. Above the primitive layer, you add a set of higher-level graphics macros and support libraries. You now are building a library of several functions that are needed for the more common graphics applications. The support libraries contain a set of functions that read the graphics parameter file introduced in Chapter 3, "The Graphics Application Environment." After all the lower levels of the DIGL are developed, you can begin to build graphics applications using various combinations of the library functions.

The main advantage of a DIGL is that once your application draws an image on any supported device, you can be assured that the representation on other supported devices is almost identical.

In all the reference detail provided in this chapter and throughout this book, whitespace is used only for readability. Spaces separating formal parameters in functions and expressions have no effect on the outcome. Remember as well that the C language is case-sensitive. Always make sure that upper- and lowercase usage is consistent with the structure of the libraries.

Appendix B, "DIGL Function Reference," summarizes all the functions that are part of the DIGL or support libraries discussed in this book. All other functions are part of the libraries specified by the ANSI C language.

Representing the DIGL Graphics State

The DIGL graphics state consists of several variables and data structures that are used to represent vector and pixel manipulations. The GRASTATE.H `include` file on your DIGL disk contains the entire state as it is implemented in C. GRASTATE.H contains three sections, which represent three different forms of state control.

DIGL Graphics Primitives

One of the fundamental decisions that you must make when you develop a graphics state representation is what type of low-level graphics operations is needed. The graphics state exists somewhere between Layers 2 and 3 (refer to Chapter 1, "Architectures, Language, and Applications," Figure 1.4).

The following code is the first section of the DIGL graphics state control file, GRASTATE.H. The variables that are part of this file are used to describe the state of a graphics application during execution.

```
*=========================================================================
==     Graphics State and device primitive keyword definitions...    ==
=========================================================================*/

/*===================== graphics primitive ========================*/

enum   PRIMITIVE {
                  GMOV=1,   /*primitive move instruction     */
                  GDRA,     /*primitive draw instruction     */
                  GPEN,     /*primitive pen select instruction*/
                  GINI,     /*primitive graphics initialize  */
                  LINE,     /*primitive graphics line type   */
                  GCLR,     /*primitive clear graphics       */
                  BELL,     /*primitive graphics/crt beeper  */
                  FOCO,     /*primitive foreground color     */
                  BKCO,     /*primitive background color     */
                  CMIX,     /*primitive color mix            */
```

```
                    REFL,       /*primitive solid rectangular fill*/
                    FTYP,       /*primitive polygon fill type    */
                    LWID        /*primitive line width           */
        };
```

In this case, I made the arbitrary decision to represent the graphics primitives with four-letter mnemonics. So far I have defined 13 different primitives as numeric constants. Their specific values are of no importance as long as each one is a unique number code. When these primitives are used later in this chapter, only their four-letter names are used as identifiers.

DIGL Device Driver Codes

Once you define which primitives will be supported—that is, defined as part of the system—you must decide which graphics devices will be by the graphics applications. The following code is the second section of the DIGL graphics state file, GRASTATE.H. It indicates the syntax used to define all the graphics devices that an application can use to draw the graphics image.

```
/*================= graphic device identification  =================*/

enum DEVICETYPE {
                    HPGL=1,     /*general purpose hp graph plot  */
                    VGACOLOR,   /*ibm pc vga color graphics      */
                    VGABW,      /*ibm pc vga black/white graphics*/
                    EGACOLOR,   /*ibm pc ega color               */
                    EGABW,      /*ibm pc ega black/white graphics*/
                    CGACOLOR,   /*ibm pc cga color graphics      */
                    CGABW,      /*ibm pc cga black/white graphics*/
                    HERCULES,   /*ibm pc cga hercules black/white*/
                    DOSVIDEO,   /*DOS video device               */
                    SUNVIDEO,   /*Sun SPARC station video        */
                    POSTSCRIPT /*postscript laser device         */
        };
```

As with names of primitives, I use arbitrary names for the devices for which I intend to write driver code. In this case, only four different types of graphics devices are defined—HPGL, DOSVIDEO, SUNVIDEO and POSTSCRIPT. The IBM PC uses several different types of graphics adapters—VGACOLOR, HERCULES, and so on—that are supported by most compilers. In this version of the video driver, they are considered subtypes of DOSVIDEO.

DIGL Graphics State Data Structures

In the last section of the graphics state, variables and data structures are used to control the information that is needed from one graphics operation to the next. This keeps interface calls between functions as simple as possible.

The following code is the third section of the graphics state control file, GRASTATE.H. It identifies the data structures and variables that the graphics application uses at runtime for the status and control of execution states.

```
/*============ graphics state parameters and data items ============*/

#define        PZERO      0   /*parameter selection constant   */
#define        PONE       1   /*parameter selection constant   */
#define        PTWO       2   /*parameter selection constant   */
#define        PTHREE     3   /*parameter selection constant   */
#define        PFOUR      4   /*parameter selection constant   */
#define        COLORLEN   32  /*max length of color name       */
#define        MAXCOLORS  17  /*maximum number of colors       */

        int        devtype      ;/*current device type           */
        int        lorigin      ;/*label origin-indicates position */
        int        maxpens      ;/*max colors selectable for device*/
        int        isotropic    ;/*indicates 'show' primitive    */
        int        filesnap     ;/*routes graphics protocol to file*/
        int        bitmap       ;/*indicates device is bit mapped */
        int        hardinit     ;/*bypass init during program spawn*/

        double     grid_mapx[3] ;/*min/max x grid parameters     */
        double     grid_mapy[3] ;/*min/max y grid parameters     */
        double     view_mapx[3] ;/*min/max x viewport select     */
        double     view_mapy[3] ;/*min/max y viewport select     */
        double     show_mapx[3] ;/*min/max x isotropic viewport  */
        double     show_mapy[3] ;/*min/max y isotropic viewport  */
        double     absol_mapx[3];/*total min/max x dimension     */
        double     absol_mapy[3];/*total min/max y dimension     */
        double     user_mapx[3] ;/*used in windowing for x scaling */
        double     user_mapy[3] ;/*used in windowing for y scaling */
        double     lastx        ;/*last x vector in user units    */
        double     lasty        ;/*last y vector in user units    */
        double     lscaledx     ;/*last x vector after scaling    */
        double     lscaledy     ;/*last y vector after scaling    */
        double     cscaledx     ;/*current x vector after scaling */
```

```
double      cscaledy      ;/*current y vector after scaling   */
double      ratiox        ;/*used in isotropic scaling        */
double      ratioy        ;/*used in isotropic scaling        */
double      iso_factx     ;/*isotropic x scaling constant     */
double      iso_facty     ;/*isotropic y scaling constant     */
double      origin[3]     ;/*loc of 0,0 with respect to x,y   */
double      scalexc1      ;/*internal scaling constant        */
double      scalexc2      ;/*internal scaling constant        */
double      scaleyc1      ;/*internal scaling constant        */
double      scaleyc2      ;/*internal scaling constant        */
double      xlabscale     ;/*x axis scale factor for labeling*/
double      ylabscale     ;/*y axis scale factor for labeling*/
double      labwidth      ;/*width of last label              */
double      labheight     ;/*height of last label             */

FILE        *GraphFile    ;/* graphics device stream pointer */

char        pramstring[80] ;/*parameter string post scaling ..*/
char        lastpram[80]   ;/*last parameter string issued    */
char        gratemp[64]    ;/*temporary graphics string       */
char        penorder[60]   ;/*internal plotter color index ref*/

static char NEWLINE[2]={'\n','\0'};/*line terminator sequence */

struct colormap
    {
       char color[COLORLEN];
    } colormap[MAXCOLORS]   ;/*internal color index reference  */

int         gridtype      ;/*plot grid identifier             */
int         graphdevice   ;/*graphics device type             */
int         plinestyle    ;/*plotting device line type        */
int         pfilltype     ;/*plotting device polyfill type    */

char        ctlfile[80]   ;/* current plot control file name */
char        ctlroot[32]   ;/* plot control file root name    */
char        ctlpath[80]   ;/* plot control pathname          */
char        plotfor[COLORLEN] ;/*plot foreground label color  */
char        plotbak[COLORLEN] ;/*plot background color        */
char        plotfont[80]  ;/*default font name                */
char        plotprim[80]  ;/*plot protocol output filename    */

int         outtofile     ;/*controls graphics output to file*/
```

Graphics Device Coordinate Representation

The variables `grid_mapx`, `grid_mapy`, `view_mapx`, and `view_mapy` are used to represent the limits of the graphics plotting surface available. They also represent the user-specified portion of the surface that is used for a graphics operation. Figure 5.1 is an example of `grid_map` versus `view_map`.

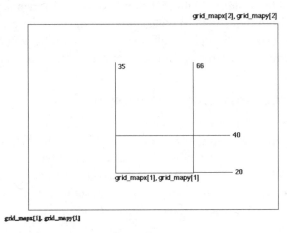

Figure 5.1. An example of `grid_map` *versus* `view_map`.

The `grid_map` array structure represents the absolute limits of the currently selected graphics device. The minimum value is contained in element 1 of each array, and the maximum value is contained in element 2. For example, if the DIGL driver defined an HP plotter as the current graphics device, the contents of `grid_mapx[1]` and `grid_mapy[1]` are values `80` and `320`, respectively. These values represent the lower left corner of the plotter paper. Likewise, the contents of `grid_mapx[2]` and `grid_mapy[2]`—values `10080` and `7520`, respectively—represent the upper right corner of the plotter paper.

If the current graphics device is an IBM PC VGA (16 color) graphics adapter, the values for the lower left corner are `0` and `0`—represented by `grid_mapx[1]` and `grid_mapy[1]`, respectively. The values for upper right corner are `640` and `480`—represented by `grid_mapx[1]` and `grid_mapy[1]`, respectively. The individual graphics drivers are responsible for setting these and other values at initialization.

The `grid_map` variables represent the absolute limits of the drawing area. However, for many graphics applications, you might want to plot a figure in one portion of the viewing area and other figures in other portions of the viewing area.

To accomplish this, represent the current user-selected drawing area in variables view_mapx and view_mapy. As Figure 5.1 shows, the actual viewing area—or *viewport*—is a subset of the absolute grid map.

The grid_map variables differ from device to device. To make the viewport-to-grid transformations device-independent, another convention must be used—a percentage of full scale. As Figure 5.1 shows, you can represent any fraction of a grid map—for example, 35% to 66% along the *x*-axis of the grid, and 20% to 40% along the *y*-axis. Through simple mathematical scaling, you can set the corresponding view_map variables, regardless of the specific graphics device.

Isotropic and Anisotropic Representations

When you draw certain geometric patterns, such as circles or polygon transformations, it is often desirable to represent the *x*- and *y*-axis units of coordinate vectors in *isotropic* units. With isotropic units, the values represent equal distances along the *x*- and *y*-axes. Because the *x*- and *y*-axes often have different maximum ranges, or resolutions, it is necessary to use a constant to adjust values along an axis. This adjustment process is called *aspect ratio control.*

To represent a true circle, the aspect ratio should equal 1. For all graphics devices, however, the aspect ratio is a fraction that usually represents a resolution larger along one axis than along the other. The variables show_mapx, show_mapy, ratiox, ratioy, iso_factx, and iso_facty are used internally by the DIGL to calculate the factors used to create isotropic units.

DIGL provides library functions that enable a user to select isotropic or *anisotropic* (having different values along the axis, not equally spaced) units. Figure 5.2 illustrates the effects of isotropic versus anisotropic units for drawing circles. An ellipse function provided in the DIGL software is used to draw two ellipses. When you draw an ellipse, if the *x* radius and *y* radius values are the same, the figure drawn is a perfect circle. On the left side of Figure 5.2, the ellipse is drawn in anisotropic mode by means of the window function of the DIGL. On the right side of Figure 5.2, the identical call to ellipse was made with isotropic units by means of the show function. (These functions are discussed later in this chapter.)

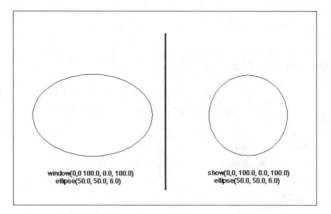

Figure 5.2. Generating ellipses and circles in Windows.

Drawing Conventions

The variables `lastx`, `lasty`, `lscaledx`, `lscaledy`, `cscaledx`, and `cscaledy` are used in the graphics state data structures to provide a single-point history in the DIGL graphics state. The single-point history represents the coordinates of the last vector drawn or moved to. This information can be used for *incremental drawing mode* and *"from to" drawing conventions.*

In incremental drawing, the coordinates of the vector represent an increment from the last point drawn. For example, the incremental vector (56,35) means to move or draw 56 units in the *x* direction by adding 56 to the contents of the last vector, represented by `lastx` in user units and by `lscaledx` in graphics device units. Similarly, the increment in the *y* direction is 35 units.

Some graphics drivers require two sets of vectors that represent a move or draw operation from vector (a,b) to vector (c,d). Because the "from to" convention is not a universal convention, DIGL controls and provides these variables to allow each graphics driver to use them if desired.

Color Conventions

In order to make application code as readable as possible, the DIGL uses descriptive names for colors that you can use. The names of the colors are loaded into the color map data structure, represented in the header file as

```
struct colormap
  {
    char color[COLORLEN];
  } colormap[MAXCOLORS];
```

The current default color names are consistent with the IBM PC color scheme:

```
colormap[1].color  <- CYAN
colormap[2].color  <- GREEN
colormap[3].color  <- BROWN
colormap[4].color  <- YELLOW
colormap[5].color  <- LIGHTRED
colormap[6].color  <- RED
colormap[7].color  <- MAGENTA
colormap[8].color  <- WHITE
colormap[9].color  <- DARKGRAY
colormap[10].color <- LIGHTBLUE
colormap[11].color <- LIGHTGREEN
colormap[12].color <- LIGHTCYAN
colormap[13].color <- GREEN
colormap[14].color <- LIGHTMAGENTA
colormap[15].color <- BLUE
colormap[16].color <- BRIGHTWHITE
```

This mapping takes place at initialization. The maximum length and number of color names is arbitrary. How this information is used depends on the specific graphics driver.

DIGL Parameter Control File Structure

The parameter file system was introduced in Chapter 3, "The Graphics Application Environment." Your DIGL disk includes the parameter file structure and a library of related functions. Here is the parameter control file, VGA.CTL, which is supported by the DIGL. In this example, the graphics application is routed to the VGA color graphics adapter for an IBM PC.

```
Contents Of VGA.CTL

;
;                       Scientific Concepts, Inc
;                           (c) 1989-93 SCI
;
GRAPDEV     //VGACOLOR
OUTTOFIL    //FALSE                          ;plot to file ?
PLOTFI      //VOID                           ;plot output file
;
GRIDTYPE    //2                              ;grid selection
LINESTYLE   //1                              ;line type setting
FILLTYPE    //1                              ;polygon fill setting
;
BAKCOL      //BLACK                          ;video background
color
FORCOL      //CYAN                           ;plot labeling color
```

Low-Level Primitive Library

So far you have defined a graphics state that consists of the parameter definitions of the low-level graphics operations that you want to perform. You have also defined the names of the graphics devices that are supported by this version of the DIGL. Now, you define and construct the low-level graphics functions that convert, translate, and route graphics operations to the graphics drivers.

The functional interface to the routines is consistent and simple. Each graphics operation requires very little actual code. Because the graphics parameters are already defined, the graphics primitive performs the conversion from user units to device units, and it routes the primitive command to the appropriate driver.

Here is the pseudocode for the primitive routine for a graphics draw operation:

Begin Draw(xval : float , yval : float)

    Call scale(xval, yval) *to convert to device units*
    if graphics device is bit-mapped CRT, then

> *convert integer device units to strings*
> *store result in internal buffer*
end if

call graphics driver(GDRA)

End Draw

Devices that are not bit-mapped, such as HPGL and PostScript drivers, might require an alternate string representation of the scaled values for output.

The following is an implementation of the Draw pseudocode in C. It is contained in the primitive library on your DIGL disk.

```
*+=============================================================================
==    void draw(double xval,double yval) : function to draw on the    ==
==    graphics page to the specified coordinates assuming pen down    ==
==    status...                                                       ==
==                                                                    ==
== Argument list:  double xval      user units in x direction         ==
==                 double yval      user units in y direction         ==
==                                                                    ==
== Return value:   void                                               ==
==                                                                    ==
== Author: Scientific Concepts, Inc.                                  ==
== Copyright (c) 1990-1993. All rights reserved worldwide.            ==
=============================================================================*/
void draw(xval, yval)
double xval;
double yval;
{

        int         idx         ;/* counter                    */
        int         sx          ;/* scaled x units             */
        int         sy          ;/* scaled y units             */

        char        *ptr        ;/* substring pointer          */
        char        stemp[17]    ;/* temporary string          */

        scale(xval,yval,&sx,&sy);
```

```
    if (! bitmap)
      {
        intstring(&sx,gratemp);
        intstring(&sy,stemp);
        ptr=gratemp;
        for (idx=0;idx<=15;idx++)
          *(ptr+idx+16)=stemp[idx];
        gratemp[34]='\0';
      }

    gracur(GDRA);

}/* end of draw */
```

Most of the primitive routines fit this profile. The graphics primitives used in the lower layers of the DIGL are contained in the file PRIMLIB.C. The corresponding file PRIMLIB.H contains the function prototypes needed to resolve forward-referencing when these functions are called from other modules. Each function is described in this section.

forecolor

Name

forecolor(char colstr[]) selects a color for the foreground in graphics mode.

Synopsis

```
void forecolor(colstr)
char colstr[];
```

Description

This function selects a color for the foreground in graphics mode from one of the colormap color names that are currently defined. If the internal names (16 total) do not match the color that the user requests, pen 2 is used by default.

Diagnostics

>   The formal string argument (`colstr`) is not modified.

>   Not all graphics devices support the maximum number of pens defined by the internal color map. In each case, the individual graphics driver decides how this exception is handled. For example, the HPGL driver pegs the maximum pen number selected at 8, which is the maximum number of pens in the carousel of an HP7550A. In the case of other plotters with six or fewer pens, the plotter might either keep the current pen or use *no pen* if the number is higher than what is permitted.

See Also

```
backcolor(char colstr[])
```

backcolor

Name

>   void `backcolor(char colstr[])` selects a color for the background in graphics mode.

Synopsis

```
void backcolor(colstr)
char colstr[];
```

Description

>   This function selects a color for the background in graphics mode from one of the internal `colormap` color names that are currently defined. If the internal names (16 total) do not match the color requested by the user, pen 2 is used.

Diagnostics

>   The formal string argument (`colstr`) is not modified.

Not all graphics devices support the maximum number of pens defined by the internal color map. In each case, the individual graphics driver decides how this exception is handled. For example, the HPGL driver pegs the maximum pen number selected at 8, which is the maximum number of pens in the carousel of an HP7550A. In the case of other plotters with six or fewer pens, the plotter might either keep the current pen or use *no pen* if the number is higher than what is permitted. This option has no meaning for devices that are not bit-mapped—for example, digital plotters. The background in that case is the color of the paper used.

See Also

```
forecolor(colstr)
```

linewidth

Name

> void linewidth(int width) sets the width of the line.

Synopsis

```
void linewidth(width)
int width;
```

Description

> This function is an integer code used by each driver to set the line width in pixel units that are unique to each driver.

Diagnostics

> The formal integer argument (width) is not modified.

This option is not recognized for pen plotters or for any other device with a fixed number of pens.

See Also

    linetype(style)

linetype

Name

void linetype(int style) selects line style type.

Synopsis

    void linetype(style)
    int style;

Description

This function selects the line style type from four internally defined line styles, or types, according to the following convention:

Integer Code	Line Produced
1	Solid line
2	Dotted line
3	Dashed line
4	Dotted and dashed line

Diagnostics

The formal integer argument (style) is not modified.

 NOTE   Line style codes outside the range of 1 to 4 are set to the minimum and maximum codes that are defined in the body of the primitive function.

See Also

    linewidth(width)

frame

Name

frame draws a box around the viewport area that is currently selected.

Synopsis

```
void frame(void)
```

Description

This function draws a box in the current line style, color, and width around the viewport area that is currently defined. frame assumes that the graphics device has been initialized. The graphics cursor is moved first to the lower corner of the user-selected portion (user_mapx, user_mapy) of the maximum plotter area that is available for the graphics device.

Diagnostics

This function requires no parameters.

This function requires that the DIGL graphics state be initialized. Otherwise, the scale and mapping equations are invalid.

See Also

```
window(xmin, xmax, ymin, ymax)
```

pencolor

Name

void pencolor(char colstr[]) selects a color for image drawing in graphics mode.

Synopsis

```
void pencolor(colstr)
char colstr[];
```

Description

This function selects a color for image drawing in graphics mode from one of the `colormap` color names that are currently defined. If the internal names (16 total) do not match the color that the user requests, pen 2 is used.

Diagnostics

The formal string argument (`colstr`) is not modified.

Not all graphics devices support the maximum number of pens defined by the internal color map. In each case, the individual graphics driver decides how this exception is handled. For example, the HPGL driver pegs the maximum pen number selected at 8, which is the maximum number of pens in the carousel of an HP7550A. In the case of other plotters with 6 or fewer pens, the plotter might either keep the current pen or use *no pen* if the number is higher than what is permitted.

See Also

```
forecolor(colstr)
```

show

Name

void show(double xmin, double xmax, double ymin, double ymax) maps the user units into the defined area for subsequent scaling in `move` and `draw` operations.

Synopsis

```
void show(xmin, xmax, ymin, ymax)
double xmin;
double xmax;
double ymin;
double ymax;
```

Description

This function maps the user units into the defined area for subsequent scaling in move and draw operations. Unlike the window primitive, show is designed to force vectors to be equidistant—that is, isotropic—on the *x*- and *y*-axes. This is needed for circles and special graphics options, such as polygon rendering, where equal distance between points is required. All subsequent scaling operations are done with isotropic constants that are calculated from aspect ratio constants. The aspect ratio constants are set independently by each graphics driver.

Diagnostics

The formal arguments are not modified.

If the viewport must be clipped, the *y*-axis viewport is adjusted by the corresponding percentage of clipping on the *x*-axis; the same ratio is applied to the *y*-axis limit. The show primitive is prevented from drawing outside the user-specified viewport.

See Also

```
window(xmin, xmax, ymin, ymax)
viewport(vxmin, vxmax, vymin, vymax)
```

pen

Name

void pen(int xint) directly selects a pen for the graphics device.

Synopsis

```
void pen(xint)
int xint;
```

Description

This function directly selects a pen for the graphics device. The pen code must be in a range consistent with the graphics device driver. The pen code is passed directly to the driver without translation.

Diagnostics

The formal parameter is left unchanged.

As with other pen color operations, the graphics device driver might not support the pen value that the user requests. The device driver overrides this request if it is outside the limits permitted.

See Also

```
forecolor(colstr)
backcolor(colstr)
```

draw

Name

void draw(double xval, double yval) draws a line on the graphics page.

Synopsis

```
void draw(xval, yval)
double xval;
double yval;
```

Description

This function draws a line on the graphics page from current coordinates (lastx, lasty) to the specified coordinates; pen down status is assumed. The formal parameters are specified in user units.

Diagnostics

The formal parameters are left unchanged.

Values outside the range of the window that the user specifies are clipped to the current viewport.

See Also

```
move(double xval, double yval)
```

gclear

Name

    `void gclear(void)` clears the entire graphics display.

Synopsis

```
void gclear(void)
```

Description

    This function clears the entire graphics display of all image data. The current background color remains.

Diagnostics

    No other change is made to the DIGL graphics state.

With devices that are not bit-mapped—for example, pen plotters—this function issues a page eject, which the specific device might or might not support.

See Also

```
ginit()
```

imove

Name

    `void imove(double xincr, double yincr)` moves the graphics cursor incrementally.

Synopsis

```
void imove(xincr, yincr)
double xincr;
double yincr;
```

Description

This function moves the virtual graphics cursor on the graphics page to the specified coordinates, assuming pen up (no draw) status. However, the move is based on an increment from the current position coordinate (lastx, lasty). Normally, this option is used for digitizer operations or polygon commands.

Diagnostics

The formal arguments are left unchanged. The internal position coordinates (lastx, lasty) are modified.

Negative values are required for pen movements to the left or down.

See Also

```
void idraw(xincr, yincr)
```

idraw

Name

void idraw(double xincr, double yincr) draws on the graphics page incrementally.

Synopsis

```
void idraw(xincr, yincr)
double xincr;
double yincr;
```

Description

This function draws on the graphics page to the specified coordinates; pen down status is assumed. However, the move is based on an increment from the last *x,y*-coordinate. Normally, this option is intended for digitizer operations or polygon commands.

Diagnostics

The formal arguments are left unchanged. The internal position coordinates (`lastx`, `lasty`) are modified.

Negative values are required for pen movements to the left or down.

See Also

```
void imove(xincr, yincr)
```

move

Name

`void move(double xval, double yval)` moves the graphics cursor to the specified coordinates.

Synopsis

```
void move(xval, yval)
double xval;
double yval;
```

Description

This function moves the graphics cursor to the specified coordinates. The inputs are assumed to be in user units; pen up status is assumed.

Diagnostics

The formal parameters are left unchanged.

In some cases, the graphics drivers remove successive move operations automatically. This is especially true of electromechanical devices, or in cases where the I/O channel is slow—for example, serial interfaces.

See Also

```
void draw(double xval, double yval)
```

ginit

Name

void ginit() initializes a graphics device to a known state.

Synopsis

```
void ginit()
```

Description

This function initializes a graphics device to a known state. The primitive sets the viewport to the maximum area defined for the device. It sets the window to a default of the same region of coverage. The line style is set to solid.

Diagnostics

No formal parameters are required, but this routine does initialize the graphics state to common default values.

This routine is automatically called during parameter file initialization to set the internal scale parameters. User units are reestablished by the application with subsequent viewport and window calls.

See Also

```
viewport(zero, maxnum, zero, maxnum)
window(zero, maxnum, zero, maxnum)
move(zero, zero)
linetype(intstyle)
```

parseparm

Name

void parseparm(int parnum) parses a string and adds to the paramstring for output to a graphics device.

Synopsis

```
void parseparm(parnum)
int parnum;
```

Description

This function parses a string and adds to the paramstring for output to a graphics device. A globally visible buffer (gratemp) is used to keep track of the string equivalent of each parameter that is required by a graphics primitive. The parameters are contained in gratemp in 16-character blocks. This routine removes the parameter block specified by parnum, and appends it to the current parameter buffer (paramstring).

Diagnostics

The formal parameter is not modified by this routine.

The user should not call this routine directly. The contents of paramstring should not be modified or referenced directly by application routines.

See Also

```
void gracur()
```

gracur

Name

gracur(int primitive) selects and sends a graphics primitive to a device driver.

Synopsis

```
void gracur(primitive)
int primitive;
```

Description

This function selects and sends a graphics primitive to a device driver by using an integer code for a primitive. The graphics state defines the primitive codes in the GRASTATE.H file.

Diagnostics

The formal argument for the graphics primitive is not changed.

The graphics device currently selected by the application might not support the primitive code that the formal argument identifies.

See Also

parseparm

viewport

Name

void viewport(double xmin, double xmax, double ymin, double ymax) defines a subset of the drawing area.

Synopsis

```
void viewport(xmin, xmax, ymin, ymax)
double xmin;
double xmax;
double ymin;
double ymax;
```

Description

This function defines a subset of the drawing area that the user defines for scaling and coordinate control. The resulting graphics image is restricted to this area by clipping that is built into the equation for scaling. The formal parameters represent the drawing area as a percentage of the full scale.

Diagnostics

Formal parameters are left unchanged, but they should be in the range of 0 to 100, where xmin is less than xmax, and ymin is less than ymax.

> Values less than 0 percent or greater than 100 percent are ignored. Each call to viewport automatically resets the active window.

See Also

```
window(double xmin, double xmax, double ymin, double ymax)
scale(double userx, double usery, int scalex, int scaley)
```

window

Name

```
void window(double xmin, double xmax, double ymin, double ymax)
```
maps the user units into the defined area.

Synopsis

```
void window(xmin, xmax, ymin, ymax)
double xmin;
double xmax;
double ymin;
double ymax;
```

Description

This function maps the user units into the defined area for subsequent scaling in graphics operations. The user-specified minimum and maximum values can be any legal floating-point number; this includes the full range of negative values.

Diagnostics

The formal parameters are left unchanged. For the minimum and maximum values, xmin is less than xmax, and ymin is less than ymax.

113

The window functions should be called as soon as possible after the viewport is reset.

See Also

```
viewport(double xmin, double xmax, double ymin, double ymax)
scale(double userx, double usery, int scalex, int scaley)
```

scale

Name

```
void scale(double userx, double usery, int scalex, int scaley)
```
scales user input.

Synopsis

```
void scale(userx, usery, scalex, scaley)
double userx;
double usery;
int *scalex;
int *scaley;
```

Description

This function takes input user units (userx, usery) and scales it consistent with the limits of the viewport and window. The calculated values are restricted to the limits—that is, the minimum and maximum ranges—of the *x*- and *y*-axes. This restriction is one method for clipping the supplied values. The scaled values are returned as (scalex, scaley).

Diagnostics

The formal parameters scalex, scaley are changed based on current viewport and window parameters.

Scale calculations are based on the constant scale factors that are calculated at each viewport setting. If a graphics primitive is called after a viewport change and prior to a window or show function, unpredictable results may occur.

See Also

```
void move(double xval, double yval)
void draw(double xval, double yval)
```

digbeep

Name

    void `digbeep()` sounds the beeper of the current graphics device.

Synopsis

```
void digbeep()
```

Description

This function sounds the beeper—an audible alarm—of the current graphics device. Each graphics driver is responsible for implementing this command.

Diagnostics

No formal parameters are required.

Some graphics devices do not support this command. It is an audible alarm for the purpose of alerting an operator.

See Also

```
ginit()
```

MACROLIB.C

Now that you have a set of basic graphics primitives, you can build higher-level routines on top of them.

arc

Drawing an arc is a simple matter of converting angle information supplied in degrees to Cartesian coordinates. You must specify the resolution of the arc to determine how smooth the appearance should be. The term *segment* refers to the number of degrees of resolution required to subdivide the arc. For example, Figure 5.3 shows an arc of 180 degrees—in other words, a semicircle—with varying degrees of resolution. The degree of resolution is defined by the *segment size.*

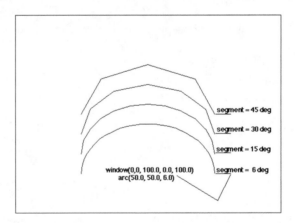

Figure 5.3. Examples of arc drawing.

Name

```
void arc(double centerx, double centery, double radius, double
startang, double stopang, double segment) draws an arc centered at
(centerx, centery).
```

Synopsis

```
void arc(centerx, centery, radius, startang, stopang,
    segment)
double centerx;
```

```
double centery;
double radius;
double startang;
double stopang;
double segment;
```

Description

This function draws an arc centered at (`centerx`, `centery`). The radius is in user units. Degrees are used for the start angle (`startang`), stop angle (`stopang`), and segment size (`segment`). The segment size defines the resolution of the arc.

Diagnostics

The formal parameters are left unchanged. The graphics cursor is assumed to be at the center.

Isotropic units should be used to avoid circles that are egg-shaped.

See Also

```
void circle(double radius, double segment)
void ellipse(Xradius, Yradius, Segment)
```

ellipse

The algorithm for the ellipse function is based on multiple calls to the `arc` function.

Name

`void ellipse(double Xradius, double Xradius, double segment)` draws an ellipse at the current position.

Synopsis

```
void ellipse(Xradius, Yradius, Segment)
double Xradius;
double Yradius;
double Segment;
```

Description

This function draws an ellipse at the current position. The `segment size` parameter defines the resolution of the arc used. Unlike the `circle` macro, this routine does not assume or require isotropic units (see the `show` function).

Diagnostics

The formal parameters are left unchanged.

> The size of the `segment` parameter determines how much time is required to generate the ellipse.

See Also

```
void circle(double radius, double segment)
void arc(double centerx, double centery, double radius, double
startang, double stopang, double segment)
```

circle

The algorithm for the `circle` function is based on multiple calls to the `arc` function.

Name

```
void circle(double radius, double segment)
```
draws a circle.

Synopsis

```
void circle(radius, segment)
double radius;
double segment;
```

Description

This function draws a circle that is centered at the current graphics cursor position. The radius is in user units. The segment size (`segment`) defines the resolution of the arc.

Diagnostics

The formal parameters are left unchanged. Isotropic units are used to avoid eggs for circles.

The size of the `segment` parameter determines how much time is required to generate the circle.

See Also

```
void arc(double centerx, double centery, double radius, double
startang, double stopang, double segment)
```

box

Name

`void box(width, height)` draws a box.

Synopsis

```
void box(width, height)
double width;
double height;
```

Description

This function draws a box whose width and height are specified by the user. The last user coordinates of *x,y* are at the lower left corner of the box. The graphics cursor is positioned at the lower left corner of the box when the drawing is completed.

Diagnostics

The formal parameters are left unchanged.

If the coordinates of the current graphics cursor (`lastx`, `lasty`) are near the borders of the viewing area, the box is clipped along the edges.

119

See Also

```
frame()
```

rectgrid

Grids are commonly used as backgrounds. They make it easier to read graph data that is in the form of linear plots. Figure 5.4. shows several forms of linear grids that the DIGL provides.

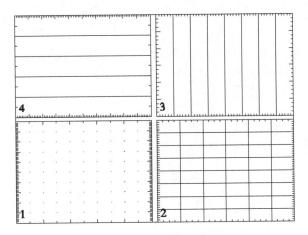

Figure 5.4. Examples of linear grids.

Name

> void rectgrid(int xmajor, int xminor, int ymajor, int yminor, int gridtype, int evenwindow) draws a rectangular grid.

Synopsis

```
void rectgrid(xmajor, xminor, ymajor, yminor, gridtype,
    evenwindow)
int xmajor;
int xminor;
int ymajor;
int yminor;
int gridtype;
int evenwindow;
```

Description

This function draws a rectangular grid within the specified viewport. Ticks are spaced automatically within the viewport to accommodate grid labeling. This function has a built-in feature that enables you to alternate the directions in which the ticks are drawn. It draws tick marks from left to right in one direction, and from right to left in the other direction. On completion, `rectgrid` also resets the window to its initial values.

Diagnostics

The formal parameters are left unchanged.

The formal parameters `xmajor`, `xminor`, `ymajor`, and `yminor` must be greater than or equal to 1 in order to prevent division by zero.

See Also

```
void polargrid(xmajor, xminor, ymajor, yminor, segment)
```

polargrid

Polar grids are commonly used as backgrounds. They make it easier to read graph data that is in the form of polar plots. Figure 5.5 shows a form of a polar grid that the DIGL provides.

Name

```
void polargrid(int xmajor, int xminor, int ymajor, int yminor,
double segment) draws a polar grid.
```

Synopsis

```
void polargrid(xmajor, xminor, ymajor, yminor, segment)
int xmajor;
int xminor;
int ymajor;
int yminor;
double segment;
```

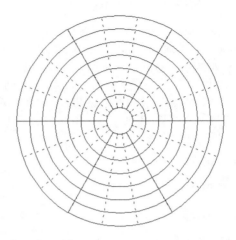

Figure 5.5. Example of a polar grid.

Description

This function draws a polar grid within the selected viewport. The major and minor tick marks are drawn as specified. The `polargrid` function automatically sets up an isotropic display at the specified radial coordinates. It draws the *x*-axis grid lines. With polar grids, the x-axis grid lines are drawn as radial lines from the largest outer circle to the smallest inner circle (see Figure 5.6). Minor ticks are drawn as dotted lines.

Diagnostics

The formal parameters are not modified, but they must be consistent with the viewport area for isotropic units.

The formal parameters `xmajor`, `xminor`, `ymajor`, and `yminor` must be greater than or equal to 1 in order to prevent division by zero.

See Also

```
void circle(double radius, double segment)
void ellipse(Xradius, Yradius, Segment)
```

Extended Application Graphics Support Libraries

DIGL has been extended to provide support for parameter file control and for the 2-D polygon transformations discussed in Chapter 4, "Graphics Visualization." These libraries are discussed in detail in this section.

POLYLIB.H

The polygon support library contains applications that render polygons. This library is used to control and display any graphics figure that can be represented as a polygon. This includes polygons that represent stroke tables for characters or any other user-defined figures.

In this section, I describe the functions of the 2-D polygon library POLYLIB.C and its corresponding header file POLYLIB.H. Listing 5.1 is of the 2-D polygon library data structures as they are defined in the POLYLIB. Hfile.

Listing 5.1. POLYLIB.H library data structures.

```
/*====================================================================
== DIGL polygon primitive library function header and prototypes    ==
==                                                                   ==
==                                                                   ==
== Author: Scientific Concepts, Inc.                                 ==
== Copyright (c) 1990-1993. All rights reserved worldwide.           ==
=====================================================================*/


/*================= Data Structures and Definitions ================*/


#define MAXRSIZE    250            /* maximum row size of polygons   */
#define PI          3.141592654    /* conversion of degrees to radian*/
#define DEGTORAD    PI/180.0       /* conversion of degrees to radian*/
```

continues

123

Listing 5.1. continued

```
/*============================ Macros =============================*/


typedef struct twodmatrix_st     /* structure for 2-D matrix row,col*/
  {
    int    mrows;                /* Number of rows in matrix        */
    int    mcols;                /* Number of columns in matrix     */
    double melem[MAXRSIZE][3];   /* First line table item           */
  } TWODMATRIX;

typedef struct sml2dmatrix_st    /* structure for 2-D matrix row,col*/
  {
    int    mrows;                /* Number of rows in matrix        */
    int    mcols;                /* Number of columns in matrix     */
    double melem[3][3];          /* First line table item           */
  } SML2DMATRIX;


/*====================== Global Variables==========================*/


    static SML2DMATRIX rotatemat=    { 3,3,
                                       0.0, 0.0, 0.0,
                                       0.0, 0.0, 0.0,
                                       0.0, 0.0, 1.0
                                     };

    static SML2DMATRIX translatemat={ 3,3,
                                       1.0, 0.0, 0.0,
                                       0.0, 1.0, 0.0,
                                       0.0, 0.0, 1.0
                                     };

    static SML2DMATRIX scalemat=     { 3,3,
                                       0.0, 0.0, 0.0,
                                       0.0, 0.0, 0.0,
                                       0.0, 0.0, 1.0
                                     };
```

```
        static SML2DMATRIX shearmat=    { 3,3,
                                          0.0, 0.0, 0.0,
                                          0.0, 0.0, 0.0,
                                          0.0, 0.0, 1.0
                                        };

        static SML2DMATRIX reflectmat=  { 3,3,
                                          0.0, 0.0, 0.0,
                                          0.0, 0.0, 0.0,
                                          0.0, 0.0, 1.0
                                        };


/*====================== Function Prototypes =======================*/

int getpoly()                   ;/* read polygon data file into mat*/
void drawipoly()                ;/* draw current poly in increment */
void drawapoly()                ;/* draw current poly in absolute  */
void centerpoly()               ;/* center current polygon         */
void matrixrotat()              ;/* 2-D matrix rotation            */
void matrixtrans()              ;/* 2-D matrix translation         */
void matrixscale()              ;/* 2-D matrix scale               */
void matrixreflect()            ;/* 2-D matrix reflection          */
void matrixshear()              ;/* 2-D matrix shear               */
void mamul2D()                  ;/* General purpose matrix multiply*/
void framepoly()                ;/* find min/max extents of polygon*/
void atoipoly()                 ;/* convert from absolute to incr. */
```

POLYLIB.C

The following functions manipulate polygons and render graphics images that you can customize at runtime. Customization permits rotation, scaling, and distortions along either the *x*- or the *y*-axis.

125

matrixrotate

Name

void matrixrotate(mata, mares, angle) performs the 2-D matrix rotation operation.

Synopsis

```
void matrixrotate(mata, mares, angle)
TWODMATRIX *mata;
TWODMATRIX *mares;
double angle;
```

Description

This function performs the 2-D matrix rotation operation. The rotation is through a user-specified angle measured in degrees.

Diagnostics

Matrix A (mata) is rotated through an angle; the result is placed in the result matrix (mares). This routine assumes that all the matrices conform to the dimension constraints on matrix multiplication (see Chapter 4, "Graphics Visualization and Transformations").

Pointers to the addresses of these arrays are used. All transformation functions use globally visible transform matrix data in the implementation of transform operations. The operations require matrix multiply operations after the values of the matrix elements are set to 1, 0, or a user-specified value.

See Also

transformmul2D(mata, &rotatemat, mares)

matrixreflect

Name

void matrixreflect(mata, mares, xreflect, yreflect) performs the 2-D matrix reflection operation.

Synopsis

```
void matrixreflect(mata, mares, xreflect, yreflect)
TWODMATRIX *mata;
TWODMATRIX *mares;
int xreflect;
int yreflect;
```

Description

This function performs the 2-D matrix reflection operation. The axis selections (`xreflect`, `yreflect`) are specified by the user. These values must be set to 1 or 0—TRUE or FALSE—to determine whether the corresponding reflection operation will be done. Reflection operations can be performed independently on the *x*-axis or the *y*-axis.

Diagnostics

Matrix A (`mata`) is reflected about the specified axis; the result is placed in the result matrix (`mares`). This routine assumes that all the matrices conform to the dimension constraints on matrix multiplications (see Chapter 4).

Pointers to the addresses of these arrays are used. All transformation functions use the globally visible transform matrix data in the subsequent matrix multiply operations.

See Also

```
transformmul2D(mata, &rotatemat, mares)
```

matrixshear

Name

void `matrixshear(mata, mares, xshear, yshear)` performs the 2-D matrix shear operation.

Synopsis

```
void matrixshear(mata, mares, xshear, yshear)
TWODMATRIX *mata;
TWODMATRIX *mares;
double xshear;
double yshear;
```

Description

This function performs the 2-D matrix shear operation. The shear values (xshear, yshear) are specified by the user. Shear operations can be performed independently on the *x*-axis or the *y*-axis.

Diagnostics

Matrix A (mata) sheared as specified. The result is placed in the result matrix (mares). This routine assumes that all the matrices are compatible with dimension constraints on matrix multiplications (see Chapter 4).

Pointers to the addresses of these arrays are used. All transformation functions use the globally visible transform matrix data in the subsequent matrix multiply operations.

See Also

```
transformmul2D(mata, &rotatemat, mares)
```

matrixtranslate

Name

void matrixtranslate(mata, mares, xtrans, ytrans) performs the 2-D matrix translation operation.

Synopsis

```
void matrixtranslate(mata, mares, xtrans, ytrans)
TWODMATRIX *mata;
TWODMATRIX *mares;
double xtrans;
double ytrans;
```

Description

This function performs the 2-D matrix translation operation. The translation values (xtrans, ytrans) are specified by the user. Translation operations can be performed independently on the *x*-axis or *y*-axis.

Diagnostics

Matrix A (mata) is translated as specified. The result is placed in the result matrix (mares). This routine assumes that all the matrices conform to the dimension constraints on matrix multiplications (see Chapter 4).

Pointers to the addresses of these arrays are used. All transformation functions use the globally visible transform matrix data in the subsequent matrix multiply operations.

See Also

```
transformmul2D(mata, &rotatemat, mares)
```

matrixscale

Name

```
void matrixscale(mata, mares, xscale, yscale) performs the 2-D
matrix scaling operation.
```

Synopsis

```
void matrixscale(mata, mares, xscale, yscale)
TWODMATRIX *mata;
TWODMATRIX *mares;
double xscale;
double yscale;
```

Description

This function performs the 2-D matrix scaling operation. The translation values (xscale, yscale) are specified by the user. Scaling operations can be performed independently on the *x*-axis or the *y*-axis.

Diagnostics

> Matrix A (`mata`) is scaled as specified. The result is placed in the result matrix (`mares`). This routine assumes that all the matrices conform to the dimension constraints on matrix multiplications (see Chapter 4).

> Pointers to the addresses of these arrays are used. All transformation functions use the globally visible transform matrix data in the subsequent matrix multiply operations.

See Also

```
transformmul2D(mata, &rotatemat, mares)
```

transformmul2D

Name

> void `transformmul2D(mata, matb, mares)` performs a specialized 2-D matrix multiplication operation.

Synopsis

```
void transformmul2D(mata, matb, mares)
TWODMATRIX *mata;
SML2DMATRIX *matb;
TWODMATRIX *mares;
```

Description

> This function performs a specialized 2-D matrix multiplication operation. This function assumes that a 2-D multiplication is to be performed with homogeneous coordinates. It further assumes that the third column of the large input matrix is set to 1.0 before the multiplication.

Diagnostics

> Matrix A (`mata`) is multiplied by matrix B. The result is placed in the result matrix (`mares`). Matrix B must be a square 2x2 homogeneous matrix. This routine assumes that all the matrices conform to the dimension constraints on matrix multiplications (see Chapter 4).

The data of the third column of matrix A are replaced by the constant 1.0 before the multiplication. Pointers to the addresses of these arrays are used. All transformation functions use the globally visible transform matrix data in the subsequent matrix multiply operations.

See Also

```
void matrixscale(mata, mares, xscale, yscale)
```

atoipoly

Name

> void atoipoly(TWODMATRIX *poly,TWODMATRIX *temp) converts a polygon from absolute to incremental coordinates.

Synopsis

```
void atoipoly(poly, temp)
TWODMATRIX *poly;
TWODMATRIX *temp;
```

Description

> This function converts a polygon—specified by the polygon array—in absolute coordinates to a polygon in incremental drawing mode. The algorithm that converts the polygon data to incremental mode redefines each coordinate in the polygon array by subtracting the previous point from the current point for the entire array. The result is placed in the temp array.

Diagnostics

> The original polygon array (poly) is left unchanged.

This function should be used as only a one-time conversion from absolute to incremental coordinates.

See Also

```
int getpoly(fname, poly)
```

framepoly

Name

```
void framepoly(TWODMATRIX *poly, double *xmin, double *xmax,
double *ymin, double *ymax)
```
finds the frame or bounding box of a polygon.

Synopsis

```
void framepoly(poly, xmin, xmax, ymin, ymax)
TWODMATRIX *poly;
double *xmin;
double *xmax;
double *ymin;
double *ymax;
```

Description

This function uses the incremental drawing mode to find the frame or bounding box of a polygon. The frame is defined by the upper and lower left corners of the rectangle—it is consistent with the axes of the coordinate system—that would exactly enclose it. This function is used for polygon autoscale features before drawing.

Diagnostics

The frame calculation is based on an origin relative to coordinates (0,0).

The data for the polygon must be in the incremental mode for the algorithm to work.

See Also

```
void atoipoly(TWODMATRIX *poly, TWODMATRIX *temp)
```

centerpoly

Name

void centerpoly(TWODMATRIX *poly, double *centerx, double *centery) finds the geometric center of a polygon.

Synopsis

```
void centerpoly(poly, centerx, centery)
TWODMATRIX *poly;
double *centerx;
double *centery;
```

Description

This function finds the geometric center of a polygon. The coordinates that are returned (centerx, centery) are used in translating polygons to the origin before rotation. This creates a spin-in-place effect.

Diagnostics

The polygon data is left unchanged.

Various transformations affect the coordinates of the geometric center. This routine should be called any time when a transformation is done and you want the coordinates of the new geometric center.

See Also

```
int getpoly(fname, poly)
```

drawapoly

Name

drawapoly(TWODMATRIX *poly) draws a polygon by means of the absolute drawing mode.

Synopsis

```
void drawapoly(poly)
TWODMATRIX *poly;
```

Description

This function draws a polygon from a data file on the graphics screen by means of the absolute drawing mode. The polygon is specified by the `polygon` array. The following conventions are used:

1. The polygon array is 2-D (i,j). i is sized at the value 3. polygon(1,*) is the x-vector, and polygon(2,*) is the y-vector. polygon(3,*) indicates the pen movement.

2. For the pen movement, −1 is move, and +1 is draw.

3. `polysize` indicates the number of three-element vector groups.

Diagnostics

The formal parameter is left unchanged. Polygon data must conform to the format specified in Chapter 4.

The data in this format are not to be used in various 2-D transformation routines—such as scale, translate, rotate, and shear—that are supplied in DIGL.

See Also

```
int getpoly(fname, poly)
void drawipoly(TWODMATRIX *poly)
```

drawipoly

Name

void `drawipoly(TWODMATRIX *poly)` draws a polygon by means of the incremental drawing mode.

Synopsis

```
void drawipoly(poly)
TWODMATRIX *poly;
```

Description

This function draws a polygon from a data file on the graphics screen by means of the incremental drawing mode. The polygon is specified by the polygon array. The following conventions are used:

1. The polygon array is 2-D (i,j). i is sized at the value 3. polygon(1,*) is the x-vector, and polygon(2,*) is the y-vector. polygon(3,*) indicates the pen movement.

2. For the pen movement, -1 is move, and $+1$ is draw.

3. polysize indicates the number of three-element vector groups.

Diagnostics

The formal parameter is left unchanged. Polygon data must conform to the format specified in Chapter 4.

The data in this format are incremental; each vector represents an offset from the previous graphics coordinates.

See Also

```
int getpoly(fname, poly)
void drawapoly(TWODMATRIX *poly)
```

getpoly

Name

```
int getpoly(char fname[], TWODMATRIX *poly) reads a polygon file.
```

Synopsis

```
int getpoly(fname, poly)
char fname[];
TWODMATRIX *ply;
```

Description

This function reads a polygon file from disk into the user-specified polygon matrix (poly).

Diagnostics

The filename (`fname`) that the user specifies must contain all the path information necessary to locate the file. The data are assumed to be in the polygon format specified in Chapter 4.

The DIGL uses a fixed constant (`MAXRSIZE`) for the size of the 2-D polygon array. If the number of points in the polygon data file exceeds this amount, the figure is truncated.

See Also

```
int framepoly()
void drawipoly(TWODMATRIX *poly)
```

PARAMLIB.H

A minimal parameter file support library is used in the graphics applications presented at the end of this chapter. In this section, I describe the functions of the parameter file support library (PARAMLIB.C) and its corresponding header file (PARAMLIB.H). Listing 5.2 is of the parameter file support library data structures as they are defined in the PARAMLIB.H file.

Listing 5.2. PARAMLIB.H library data structures.

```
/*====================================================================
== DIGL Graphics parameter file support library function prototypes ==
==                                                                  ==
== Author: Scientific Concepts, Inc.                                ==
== Copyright (c) 1990-1993. All rights reserved worldwide.          ==
=====================================================================*/

/* Function prototypes defined ...                                  */


void init_plotcom()             ;/* default initialization          */
int keyword()                   ;/* keyword parser                  */
```

```
int get_plotspec()            ;/* read plot control file        */
int initdevice()              ;/* initialize graphics device    */
int graphinit()               ;/* read parameter file and init  */
void graphicsend()            ;/* end graphics operations        */
```

PARAMLIB.C

The following functions are used to read and interpret data supplied in the form of the parameter files discussed in Chapters 3 and 4. The functions provide operations that parse the ASCII parameter files, search for keywords, and convert ASCII values into data types defined in the GRASTATE.H file.

get_plotspec

Name

> int get_plotspec(plotd, plotf, quiet, NewPlot) reads a plot control file.

Synopsis

```
int get_plotspec(plotd, plotf, quiet, NewPlot)
char plotd[];
char plotf[];
int quiet;
int NewPlot;
```

Description

> This function reads and parses a user-specified plot control file specification. This function also initializes the DIGL graphics state based on the contents of the parameter file.
>
> plotd represents the name of the directory in which the parameter file is located.
>
> plotf represents the name of the parameter file.
>
> quiet is a flag that instructs the function to output debug information to the standard output device—normally the CRT or video screen—when it is set to a value greater than zero.

NewPlot instructs the function to initialize the graphics device when its value is greater than zero.

Diagnostics

The formal parameters are left unchanged. A completion code is returned to indicate success or failure of this operation.

The parameter file keywords and delimiters must conform to the format specified in Chapter 4.

See Also

```
int initdevice()
graphinit()
```

keyword

Name

int keyword(NewPlot, srec, syntaxerr) parses a parameter file record.

Synopsis

```
int keyword(NewPlot, srec, syntaxerr)
int NewPlot;
char srec[];
int *syntaxerr;
```

Description

This function parses the user-specified parameter file record and sets the contents of the DIGL graphics state accordingly.

NewPlot instructs the function to initialize the graphics device when its value is greater than zero.

screc represents the current string record read from the parameter file.

syntaxerr is the integer code generated by the function when syntax errors are found in the parameter file.

Diagnostics

The parameter file record string is parsed on each call to keyword. Values are used to reset portions of the DIGL graphics state.

The parameter file keywords and delimiters must conform to the format specified in Chapter 4.

See Also

```
int initdevice()
graphinit()
```

init_plotcom

Name

init_plotcom(NewPlot) initializes variables in the DIGL.

Synopsis

```
void init_plotcom(NewPlot)
int NewPlot;
```

Description

This function initializes critical variables in the DIGL graphics state to control the requirements for graphics or plot applications. NewPlot instructs the function to initialize the graphics device when its value is greater than zero.

Diagnostics

The formal parameter is left unchanged. A few variables of the DIGL graphics state are set initially to default values. The default values are supplied by the init_plotcom function, which is called at the beginning of the parameter file read process. These values are

Output to file	FALSE
Graphics device	VGACOLOR;
Line stype	1
Line type	1

Foreground color	`CYAN`
Background color	`BLACK`
Plot primitive file	`DIGL.OUT`
Color map	`DIGL 16-color map (IBM PC standard)`

If a problem is encountered when the parameter file is read and parsed, this routine ensures that a few critical DIGL values are left in a known, safe state.

See Also

```
int initdevice()
graphinit()
```

initdevice

Name

    int initdevice(NewPlot) initializes a graphics device.

Synopsis

```
int initdevice(NewPlot)
int NewPlot;
```

Description

    This function initializes a graphics device, depending on requirements of the DIGL graphics state. `NewPlot` instructs the function to initialize the graphics device when its value is greater than zero.

Diagnostics

    Depending on the value of the mode set by the formal parameter (`NewPlot`), initialization can be partial or complete.

The plot or graphics options of the DIGL graphics state must be initialized. Otherwise, unpredictable behavior might result.

See Also

```
int initdevice()
init_plotcom()
```

graphinit

Name

graphinit() reads a parameter file and initializes a graphics device.

Synopsis

```
int graphinit(Fdir, Fname)
char Fdir[];
char Fname[];
```

Description

This function reads a parameter file and initializes a graphics device in one complete step.

Fdir represents the name of the directory in which the primitive file is located.

Fname represents the name of the graphics primitive file.

Diagnostics

The formal parameters are left unchanged. A completion code is returned to control the rendering process.

The plot or graphics options of the DIGL graphics state must be initialized. Otherwise, unpredictable behavior might result.

See Also

```
int initdevice()
init_plotcom()
```

graphicsend

Name

void graphicsend() signals the end of a graphics program.

Synopsis

void graphicsend()

Description

This function signals the end of a graphics program. It closes the graphics device or resets the device status. Depending on the type of graphics device used, this routine varies. In the case of video drivers, for example, the graphicsend routine causes the graphics application to pause for a user keypress before it terminates.

Diagnostics

The DIGL graphics state is cleared upon execution of this routine. In the case of file output, this routine provides for final character output.

> The plot or graphics options of the DIGL graphics state must be initialized. Otherwise, unpredictable behavior might result.

See Also

int initdevice()
graphinit()

Designing Graphics Device Drivers

The DIGL device driver performs the final conversion of graphics operations to the appropriate device units and mnemonics. Consider the following pseudocode for the driver:

Begin `GraphicsDriver(Primitive : integer)`

    if (Primitive = `Initialize`*), then*
            perform any required initialization
    if (Primitive = `Draw`*), then*
            assemble draw data and mnemonics

    .

    .

    .

    if (Primitive = `Move`*), then*
            assemble move data and mnemonics
            Route driver mnemonics to device
  End `GraphicsDriver`

In case you are wondering how to handle cases where a primitive feature is not supported by a particular library, the answer is implied in the pseudocode— if the feature is not supported, the driver ignores the command. For example, a `color` primitive routed to a black-and-white driver is dropped in the bit bucket.

HPGL

Fortunately, all DIGL drivers follow the same basic format. The HPGL driver is implemented by the routine `hpplot_drv` on the DIGL disk file DRIVRLIB.C. The following code fragment from the HPGL driver illustrates how the pseudocode is implemented in C:

.

.

.

```c
if (primative==GINI)
  {
    if (hardinit)
      {
        strcpy(pramstring,"IN;IN;SC;PG;SP1;");
        lastpram[0]='\0';
        oktosend=1;
      }
  }
```

```
        else if (primative==GDRA)
          {
            if (((pramstring[0]=='P')&&(pramstring[1]=='U'))||
                ((pramstring[0]=='S')&&(pramstring[1]=='P')))
              {
                strcpy(pramstring,lastpram);
                sjoin(pramstring,"PD;PA");
              }
            else
              {
                strcpy(pramstring,lastpram);
                sjoin(pramstring,"PA");
              }
            parseparm(PONE);
            sjoin(pramstring,",");
            parseparm(PTWO);
            sjoin(pramstring,";");
            lastpram[0]='\0';
            oktosend=1;
          }
        else if (primative==GMOV)
          {
            strcpy(pramstring,"PU");
            parseparm(PONE);
            sjoin(pramstring,",");
            parseparm(PTWO);
            sjoin(pramstring,";");
            strcpy(lastpram,pramstring);
            oktosend=0;
          }
        .
        .
        .


/*++++++++++++++++++++++++++++++++++++++++++++++++++++++++++++++++++++++++
++ Check to see if last parameter was a move only instruction.      ++
++ If so, and the current parameter is a 'non move', execute it...  ++
++++++++++++++++++++++++++++++++++++++++++++++++++++++++++++++++++++++++++*/

        if (oktosend) graphout();

}/* end of hpplot_drv */
```

Several string operations are required to parse and assemble the string mnemonics required by the HPGL. The non-ANSI string functions that are used are supplied on the DIGL disk; they are described in Appendix A.

PostScript

The PostScript driver is similar to the HPGL except for the rather verbose nature of the PostScript language syntax. The driver for it is included in the DRIVRLIB.C file.

Video Control

Unlike the HPGL and PostScript drivers, the video drivers are dependent on the system and the compiler. Video drivers for DOS and UNIX are discussed in Appendix D.

Designing Graphics Applications Design

Now that you have built the lower layers of the DIGL, you can examine some applications that are simple to moderately complex. Note that the applications are completely free of any device-specific graphics commands. In addition, because of the context, it is easy to determine the meaning of the graphics commands by the names of the commands and the data supplied as part of the formal parameters to the functions.

BOX.C

All the DIGL applications follow the same basic program structure. The BOX.C program from the DIGL disk is shown in Listing 5.3.

Listing 5.3. The BOX.C program.

```
/*+==================================================================
== Box: Graphics program to draw a box on graphics device ...        ==
==                                                                   ==
== Author: Scientific Concepts, Inc.                                 ==
== Copyright (c) 1990-1993. All rights reserved worldwide.           ==
=================================================================*/


#include "syshead.h"



/*================= Data Structures and Definitions =================*/



/*=========================== Macros ==============================*/

/*======================* Global Variables ========================*/



/*==================+====== Function Prototypes ====================*/



/*======================= Begin Main Program ======================*/

int main()
{
      int          Errc              ;/* "status code              */

      char         ParamFile[80]     ;/* polygon data filename     */


/*++++++++++++++++++++++++++++++++++++++++++++++++++++++++++++++++++++
++ Get name of graphics parameter file from user...                  ++
++++++++++++++++++++++++++++++++++++++++++++++++++++++++++++++++++++*/

      printf("\nEnter name of graphics parameter file: ");
      scanf("%s",ParamFile);
```

```
/*+++++++++++++++++++++++++++++++++++++++++++++++++++++++++++++++++++++++++
++ Initialize graphics device and set viewport...                       ++
+++++++++++++++++++++++++++++++++++++++++++++++++++++++++++++++++++++++++*/

      Errc = GraphInit(" ",ParamFile);

      if (Errc == 0)
        {
          viewport(0.0,100.0,0.0,100.0);
          window(-100.0,100.0,-100.0,100.0);
          frame();

/*+++++++++++++++++++++++++++++++++++++++++++++++++++++++++++++++++++++++++
++ Draw box at center of viewport.                                      ++
+++++++++++++++++++++++++++++++++++++++++++++++++++++++++++++++++++++++++*/

          move(0.0, 0.0);
          box(25.0, 50.0);

          GraphicsEnd();

        }

}/* End of main */
```

The box program draws a box 25 units wide by 50 units high. This example is not very exciting, but it is short and illustrates well the basic concepts of the DIGL, such as device initialization and graphics mode termination. The structure also illustrates how to organize include files and local and global variables.

Your first look at device independence is when the box program asks for the name of a parameter. There are five parameter files located in the DATA subdirectory on the DIGL disk. Three of those files are

■ VGA.CTL for output to the IBM PC screen in VGA mode

■ POST.CTL for output to a disk file named POST.PRT

■ HPGL.CTL for output to a disk file named HPGL.PLT

If you answer the question with the parameter filename VGA.CTL, your monitor displays the program output. Figure 5.6 shows the output from the BOX.C program.

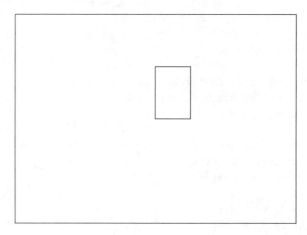

Figure 5.6. Output from the BOX.C program.

If you answer the question with the parameter filename POST.CTL, a file called POST.PRT is created. POST.PRT has the following contents:

```
%!PS-Adobe-1.0 ==* SCI 1993 ==*
%%CreationDate:
%Macros
/dr {lineto} def
/mo {moveto} def
/st {stroke} def
/sg {setgray} def
/cp {closepath} def
/sh {show} def
%Initialize
%%BoundingBox: 0 0 612 792
/Helvetica findfont
18 scalefont setfont
0 sg
1 1 scale
1 setlinewidth
612 0 translate
90 rotate
```

```
50.0 50.0 mo [] 0 setdash 50.0 50.0 mo 730.0 50.0 dr 730.0 570.0 dr
50.0 570.0 dr 50.0 50.0 dr 390.0 310.0 mo 390.0 310.0 mo 475.0 310.0
dr 475.0 440.0 dr 390.0 440.0 dr 390.0 310.0 dr
st
showpage
```

If you answer the question with the parameter filename HPGL.CTL, a file called HPGL.PLT is created. HPGL.PLT has the following contents:

```
IN;IN;SC;PG;SP1;PU80,320;LT;PU;SP0;PU80,320;PD;PA10080,320;PD;PA10080,7520;PA80,
7520;PA80,320;PU5080,3920;PD;PA6330,3920;PD;PA6330,5720;PA5080,5720;PA5080,3920;
```

The contents of the HPGL or PostScript files can be copied to devices or software that are compatible with the graphics protocol.

SIMPLE.C

In the next example, you experiment with the isotropic and anisotropic units that are discussed earlier in this chapter. The SIMPLE.C program from the DIGL disk is shown in Listing 5.4.

Listing 5.4. The SIMPLE.C program.

```
/*+=================================================================*
== Simple: Simple graphics program to draw concentric circle     ==
== test pattern on graphics device ...                           ==
==                                                               ==
== Author: Scientific Concepts, Inc.                             ==
== Copyright (c) 1990-1993. All rights reserved worldwide.       ==
=================================================================*/


#include "syshead.h"



/*================= Data Structures and Definitions =================*/



/*=========================== Macros ===============================*/
```

Listing 5.4. continued

```
/*========================= Global Variables  =======================*/



/*======================= Function Prototypes =======================*/



/*======================= Begin Main Program =======================*/

int main()
{
      int         Errc           ;/* "status code               */

      double      CirRes         ;/* "resolution of circle      */
      double      CirRad         ;/* "resolution of circle      */

      char        ParamFile[80]  ;/* polygon data filename       */


/*+++++++++++++++++++++++++++++++++++++++++++++++++++++++++++++++++++++++
++ Get name of graphics parameter file from user...               ++
+++++++++++++++++++++++++++++++++++++++++++++++++++++++++++++++++++++++++*/

      printf("\nEnter name of graphics parameter file: ");
      scanf("%s",ParamFile);

/*+++++++++++++++++++++++++++++++++++++++++++++++++++++++++++++++++++++++
++ Initialize graphics device and set viewport...                 ++
+++++++++++++++++++++++++++++++++++++++++++++++++++++++++++++++++++++++++*/

      Errc = GraphInit(" ",ParamFile);

      if (Errc == 0)
        {
          viewport(0.0,100.0,0.0,100.0);
          show(0.0,300.0,0.0,300.0);
          frame();
```

```
/*+++++++++++++++++++++++++++++++++++++++++++++++++++++++++++++++++++++++++
++ Calculate and draw "simple" figure...                                ++
+++++++++++++++++++++++++++++++++++++++++++++++++++++++++++++++++++++++++*/

          CirRes = 5.0;

          for (CirRad = 10.0; CirRad < 100.00; CirRad = CirRad + 5.0)
            {
              forecolor("GREEN");
              move(0.0 + CirRad, 150.0);
              circle(CirRad,CirRes);

              forecolor("YELLOW");
              move(300.0 - CirRad, 150.0);
              circle(CirRad,CirRes);

              forecolor("CYAN");
              move(150.0 , 0.0 + CirRad);
              ellipse(70.0, CirRad, CirRes);

              forecolor("BLUE");
              move(150.0 , 300.0 - CirRad);
              ellipse(70.0, CirRad, CirRes);
            }

          GraphicsEnd();

      }

}/* End of main */
```

This program draws a series of concentric circles and ellipses in the colors green, yellow, cyan, and blue. Figure 5.7 shows the output from the SIMPLE.C program.

GLOBES.C

The GLOBES.C program illustrates more of the features of the DIGL. Calculations of longitude and latitude lobes are graphically depicted in a series of four viewports at different locations on the screen. The GLOBES.C program from the DIGL disk is shown in Listing 5.5.

151

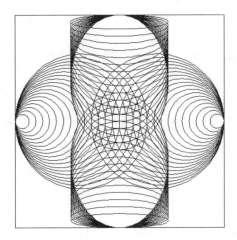

Figure 5.7. Output from the SIMPLE.C program.

Listing 5.5. The GLOBES.C program.

```
/*+==================================================================
== Globes: Program to draw four views of a globe on graphics     ==
== device ...                                                    ==
==                                                               ==
== Author: Scientific Concepts, Inc.                             ==
== Copyright (c) 1990-1993. All rights reserved worldwide.       ==
==================================================================*/

#include "syshead.h"


/*================= Data Structures and Definitions =================*/


/*=========================== Macros ===============================*/

/*======================= Global Variables =========================*/



/*====================== Function Prototypes =======================*/

void DrawGlobe(double tilt, char color[]);
```

```c
/*======================= Begin Main Program =======================*/

int main()
{
    int             Errc            ;/* status code             */

    char            ParamFile[80]   ;/* polygon data filename   */


/*++++++++++++++++++++++++++++++++++++++++++++++++++++++++++++++++++++
++ Get name of graphics parameter file from user...              ++
++++++++++++++++++++++++++++++++++++++++++++++++++++++++++++++++++++*/

    printf("\nEnter name of graphics parameter file: ");
    scanf("%s",ParamFile);

/*++++++++++++++++++++++++++++++++++++++++++++++++++++++++++++++++++++
++ Initialize graphics device and set viewport...               ++
++++++++++++++++++++++++++++++++++++++++++++++++++++++++++++++++++++*/

    Errc = GraphInit(" ",ParamFile);

    if (Errc == 0)
      {
        viewport(0.0,48.0,0.0,48.0);
        DrawGlobe(65.0,"MAGENTA");

        viewport(00.0,48.0,52.0,100.0);
        DrawGlobe(-65.0,"YELLOW");

        viewport(52.0,100.0,0.0,48.0);
        DrawGlobe(45.0,"GREEN");

        viewport(52.0,100.0,52.0,100.0);
        DrawGlobe(-45.0,"LIGHTBLUE");

        viewport(36.75,56.75,40.0,60.0);
        DrawGlobe(-15.0,"CYAN");

        GraphicsEnd();

      }
```

continues

Listing 5.5. continued

```
}/* End of main */

/*====================================================================
== void DrawGlobe(double tilt) : Function to draw globe at        ==
== specified tilt angle...                                        ==
==                                                                ==
== Argument list:  double        tilt angle                       ==
==                 double        color of globe                   ==
==                                                                ==
== Return value:   void                                           ==
==                                                                ==
=====================================================================*/
void DrawGlobe(double tilt, char globecolor[])
{
        int         idx1          ;/* index counter             */
        int         idx2          ;/* index counter             */
        int         NumLobes = 20  ;/* number of circles        */
        int         LatPenstat    ;/* latitude pen control code  */
        int         LongPenstat   ;/* latitude pen control code  */

        double      xcoor         ;/* origin coordinates         */
        double      ycoor         ;/* origin coordinates         */
        double      radius        ;/* globe radius               */
        double      elevation     ;/* elevation in degrees       */
        double      azimuth       ;/* azimuth in degrees         */
        double      xpos          ;/* temp                       */
        double      ypos          ;/* temp                       */
        double      costilt       ;/* cosine of tilt angle       */
        double      sintilt       ;/* sine of tilt angle         */
        double      pi            ;/* pi constant                */

        show(0.0,600.0,0.0,600.0);
        forecolor(globecolor);

        frame();

        xcoor = 300.0;
        ycoor = 300.0;
        radius = 250.0;
```

```
/*+++++++++++++++++++++++++++++++++++++++++++++++++++++++++++++++++++++++
++ draw a '+' at origin...                                            ++
+++++++++++++++++++++++++++++++++++++++++++++++++++++++++++++++++++++++*/

      forecolor("BRIGHTWHITE");
      move(xcoor-10.0,ycoor);
      draw(xcoor+10.0,ycoor);
      move(xcoor,ycoor-10.0);
      draw(xcoor,ycoor+10.0);


/*+++++++++++++++++++++++++++++++++++++++++++++++++++++++++++++++++++++++
++ draw outer circle...                                               ++
+++++++++++++++++++++++++++++++++++++++++++++++++++++++++++++++++++++++*/

      forecolor(globecolor);

      move(xcoor+radius,ycoor);
      pi=3.14159265;
      for (idx1=1; idx1 <=100; idx1++)
        draw(xcoor+radius*cos(idx1*2*pi/100),
        ycoor+radius*sin(idx1*2*pi/100));


/*+++++++++++++++++++++++++++++++++++++++++++++++++++++++++++++++++++++++
++ draw latitudes and longitudes...                                   ++
+++++++++++++++++++++++++++++++++++++++++++++++++++++++++++++++++++++++*/

      tilt=tilt*pi/180;
      costilt=cos(tilt);
      sintilt=sin(tilt);

      LatPenstat=0;
      LongPenstat=0;
      for (idx1=1; idx1 <= NumLobes; idx1++)
        {
          elevation=pi/2-pi/NumLobes*idx1;
          move(xcoor,ycoor+radius*(sin(elevation)*costilt -
              cos(elevation)*sintilt));
          for (idx2=1; idx2 <= 100; idx2++)
            {
```

continues

Listing 5.5. continued

```
            azimuth=idx2*2*pi/100;
            if(sin(elevation)*sintilt +
              cos(elevation)*cos(azimuth)*costilt >= 0.0)
              {
                xpos=xcoor+radius*cos(elevation)*sin(azimuth);
                ypos=ycoor+radius*(sin(elevation)*costilt -
                  cos(elevation)*cos(azimuth)*sintilt);
                if (LongPenstat)
                  draw(xpos,ypos);
                else
                  move(xpos,ypos);
                LongPenstat=1;
              }
          else
            LongPenstat=0;
      }

    azimuth=idx1*pi/NumLobes;
    move(xcoor,ycoor+radius*costilt);
    for (idx2=1; idx2 <= 100; idx2++)
      {
        elevation=pi/2-idx2*2*pi/100;
        if(sin(elevation)*sintilt +
          cos(elevation)*cos(azimuth)*costilt >= 0.0)
          {
            xpos=xcoor+radius*cos(elevation)*sin(azimuth);
            ypos=ycoor+radius*(sin(elevation)*costilt -
                cos(elevation)*cos(azimuth)*sintilt);
            if (LatPenstat)
              draw(xpos,ypos);
            else
              move(xpos,ypos);
            LatPenstat=1;
          }
      else
        LatPenstat=0;
    }
  }


}/* End of DrawGlobe */
```

The SIMPLE.C program is shown in Figure 5.8. The program uses the viewport command to partition the screen into 5 different sections. The fifth section illustrates that a viewport can be any number in the range of 0 to 100%!

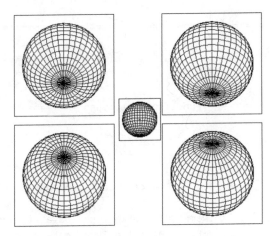

Figure 5.8. Output from the GLOBES.C Program.

POLY2D.C

I discussed polygon operations in detail in the last two chapters. The POLY2D.C program is a self-contained program that reads and displays a 2-D polygon. Sample 2-D polygon files are provided on the DIGL disk; they have a .POG extension. The POLY2D.C program from the DIGL disk is shown in Listing 5.6.

Listing 5.6. The POLY2D.C program.

```
/*===================================================================*
== Poly2d: Program to read a 2D polygon file and display the       ==
== figure ...                                                      ==
==                                                                 ==
== Author: Scientific Concepts, Inc.                               ==
== Copyright (c) 1990-1993. All rights reserved worldwide.         ==
====================================================================*/


#include "syshead.h"
```

continues

Listing 5.6. continued

```
/*================= Data Structures and Definitions ================*/



/*============================ Macros ============================*/

/*=====================* Global Variables=======================*/


/*===================== Function Prototypes =====================*/


int main()
{
        int             Errc            ;/* status of polygon read/transl.*/

        char            PlotName[80]  ;/* polygon data file name        */
        char            ParamFile[80] ;/* polygon data file name        */

        double          Wxmin           ;/* window x minimum              */
        double          Wxmax           ;/* window x maximum              */
        double          Wymin           ;/* window y minimum              */
        double          Wymax           ;/* window y maximum              */

        double          Xbias           ;/* expansion factor in X direction*/
        double          Ybias           ;/* expansion factor in Y direction*/

        TWODMATRIX      Polygon         ;/* test polygon structure        */

/*+++++++++++++++++++++++++++++++++++++++++++++++++++++++++++++++++++++++
++ Get name of 2D polygon data file and graphics parameter file     ++
++ from user.                                                        ++
+++++++++++++++++++++++++++++++++++++++++++++++++++++++++++++++++++++++*/

        printf("\nEnter name of 2D polygon data file: ");
        scanf("%s",PlotName);

        printf("\nEnter name of graphics parameter file: ");
        scanf("%s",ParamFile);
```

```
         Errc=getpoly(PlotName,&Polygon);

         if (Errc == 0) Errc = GraphInit(" ",ParamFile);



/*+++++++++++++++++++++++++++++++++++++++++++++++++++++++++++++++++++++
++ Initialize graphics and display results...                      ++
+++++++++++++++++++++++++++++++++++++++++++++++++++++++++++++++++++++++*/

         if (Errc == 0)
           {
             framepoly(&Polygon, &Wxmin, &Wxmax, &Wymin, &Wymax);
             viewport(0.0,100.0,0.0,100.0);

             Xbias = (Wxmax - Wxmin)/2.0;
             Ybias = (Wymax - Wymin)/2.0;

             window(Wxmin-Xbias, Wxmax+Xbias, Wymin-Ybias, Wymax+Ybias);

             frame();

             move(Wxmin + Xbias/2.0 , Wymin + Ybias/2.0);
             drawipoly(&Polygon);

             GraphicsEnd();

           }
         else
           printf("\nError reading polygon - process aborted!\n");

         return;

}/*End of main */
```

Figure 5.9 shows the output from the POLY2D.C program that is based on the input from the MIG25.POG polygon file.

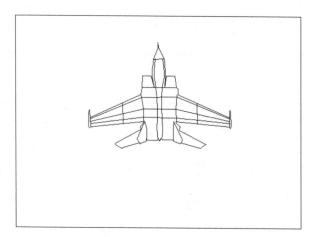

Figure 5.9. Output from the POLY2D.C program.

Summary

The main advantage of device independence in the DIGL is ensuring that graphical representation among different supported devices is consistent and identical. This chapter examines an implementation of the DIGL. The DIGL graphics state consists of several variables and data structures used to represent vector and pixel manipulation of the DIGL model.

Some of the most basic and fundamental decisions in developing a graphics state representation are what types of low-level graphics operations are needed, which graphics devices will be supported, and what variables and data structures will be used to control information from one graphics operation to the next. Once these decisions are made, you can define and construct the low-level graphics functions you need to convert, translate, and route graphics operations to the graphics drivers.

DIGL has been extended to provide support for parameter file control with a polygon support library, POLYLIB.H, and its corresponding header file, POLYLIB.C. These can be used for several applications, including polygon rendering and display of stroke fonts.

The next chapters explore options for providing automated menu interfaces to graphics applications and parameter files, and provide you with some insight into extending this package for more advanced applications.

A DESIGN PROTOTYPE FOR TEXT-BASED POP-UP WINDOWS

This chapter focuses on the user interface, in particular, the techniques required to design custom text-based pop-up window libraries. A prototype for a pop-up window system is presented, with a library of calls that are sufficient for developing and testing pop-up window generation. Some of the code samples that are supplied with your DIGL disk are examined to make it easier for you to extend the pop-up window library if you want.

Although this discussion does not presume a particular platform, some examples rely on DOS and similar memory-mapped configurations. Even if you plan to use off-the-shelf window libraries such as X Windows, the information in this chapter is useful.

Text-Based Pop-Up Windows

A *text-based* pop-up window is a window that consists entirely of ASCII text characters, including the DOS extended graphics character set. The window is *virtual* in the sense that its contents are well-defined but its exact location may be decided at runtime. The term *pop-up* refers to the fact that the window partially or fully covers what was previously on the screen only when it is open. When the window is closed, whatever it covered is left unchanged.

To provide the speed necessary for pop-up windows, several low-level functions must be used. Fortunately, in the DOS world calls are already defined for access to the BIOS to assist in performing many of these features. You merely need to organize these requirements into the form of a layered library, which enables the generation of higher-level programs that demonstrate these techniques.

You approach the design of text-based pop-up windows in much the same manner as in developing the DIGL graphics model. Figure 6.1 illustrates a layered model of a pop-up window menu library. As with the DIGL graphics library, I implement the pop-up window menu library from the bottom up.

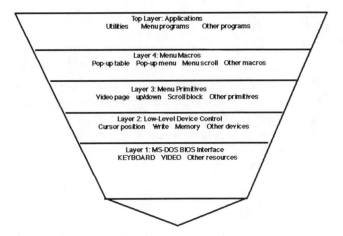

Figure 6.1. DOS menu library model.

Layer 1 contains DOS BIOS routines. In Layer 2, driver routines that perform keyboard input operations, cursor positioning, and mouse status checks in real-time can be implemented. In Layer 3, you create higher-level functions that increment the video page, scroll areas of text, and draw the components used for drawing menu and table boxes. High-level user input prompt routines that check for special functions and edit keys can also be created here. Layer 4 is used to create functions that draw window and menu boxes with special highlighting detail for titles and edit fields. In the top layer, you create applications that interact with the window library.

Keyboard and Input Control

Regardless of how objects are displayed on the screen, some method of interacting with the user is necessary for control of the application. Simple methods of waiting for user input are not sufficient. The application must be free to check for mouse or keyboard input without waiting to perform select activities in the background; this is called *task suspension*. This implies that yet another higher-level function must be used to handle any type of user input as an event.

Event Handling Options

Once information is displayed, you must decide what action needs to be taken. A keystroke or mouse click can tell the window library what has happened in relation to the data displayed. This type of event recognition can have the form of scroll bars. In the DOS model, you can handle event recognition by waiting for and processing a keyboard or mouse event. At the highest level of interface with the GUI library, you need to supply information about only the window elements, location, and event processing.

Video Page Control

Before you can develop a set of specifications and performance requirements for controlling the video text page, you must describe the DOS memory map structure. In standard DOS configurations, the memory map consists of standard address locations reserved for the operating system and user data space; some areas are reserved specifically for DOS. Figure 6.2 shows a typical memory map of a standard DOS configuration. The BIOS is located at hexadecimal location 400. Recall that the BIOS consists of several functions around which various I/O operations can be performed. Note that some areas in the DOS memory map are reserved specifically for DOS.

0x0000	Interrupt vectors
0x0400	BIOS
	DOS kernel
	Device drivers
	COMMAND.COM
0xA0000	Program area
	Display memory
0xC8000	
	Additional BIOS services
0xCC000	
0xE0000	
0xFFFFF	Reserved for BIOS

Figure 6.2. A typical DOS memory map.

Video Starts at B0000h

Because the pop-up windows are text-based, the high-resolution graphics plane is not used for individual pixel control. Instead, the video pages reside at a fixed segment address—B0000h through B0F9Fh.

> DOS video memory consists of character/attribute byte pairs. The attribute byte controls the background and foreground colors. It also determines whether character blinking is turned on or off. That's why the F9Fh number (3999 in decimal notation) is twice the size of 80×25. The characters are at every other byte position in memory.

By using text video maps, you can exploit the advantages of speed and simplicity—provided that your language of choice enables you to write to and read from memory locations directly. The effect of real-time window popping is achieved by switching between video pages. Depending on the video adapter you use, up to four video pages are available. Each page is offset from the base page (page 0) by the total number of bytes per page—F9F (hexadecimal notation for 80×25×2).

Lower-Level Video Operations

You can expand the basic text-based window support library from block read-write operations by adding the following low-level functions. In this chapter, I don't implement every routine, but I do implement enough of the lower-level routines to enable you to add additional functions.

- ■ ReadFromMemory(), WriteToMemory() respectively reads from or writes to video memory directly.

- ■ GetVideoPage(), SetVideoPage() controls the video page that you are reading from and writing to, respectively.

- ■ GetCursorPosition(), SetCursorPosition() respectively returns the location values or moves the cursor to a specified *x,y* position.

- ■ GetAttributeByte(), SetAttributeByte() respectively gets or sets the attribute of a character at a row or column location on the current page.

- ScrollBlock() moves a block of video character data up or down.

- GetAttributeCharacter(), SetAttributeCharacter() respectively reads or writes a character at a row or column location on the current page.

- ReadString(), WriteString() uses previous lower-level calls to read or write, respectively, a character string to a specified row and column on the current video page.

Built on top of these four routines are higher-level calls for drawing boxes by using DOS graphics characters and color control. To complete the DOS-based GUI, add routines for mouse control and keyboard monitoring; also add extended prompt routines that permit keyboard editing. Finally—several thousand lines of code later—the text-based GUI is complete!

Menu Structure and Representation

Now you understand the lower-level tools used to display boxes and text. In your applications, you will use a window conceptual model. The basic window structure is simply a rectangular area in which text data is displayed. When you make calls to the window library, you specify what the information is, where you want it displayed, what color you want for borders, and so on. You can define two types of window or box structures to implement in the library prototype. Figure 6.3 shows the structure of a simple window.

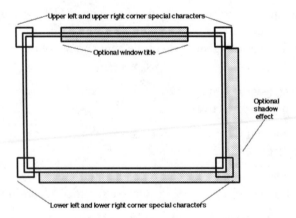

Figure 6.3. Structure of a simple window.

The form of the window is a rectangular area framed by some type of border. By using the special line-drawing characters provided by the DOS character set, you can easily draw this type of box. Special characters are used for the corners. In addition, you can include an optional title, which is centered along the top of the window. This technique is commonly used in many DOS-based utilities.

The optional shadow area is used to create the illusion that the window box is raised above the text it covers. Creating a shadow area, however, is not as simple as drawing a gray rectangle offset from the window and overlaying the window. To produce a shadow, the text below the shadow must still be readable. You accomplish this by reading the data in the shadow area and by changing the color attributes to a gray background. This seems like a lot of work for a cute effect, but it's worth the effort.

Figure 6.4 shows that you can enhance a simple box. In this case, you reserve a special area for a title. This might represent, for example, a submenu title of a menu. You also need to define additional special characters to allow for joints in the menu structure.

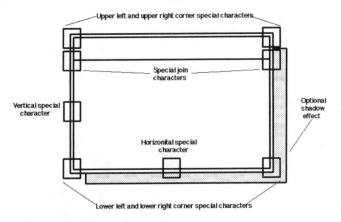

Figure 6.4. Structure of an enhanced window.

Pop-Up Window Library for DOS

So far I have described some low-level library operations and introduced high-level windows. Now all you need is the code to implement them. You know what you want your menu library prototype to be able to do, so you can begin to implement library functions that accomplish those tasks. Start by defining the constants, macros, and data structures that you need. Follow this with functional interface descriptions that represent the options that I have described.

Data Structures

The DIGL disk includes a file called MSCMELIB.H (see Listing 6.1), which contains the structures and prototypes needed to support the menu examples discussed later in this chapter.

Listing 6.1. PC pop-up window library function header and prototypes.

```
/*======================================================================
== PC pop-up window library function header and prototypes         ==
==                                                                 ==
== Author: Scientific Concepts, Inc.                               ==
== Copyright (c) 1990-1993. All rights reserved worldwide.         ==
======================================================================*/


/*================= Data Structures and Definitions ================*/


#define MAXPAGE    8              /* maximum number of video pages  */

#define PAGE0      0              /* video page number              */
#define PAGE1      1              /* video page number              */
#define PAGE2      2              /* video page number              */
#define PAGE3      3              /* video page number              */

#define VBBLACK    0              /* color background definition     */
#define VBBLUE     16             /* color background definition     */
#define VBGREEN    32             /* color background definition     */
#define VBCYAN     48             /* color background definition     */
#define VBRED      64             /* color background definition     */
#define VBMAGENTA  80             /* color background definition     */
#define VBBROWN    96             /* color background definition     */
#define VBWHITE    112            /* color background definition     */
```

```
#define VFBLACK      0           /* color foreground definition  */
#define VFBLUE       1           /* color foreground definition  */
#define VFGREEN      2           /* color foreground definition  */
#define VFCYAN       3           /* color foreground definition  */
#define VFRED        4           /* color foreground definition  */
#define VFMAGENTA    5           /* color foreground definition  */
#define VFBROWN      6           /* color foreground definition  */
#define VFWHITE      7           /* color foreground definition  */
#define VFGRAY       8           /* color foreground definition  */
#define VFLIBLUE     9           /* color foreground definition  */
#define VFLIGREEN    10          /* color foreground definition  */
#define VFLICYAN     11          /* color foreground definition  */
#define VFLIRED      12          /* color foreground definition  */
#define VFLIMAGEN    13          /* color foreground definition  */
#define VFYELLOW     14          /* color foreground definition  */
#define VFBRWHITE    15          /* color foreground definition  */


#define TABSIZE      10          /* maximum # of lines in table  */


typedef unsigned    TWOBWORD;    /* signed 16 integer            */

typedef struct boxdef_st         /* structure for box attributes */
  {
    char   uleft;                /* upper left corner box char   */
    char   uljoin;               /* upper left joined box char   */
    char   uright;               /* upper right corner box char  */
    char   urjoin;               /* upper right joined box char  */
    char   lleft;                /* lower left corner box char   */
    char   lright;               /* lower right corner box char  */
    char   horiz;                /* horizontal line box char     */
    char   vert;                 /* vertical line box char       */
  } BOXDEF;

typedef struct table_st          /* structure for table          */
  {
    char    title[80];           /* title of table data          */
    char    *lines[TABSIZE];     /* pointer to table data        */
  } TABLE;
```

continues

169

Listing 6.1. continued

```
/*============================= Macros ===============================*/


#define SETBLINK(a) (a=a¦0x80)      /* set blink bit of word         */
#define RESETBLINK(a) (a=a&0x7f)    /* reset blink bit of word       */


#define SETFAROFFSET(a,b)       ((*(unsigned *)&a) = b)
#define SETFARSEGMENT(a,b)      ((*(((unsigned *)&a)+1)) = b)
#define SETFARPOINTER(a,b,c)    (SETFARSEGMENT(a,b),SETFAROFFSET(a,c))
#define GETFARPOFFSET(a)        ((*(unsigned *)&a))
#define GETFARPSEGMENT(a)       ((*(((unsigned *)&a)+1)))


/*======================* Global Variables=========================*/


    static BOXDEF SINGLE =
      {
        218,                        /* upper left corner box char    */
        195,                        /* upper left joined box char     */
        191,                        /* upper right corner box char    */
        180,                        /* upper right joined box char    */
        192,                        /* lower left corner box char     */
        217,                        /* lower right corner box char    */
        196,                        /* horizontal line box char       */
        179                         /* vertical line box char         */
      };

    static BOXDEF DOUBLE =
      {
        201,                        /* upper left corner box char     */
        204,                        /* upper left joined box char      */
        187,                        /* upper right corner box char     */
        185,                        /* upper right joined box char      */
        200,                        /* lower left corner box char      */
        188,                        /* lower right corner box char      */
        205,                        /* horizontal line box char        */
        186                         /* vertical line box char          */
      };
```

```
/*====================== Function Prototypes ======================*/

void PageUp()                  ;/* set video plane to next page  */
void PageDown()                ;/* set video plane to prev page  */
void WriteString()             ;/* write string direct to memory */
void GetSegAddrress()          ;/* get segment address for ptr   */
int GetVideoPage()             ;/* get current video page number */
void SetVideoPage()            ;/* set video page number         */
void MemCopy()                 ;/* copy section from page to page*/
void PopTable()                ;/* display a table in pop-up     */
```

The MSC portion of this file and all the filenames on the DIGL disk stand for *Microsoft Compiler*. Code contained in these files is intended for versions 5.1 through 7.0 of the Microsoft C compiler. The code could be modified to work on other compilers if you want.

Pop-Up Window Functions

This section includes reference and interface information for the window library provided on the DIGL disk. The disk includes a file called MSCMELIB.C, which contains the source code for these functions.

PopTable

Name

> PopTable(tab, row, col, fore, back, boxtype) displays a table by indexing the video page at a specified row and column.

Synopsis

```
void PopTable(tab, row, col, fore, back, boxtype)
TABLE *tab;
int row;
int col;
```

```
int fore;
int back;
BOXDEF *boxtype;
```

Description

This function displays a table at a specified row and column position, which is indicated by the variables row and col, respectively. PopTable indexes—that is, switches—to the next video page and displays the table specified by the table specification (tab). The table specification defines the border characters and the type of box (boxtype) to be drawn by using a data structure.

Diagnostics

The formal arguments are not modified.

Not all text video hardware supports the maximum number of pages defined by the data structure. Do not index beyond the maximum number of pages supported by the hardware—typically 4.

See Also

```
PageUp()
PageDown()
```

WriteString

Name

WriteString(string, row, col, fore, back, pagenum) copies a string directly to memory.

Synopsis

```
void WriteString(string, row, col, fore, back, pagenum)
char *string;
int row;
int col;
int fore;
int back;
int pagenum;
```

Description

This function writes a string directly to a user-specified row and column in memory at the user-specified video page. The user specifies the foreground and background colors.

Diagnostics

The formal arguments are not modified. The attribute bytes are set automatically, according to the required background and foreground colors.

> If row and columns extend beyond the current line or page, line wrap occurs. This can cause displays that are distorted or that write across video page boundaries.

See Also

```
PageUp()
PageDown()
```

GetSegAddress

Name

GetSegAddress(p, pseg, poff) returns the segmented address of a far pointer to PC memory.

Synopsis

```
void GetSegAddrress(p, pseg, poff)
void *p;
TWOBWORD *pseg;
TWOBWORD *poff;
```

Description

This function returns the pointer segment and the offset address, defined as two byte values that are previously described in the data structure header file.

173

Diagnostics

A special type of void pointer is cast within the routine to the special address of the PC-based far pointer of the segment and offset addresses.

As with other pointer manipulations, the misuse or inaccurate construction of pointers can cause a function to access unsafe areas of memory for read-write.

See Also

```
PageUp()
PageDown()
WriteString()
```

PageUp

Name

PageUp() indexes a text video plane to the next base page.

Synopsis

```
void PageUp()
```

Description

This function assumes a starting base page address of B800hex. It calls GetVideoPage() to find the current page number and calculates the next page, based on indexes of 1000hex. If the current page number is 3 (page 4 option base 0), page 1 is used.

Diagnostics

There are no formal arguments, but the page number is calculated locally.

As with all page-oriented functions of the DIGL, you must make sure not to exceed the number of available pages. Otherwise, information can be lost, and screens can be distorted.

See Also

    PageDown()
    GetVideoPage()

PageDown

Name

PageDown() indexes a text video plane to the previous base page.

Synopsis

    void PageDown()

Description

This function assumes that the starting base page address is B800hex. It calls GetVideoPage() to find the current page number and calculates the next page, based on indexes of 1000hex. If the current page number is 0, the page number is not decremented.

Diagnostics

There are no formal arguments, but the page number is calculated locally.

As with all page-oriented functions of the DIGL, you must make sure not to exceed the number of available pages. Otherwise, information can be lost, and screens can be distorted.

See Also

    PageUp()
    GetVideoPage()

GetVideoPage

Name

GetVideoPage() returns the page number of the current video page.

Synopsis

```
int GetVideoPage()
```

Description

This function makes a DOS BIOS call to function `0x0f` to get the video page number that is returned from register `ireg.h.bh`.

Diagnostics

An integer code that represents the page number is returned. No error code is available.

> The values that are returned are consistent with the video mode of operation and with the BIOS interrupt call for video. Consult your DOS reference manual for further assistance.

See Also

```
SetVideoPage()
PageUp()
PageDown()
```

SetVideoPage

Name

`SetVideoPage(pagenum)` indexes the current page to the next video page in the series.

Synopsis

```
void SetVideoPage(pagenum)
int pagenum;
```

Description

This function uses a user-specifed page number to index into video memory by means of the DOS BIOS call.

Diagnostics

The formal arguments are not modified.

The global constant defined for the maximum number of pages permitted (MAXPAGE) might not represent the maximum number of video pages supported by your hardware. You must ensure that the page depth is consistent with the requirements of the configuration.

See Also

```
GetVideoPage()
PageUp()
PageDown()
```

MemCopy

Name

MemCopy(fromseg, fromoff, toseg, tooff, numbytes) copies sections of memory from one segment to another by using Intel segment-based pointers.

Synopsis

```
void MemCopy(fromseg, fromoff, toseg, tooff, numbytes)
TWOBWORD fromseg;
TWOBWORD fromoff;
TWOBWORD toseg;
TWOBWORD tooff;
int numbytes;
```

Description

This function blindly copies segments of memory from one place to another using pointer manipulation. The amount of information that can be transferred is limited in byte size to that of a 2-byte integer—32767. MemCopy makes no assumptions about the validity of the addresses.

Diagnostics

The formal arguments are not modified.

This function is intended for internal use by other functions in the DIGL window library. When you specify pointer addresses, be sure that they are legal—based on the DOS memory map. Otherwise, unpredictable program behavior results.

See Also

```
PageUp()
PageDown()
```

POPUP.C

POPUP.C is a simple window utility written for DOS. It illustrates the window library and language issues that I have discussed so far. POPUP uses high-level table creation library calls to display two windows at arbitrary locations on the video screen.

Listing 6.2 is the listing of POPUP.C. Its structure is similar to those of the graphics applications presented in Chapter 5, "A Design Prototype for DIGL."

Listing 6.2. POPUP.C—DOS video test program for pop-up tables.

```
/
*+==============================================================================
== Popup: Dos video test program for "pop up" tables...                      ==
==                                                                            ==
==                                                                            ==
== Author: Scientific Concepts, Inc.                                          ==
== Copyright (c) 1990-1993. All rights reserved worldwide.                    ==
=============================================================================*/


#include "syshead.h"


/*================== Data Structures and Definitions ==================*/
```

```
/*=============================== Macros ===============================*/


    static TABLE tab1 =
      {
        "General Help Information",
        "Usage (while at page end in View): <option>",
        " <key>      Description(s) ",
        "b,-,PGUP   go back one page (or half page)",
        "  e        scroll to eof (or until key hit)",
        "  f        close file and prompt for new file",
        "  n        scroll forward one line",
        "  q,ESC    close file and quit",
        "  s        enter string to search for",
        "  t,HOME   go to top of file",
        NULL
      };


    static TABLE tab2 =
      {
        "Yet Another Table Of Information",
        "Plot—>File?:         GridLogX:       ",
        "Backgd Color:        GridLogy:       ",
        "Foregd Color:        DataLogX:       ",
        "Graphics Dev:        DataLogY:       ",
        "# Of Pens   :        GraphClr:       ",
        "Zoom        :        XANDY   :       ",
        "Auto Pen    :                        ",
        "UXmin       :        UXmax   :       ",
        "UYmin       :        UYmax   :       ",
        NULL
      };



/*====================== Function Prototypes ======================*/



/*====================== Begin Main Program ======================*/



int main()
{
```

continues

Listing 6.2. continued

```
        int        idx1        ;/* index counter              */
        int        row         ;/* row position               */
        int        col         ;/* column position            */

/
*++++++++++++++++++++++++++++++++++++++++++++++++++++++++++++++++++++++++++++++
++ Display first window at arbitrary row and column position...     ++
++++++++++++++++++++++++++++++++++++++++++++++++++++++++++++++++++++++++++++++*/

        row=3;
        col=12;

        PopTable(&tab1, row, col, VFYELLOW, VBBROWN, &SINGLE);

/
*++++++++++++++++++++++++++++++++++++++++++++++++++++++++++++++++++++++++++++++
++ Wait for user keypress and display second window offset from
   first...   ++
++++++++++++++++++++++++++++++++++++++++++++++++++++++++++++++++++++++++++++++*/

        while (!kbhit()) {;}
        idx1=getchar();
        row=8;
        col=24;
        PopTable(&tab2, row, col, VFBRWHITE, VBGREEN, &DOUBLE);

/
*++++++++++++++++++++++++++++++++++++++++++++++++++++++++++++++++++++++++++++++
++ Wait for user keypress and remove only second window...          ++
++++++++++++++++++++++++++++++++++++++++++++++++++++++++++++++++++++++++++++++*/

        while (!kbhit()) {;}
        idx1=getchar();
        PageDown();

/
*++++++++++++++++++++++++++++++++++++++++++++++++++++++++++++++++++++++++++++++
++ Wait for user keypress and first window...                       ++
++++++++++++++++++++++++++++++++++++++++++++++++++++++++++++++++++++++++++++++*/
```

```
    while (!kbhit()) {;}
    idx1=getchar();
    PageDown();


    return(0);

}/* End of Main */
```

The POPUP program defines two table data structures—tab1 and tab2. Each table is popped up and displayed on top of whatever happens to be on the video screen at the time. Figure 6.5 shows the output of a video screen after a directory list command is executed and before POPUP is run.

```
Volume in drive D is SCI
Directory of D:\DIGLLIB

X          C     1966   3-06-93   10:17a
BOX        C     2207   3-06-93   10:17a
POLY2D     C     2970   3-06-93   10:17a
FILELIB    C    17220   3-06-93   10:17a
PRIMLIB    C    32256   3-06-93   10:17a
MACROLIB   C    27948   3-06-93   10:17a
MISCLIB    C     6427   3-06-93   10:17a
POLY3D     C    30151   3-06-93   10:17a
POLYLIB    C    24130   3-06-93   10:17a
STRNGLIB   C    24177   3-06-93   10:17a
SIMPLE     C     3003   3-06-93   10:17a
SUNYILIB   C    18816   3-06-93   10:17a
GOLBES     C     7218   3-06-93   10:17a
MSCYILIB   C    12247   3-06-93   10:17a
PARAMLIB   C    17316   3-06-93   10:17a
DRIVLIB    C    23442   3-06-93   10:17a
POLYMENU   C     9474   3-06-93   10:17a
MSCWILIB   C    17245   3-07-93   10:17a
POPUP      C     3554   3-07-93   10:17a
```

Figure 6.5. Display before POPUP is run.

Figure 6.6 shows the output of the video screen after POPUP is run and before the first keystroke is made. The first table—tab1—is overlaid on the video displayed. POPUP copies the covered data to the next page and indexes the page number.

Figure 6.7 shows the output of the video screen after the user presses a key again. POPUP displays the second table screen—tab2.

Directory of D:\DIGLLIB

X	C	1966	3-06-93	10:17A
BOX	C			
POLY2D	C			
FILELIB	C			
PRIMLIB	C			
MACROLIB	C			
MISCLIB	C			
POLY3D	C			
POLYLIB	C			
STRNGLIB	C			
SIMPLE	C			
SUNVILIB	C			
GOLBES	C			
MSCVILIB	C			
PARAMLIB	C	17316	3-06-93	10:17a
DRIVRLIB	C	23442	3-06-93	10:17a
POLYMENU	C	9474	3-06-93	10:17a
MSCWILIB	C	17245	3-07-93	5:29p
POPUP	C	3554	3-07-93	5:29p

19 File(s)   4509696 bytes free

```
General Help Information
Usage (while at page end in View): <option>
<key>                Description(s)
b,-,PGUP             go back one page (or half page)
e                    scroll to eof (or until key hit)
f                    close file and prompt for new file
n                    scroll forward one line
q, ESC               close file and quit
s                    enter string to search for
t, HOME              to to top of file
```

D:\DIGLLIB>popup

Figure 6.6. First POPUP table.

Directory of D:\DIGLLIB

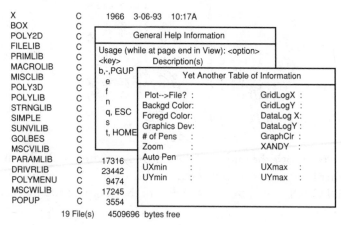

Figure 6.7. Second (cascaded) POPUP table.

Notice that the second table is cascaded and overlaid on top of the first table. Once again, POPUP copies the data to the next page and indexes the page number. At this point, the video page has been indexed twice, and all information on the previous pages copied accordingly.

The menus vanish—that is, pop down—whenever a key is pressed and the POPUP program successfully calls the PageDown function. It is not necessary to erase the data on the higher pages in memory; with each pop-up activity, the data on the lower screens are copied up.

Summary

This chapter explains many of the design issues associated with DOS memory map and BIOS interfaces, presenting the techniques that are used to design custom text-based pop-up window libraries. Both lower- and higher-level window operations are implemented to draw boxes, display text, move the cursor, provide shadow areas, and so on.

If you intend to develop a more powerful DOS-based window library, there are two paths that you can pursue:

- Extend the code provided here in order to add more features.

- Use a fully developed, off-the-shelf window library to support user interface operations.

If you are interested in other operating systems, such as UNIX, the second option is the one for you. In fact, UNIX readily supports one of the most widespread and universal windowing systems available—X Windows. Chapter 7, "High-Resolution Graphics Windows," presents a way for you to produce effects that are far more interesting with much less code and trouble.

HIGH-RESOLUTION
GRAPHICS
WINDOWS

Chapter 6, "A Design Prototype for Text-Based Pop-Up Windows," focuses exclusively on text-based window operations in DOS. Although these operations require complex memory facility, they do not require control of individual pixel elements.

This chapter focuses on more high-level window library interfaces and standards on the graphics plane. Graphics or bit-mapped windows require some of the same techniques presented in Chapter 6, but performance is more critical. However, instead of writing a bit-mapped window library (believe me, you don't want to!), this chapter uses interface calls into one of the most popular application libraries—X Windows. There are three reasons for focusing on X in this chapter:

- The X11 library is used to develop the UNIX-based video driver discussed in Appendix D, "UNIX X11 Video Drivers."

- A higher-level menu library interface such as the XView (X Window-System-based Visual/Integrated Environment for Workstations) example provided in this chapter serves as an excellent background for future menu development.

- Event handling requires careful consideration regarding which level is best for interface in the X11 library systems.

Because of the focus on X Windows, this chapter switches operating systems to UNIX where X has become a de facto standard. Many of the issues discussed apply also to window interface programming under OS/2. There are a variety of X Window look-alike support libraries available for DOS and OS/2. In fact, Microsoft Windows and X Windows share the same concept, with some differences in design and implementation due to differing architectures and operating systems.

DOS versus UNIX

Recall that DOS provides low-level access to basic video services. However, as an operating system, UNIX is more removed from lower-level CRT control. This is also true of any multitasking operating system, including OS/2.

In the DOS world, you are free to communicate directly—almost—with any device by reading and writing from the physical address map. Other than an occasional conflict with one or more *terminate-and-stay-resident* (TSR) routines—in standard DOS environments—tasks can assume uncontested control over devices and memory regions that are in fixed locations.

A TSR routine is a program that does not exit completely on termination. Once a TSR routine is activated by the operating system, it remains in memory until it is reactivated by a special interrupt or key sequence.

Chapter 6 points out that DOS provides a wide range of BIOS services that allow a single task to read and write directly—for example, video pages that are not reserved exclusively for the operating system. Although the idea of protected memory in many DOS configurations is often wishful thinking, the potential for serious problems caused by careless programming is even greater when developing and running application code in a multitasking environment. Imagine what can happen in a system in which your task is one of dozens or even hundreds competing for the same resources. In multitasking environments, one of the main goals of the operating system is to protect your program from other tasks as well as from itself. Figure 7.1 illustrates a dynamic view of memory map partitions in a multitasking operating system such as UNIX. In contrast to the simple static memory map of DOS presented in Chapter 6, Figure 7.1 illustrates a drastically different task environment structure. Not only are multiple tasks sharing one or more CPUs, but a common network protocol mechanism such as RPC (Remote Procedure Calls) can allow tasks to communicate from one workstation to another in local or remote locations.

All of this must take place while other programs or tasks may be competing for the same resources. The nature of this form of virtual mapping of video services renders the hard-coded techniques that are used in text-based DOS undesirable. Fortunately, most of the software needed to deal with this problem already exists in standard form.

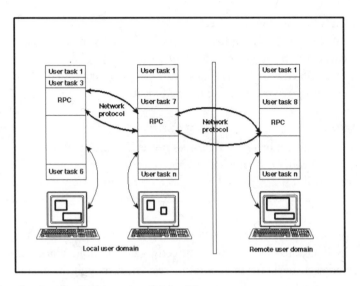

Figure 7.1. Dynamic multitasking memory model.

The X Window

The X Window is a client/server toolkit that has already been adapted to a variety of operating systems, including DOS and UNIX. As is the case for most standards, several companies support the developing and maintaining of X Window standards, including DEC, Hewlett-Packard, AT&T, and IBM.

There is good news and bad news about the wide range of support and features provided by the X Window environment. The good news is that there is a tremendous amount of documentation and support for X Window operations—from menu to graphics application development—including lots of free software. The bad news is that finding out how to do any one thing in X is frequently a complex and extremely frustrating experience.

The highest level of interface is the X View toolkit, presented in this chapter. The lowest level is represented by the graphics interface used to develop the video driver discussed in Appendix D.

Once again, you can examine the layering of the X Window system by an inverted pyramid model (see Figure 7.2). The model is similar (in principle) to the text-based model of Chapter 6. Open Look/X View in Layer 4 extends into

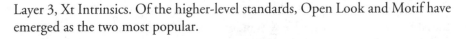

Layer 3, Xt Intrinsics. Of the higher-level standards, Open Look and Motif have emerged as the two most popular.

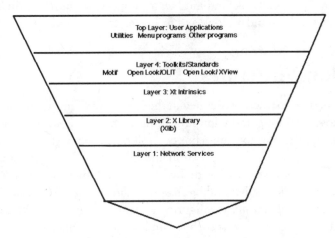

Figure 7.2. X Window toolkit library model.

This model follows the layered complexity principle of development: the lower the interface level, the more complex the software becomes. This is balanced somewhat with more control over the environment. In order to develop an X11-based video driver consistent with the procedural approach to event handling in our DIGL graphics system, you interface at the second level.

UNIX XView Toolkit

In principle, X Window applications are more complicated and extensive than the simple text-based windows of single-user environments such as DOS. High-level toolkits such as XView attempt to simplify the process of software development by encapsulating options and features into a shopping list of prefabricated objects.

In X, a display is not a fixed size entity statically located at one location in memory. In fact, a server is used in X Window systems to receive instruction and event protocols necessary to control one or more screens at a time at a variety of locations. Rather than writing to a fixed memory location to render a graphics or text box, communication protocols are used in a client/server-based procedure. As indicated in Figure 7.2, Xlib is the lowest window-level library that is used to translate data structures and events.

X View was developed by Sun Microsystems as a higher-level interface into the Xlib library to allow novice X Window developers to develop interfaces compatible with the Open Look Graphical User Interface. In short, all window operations have a similar standard look and feel using this methodology.

Window Structures

The basic viewable structures defined in the X View toolkit vary in both structure and purpose. Defining and communicating with X View windows is far more challenging than simply forming a box of scrolling lines and waiting for a keypress. There are hundreds of options for configuring buttons, boxes, lists, and text that may be selected or configured as desired. In fact, the first thing a new user may notice in using X View is that finding an option and setting the associated attributes correctly can be frustrating. Configuring a menu in this context means picking from a shopping list of objects such as windows, panels, and frames.

Event Handling Options

In simpler text-based window configurations, the notion of an event was implicit in the design. Recall from Chapter 6 that you simply popped up a window, waited for a keypress, and acted on the option selected.

In the case of X Windows, events are far more complex and can occur from a variety of sources other than the local keyboard. For example, events can occur from someone else's program that may be running on a different workstation—perhaps even in a different state! Window managers and special event handlers are needed to control the complex series of callbacks generated in an X Window environment.

Based on the structure provided by the X View toolkit, windows are defined as building blocks consisting of smaller elements or attributes. Part of the attribute setting for window objects involves specifying an event handling sequence. This usually translates into setting up a function to process the result of an event registered with another task on your behalf. Fortunately, without the need for understanding the underlying complexities of this process, all you have to do here is use the same format of the functions used in the X View programming manual examples.

POLYMENU.C

To develop a test program for the X View menu development system, I designed a parameter file read/write menu for use with the polygon application (POLY2D.C) introduced in Chapter 5, "A Design Prototype for DIGL."

DIGL has been designed to allow parameter files to be separate from the specific graphics application. Without a menu system, each parameter file must be edited with a word processor or text editor to change values. You can make this process much easier by designing a menu that allows any or all of the following actions by the user:

- Reading a user-specified parameter file

- Changing any or all of the parameter values

- Writing the parameter file to disk

Fortunately, the DIGL parameter library (PARAMLIB.C) already contains routines to read and write parameter files (GetPlotSpec and PutPlotSpec, respectively). Therefore, developing the menu utility means designing a menu layout that allows for the placement of parameter options and interactions with the user.

The X View library can be used to take care of most of these details, including the presentation of an elaborate menu panel to accomplish this task.

Designing POLYMENU.C

The X View library consists of a collection of high-level units such as

- Windows

- Frames

- Canvases

- Text windows

- Menus

- Scrollbars

191

Each of these has a large subset of attributes and data type associations that are used to define—in precise terms—the appearance and type of interaction allowed with the user. Fortunately, most of these attributes default to values that allow simple objects to be defined with just a few lines.

Because the main objective of this chapter is to introduce you to high-level window programming using libraries, the focus will be on a very small subset of the X View capabilities. The terminology used in X View is slightly different than some of the terminology developed thus far, but it is consistent with the text-based window discussions of Chapter 6.

DIGL Parameter Files

Listing 7.1, the parameter file POLYGON.CTL, is the test input into the menu utility to be developed.

Listing 7.1. POLYGON.CTL.

```
;
;                    Scientific Concepts, Inc.
;                       (c) 1989-93 SCI
;
GRAPDEV      //POSTSCRIPT
OUTTOFIL     //FALSE                      ;plot to file ?
PLOTFI       //POLY.PLT                   ;plot output file
FONT         //SIMPLXST                   ;default character font
;
GRIDTYPE     //1                          ;grid selection
LINESTYLE    //4                          ;line type setting
FILLTYPE     //1                          ;polygon fill setting
;
BAKCOL       //LIGHTGREEN                 ;video background color
FORCOL       //CYAN                       ;plot labeling color
```

Recall that reading the parameter file initializes the graphics state to the values specified in the file. In designing the menu layout of POLYMENU.C, there are three different types of data categories you can use to partition the menu:

- *String Data,* with file names such as plot output file and font
- *Selection or Choice,* with values that have a limited number of options, such as TRUE/FALSE associated with the plot-to-file option
- *List Options,* in which there are cases with a limited list of options but there are more than a few possible values, such as foreground and background colors

You can use the data categories to design a parameter layout best suited for ease of use and selection at the menu level.

Implementing POLYMENU.C

Listing 7.2 presents the program POLYMENU.C implemented with the XView library.

Listing 7.2. POLYMENU.C.

```
/*+====================================================================
== PolyMenu: Integrated polygon menu test shell...              ==
==                                                              ==
== Author: Scientific Concepts, Inc.                            ==
== Copyright (c) 1990-1993. All rights reserved worldwide.      ==
=====================================================================*/


#include <xview/xview.h>
#include <xview/frame.h>
#include <xview/panel.h>
#include <xview/notice.h>
#include <xview/cms.h>
#include <xview/tty.h>
#include <xview/font.h>
#include "syshead.h"



/*-------------------- macros / constants --------------------*/

typedef enum {OFF, ON} ONOFF;
```

continues

193

Listing 7.2. continued

```
/*---------------------- global variables -----------------------*/

     static char    POLYGON[80]="mig25.pog" ;/* polygon file to draw*/
     static char    POLYCTL[80]="polygon.ctl" ;
                                         /* polygon parameter file  */
     static char    POLYDIR[80]=" " ;/* directory of parameter file */

     static int     ForeColIdx        ;/* index of foreground color */
     static int     BackColIdx        ;/* index of background color */


/*---------------------- structures --------------------------*/



/*------------------- WINDOW RELATED CONTROL ---------------------*/

     Frame          PolyFrame         ;/* base frame for polygon menu*/
     Panel          PolyPanel         ;/* base panel for polygon menu*/

     Panel_item     PolygonName       ;/* Name of polygon to draw    */
     Panel_item     PolyFile          ;/* Poly data base file        */
     Panel_item     PolyPrim        ;/* Poly plot primitive file name*/
     Panel_item     PolyGraphDevice   ;/* Poly graphics device       */
     Panel_item     PolyFileOutput    ;/* Poly protocol output option*/
     Panel_item     PolyForeColor     ;/* Poly foreground color      */
     Panel_item     PolyBackColor     ;/* Poly background color      */
     Panel_item     PolyGrid          ;/* Poly grid selection option */
     Panel_item     PolyLineStyle     ;/* Poly line style            */

/*------------------- function prototypes -----------------------*/

void PolyQuit();
int PolySelect();
int PolyWrite();
```

```
*+=========================================================================
== program main: Polygon parameter file menu...                         ==
== Author: Scientific Concepts, Inc.                                    ==
== Copyright (c) 1990-1993. All rights reserved worldwide.              ==
=========================================================================*/
int main()
{

     int         errc         ;/* error code                   */
     int         Quiet        ;/* mode of plot control read funct*/
     int         NewPlot      ;/* indicates if new plot drawn   */



/*++++++++++++++++++++++++++++++++++++++++++++++++++++++++++++++++++++++++
++ Read parameter file to preset values...                            ++
++++++++++++++++++++++++++++++++++++++++++++++++++++++++++++++++++++++++*/

     Quiet=1;
     NewPlot=1;

     errc = get_plotspec(" ", POLYCTL,Quiet,NewPlot);
     if (errc != 0)
       puts("\n* Warning *: Could not read parameter file");

/*++++++++++++++++++++++++++++++++++++++++++++++++++++++++++++++++++++++++
++ Display main menu mask...                                          ++
++++++++++++++++++++++++++++++++++++++++++++++++++++++++++++++++++++++++*/


     PolyFrame = (Frame)xv_create(NULL, FRAME,
             FRAME_NO_CONFIRM, TRUE,
             FRAME_INHERIT_COLORS, TRUE,
             FRAME_LABEL, "POLYMENU - Polygon Menu Test Program",
             NULL);

     PolyPanel = (Panel) xv_create(PolyFrame, PANEL, NULL);

     PolyFile  = xv_create(PolyPanel, PANEL_TEXT,
             PANEL_NEXT_ROW, -1,
             PANEL_LABEL_STRING, "Parameter File Name",
```

continues

195

Listing 7.2. continued

```
            PANEL_VALUE,            POLYCTL,
            PANEL_VALUE_DISPLAY_LENGTH, 50,
            PANEL_VALUE_X,          200,
            PANEL_NOTIFY_PROC,      PolySelect,
            NULL);


    PolygonName = xv_create(PolyPanel, PANEL_TEXT,
            PANEL_NEXT_ROW, -1,
            PANEL_LABEL_STRING, "Polygon File Name",
            PANEL_VALUE,            POLYGON,
            PANEL_VALUE_DISPLAY_LENGTH, 50,
            PANEL_VALUE_X,          200,
            PANEL_NOTIFY_PROC,      PolySelect,
            NULL);

    PolyPrim  = xv_create(PolyPanel, PANEL_TEXT,
            PANEL_NEXT_ROW, -1,
            PANEL_LABEL_STRING, "Plot Output File",
            PANEL_VALUE,            plotprim,
            PANEL_VALUE_DISPLAY_LENGTH, 50,
            PANEL_VALUE_X,          200,
            PANEL_NOTIFY_PROC,      PolySelect,
            NULL);


    PolyFileOutput = xv_create(PolyPanel, PANEL_CHOICE,
            PANEL_LABEL_STRING,  "Output To File?",
            PANEL_NEXT_ROW,         20,
            PANEL_VALUE,            filesnap,
            PANEL_VALUE_X,          200,
            PANEL_CHOICE_STRINGS,"NO",
                                 "YES",
                                 NULL,
            PANEL_NOTIFY_PROC,      PolySelect,
            NULL);

    PolyGrid = xv_create(PolyPanel, PANEL_CHOICE,
            PANEL_LABEL_STRING,  "Grid Type",
```

```
        PANEL_NEXT_ROW,        -1,
        PANEL_VALUE,           gridtype,
        PANEL_VALUE_X,         200,
        PANEL_CHOICE_STRINGS,"NO GRID",
                               "DOTS ONLY",
                               "MESH",
                               "VERTICAL",
                               "HORIZONTAL",
                               NULL,
        PANEL_NOTIFY_PROC,     PolySelect,
        NULL);


PolyLineStyle = xv_create(PolyPanel, PANEL_CHOICE,
        PANEL_LABEL_STRING,  "Line Style",
        PANEL_NEXT_ROW,        -1,
        PANEL_VALUE,           plinestyle - 1,
        PANEL_VALUE_X,         200,
        PANEL_CHOICE_STRINGS,"SOLID",
                               "DOTTED",
                               "DASHED",
                               "DOTS AND DASHES",
                               NULL,
        PANEL_NOTIFY_PROC,     PolySelect,
        NULL);


PolyGraphDevice = xv_create(PolyPanel, PANEL_CHOICE,
        PANEL_LABEL_STRING,  "Graphics Device Options",
        PANEL_NEXT_ROW,        -1,
        PANEL_VALUE_X,         200,
        PANEL_CHOICE_STRINGS,"HPGL",
                               "VGACOLOR",
                               "SUNVIDEO",
                               "POSTSCRIPT",
                               NULL,
        PANEL_NOTIFY_PROC,     PolySelect,
        NULL);


PolyForeColor = xv_create(PolyPanel, PANEL_LIST,
        PANEL_LABEL_STRING,  "Foreground",
```

continues

197

Listing 7.2. continued

```
                PANEL_NEXT_ROW,     20,
                PANEL_VALUE_X,      200,
                PANEL_NOTIFY_PROC,  PolySelect,
                PANEL_LIST_STRINGS, "BLACK","CYAN",
                                    "GREEN","BROWN","YELLOW",
                                    "LIGHTRED","RED","MAGENTA","WHITE",
                                    "DARKGRAY","LIGHTBLUE","LIGHTGREEN",
                                    "LIGHTCYAN","GREEN","LIGHTMAGENTA",
                                    "BLUE", "BRIGHTWHITE",
                                    NULL,
            NULL);


    PolyBackColor = xv_create(PolyPanel, PANEL_LIST,
            PANEL_LABEL_STRING, "Background",
            PANEL_VALUE_X,      470,
            PANEL_LIST_STRINGS, "BLACK","CYAN",
                                "GREEN","BROWN","YELLOW",
                                "LIGHTRED","RED","MAGENTA","WHITE",
                                "DARKGRAY","LIGHTBLUE","LIGHTGREEN",
                                "LIGHTCYAN","GREEN","LIGHTMAGENTA",
                                "BLUE", "BRIGHTWHITE",
                                NULL,
            PANEL_NOTIFY_PROC,  PolySelect,
            NULL);



    (void) xv_create(PolyPanel, PANEL_BUTTON,
            PANEL_LABEL_STRING,  "Write Parameter File",
            XV_X,                125,
            XV_Y,                450,
            PANEL_NOTIFY_PROC,   PolyWrite,
            NULL);


    (void) xv_create(PolyPanel, PANEL_BUTTON,
            PANEL_LABEL_STRING,  "Exit Polygon Menu System",
            PANEL_NOTIFY_PROC,   PolyQuit,
            NULL);
```

```
/*++++++++++++++++++++++++++++++++++++++++++++++++++++++++++++++++++++++++
++ Sub menu control loop...                                            ++
++++++++++++++++++++++++++++++++++++++++++++++++++++++++++++++++++++++++++*/
      window_fit(PolyFrame);
      xv_main_loop(PolyFrame);


/*++++++++++++++++++++++++++++++++++++++++++++++++++++++++++++++++++++++++
++ Exit and restore CRT to main video page...                          ++
++++++++++++++++++++++++++++++++++++++++++++++++++++++++++++++++++++++++++*/


}/* end of main */

/*+=====================================================================
== int PolySelect: Process event from polygon menu selection...       ==
== Author: Scientific Concepts, Inc.                                  ==
== Copyright (c) 1990-1993. All rights reserved worldwide.            ==
=====================================================================*/
int PolySelect(item, event)
Panel_item item;
Event *event;
{
      char          ItemName[82]       ;/* name of item event     */
      char          ItemSval[82]       ;/* item value (string)    */

      int           ChoiceVal          ;/* value of keypress      */
      int           idx                ;/* loop counter           */


      strcpy(ItemName , (char *)xv_get(item, PANEL_LABEL_STRING));

      if (spos(ItemName, "Plot Output File") > 0)
        {
          strcpy(plotprim , (char *)xv_get(item, PANEL_VALUE));
        }
      else if (spos(ItemName, "Polygon File Name") > 0)
        {
          strcpy(POLYGON , (char *)xv_get(item, PANEL_VALUE));
        }
      else if (spos(ItemName, "Parameter File Name") > 0)
        {
```

continues

199

Listing 7.2. continued

```
          strcpy(POLYCTL , (char *)xv_get(item, PANEL_VALUE));
      }
    else if (spos(ItemName, "Foreground") > 0)
      {
        idx=0;
        ForeColIdx = -1;
        plotfor[0]='\0';
        while ((idx < MAXCOLORS) && (ForeColIdx < 0))
          {
            if (xv_get(PolyForeColor, PANEL_LIST_SELECTED, idx))
              {
                ForeColIdx = idx;
                strcpy(plotfor , xv_get(PolyForeColor,
                  PANEL_LIST_STRING, ForeColIdx));
              }
            idx++;
          }
      }
    else if (spos(ItemName, "Background") > 0)
      {
        idx=0;
        BackColIdx = -1;
        plotbak[0]='\0';
        while ((idx < MAXCOLORS) && (BackColIdx < 0))
          {
            if (xv_get(PolyBackColor, PANEL_LIST_SELECTED, idx))
              {
                BackColIdx = idx;
                strcpy(plotbak , xv_get(PolyBackColor,
                  PANEL_LIST_STRING, BackColIdx));
              }
            idx++;
          }
      }
    else if (spos(ItemName, "Output To File?") > 0)
      {
        filesnap =  (int) xv_get(item, PANEL_VALUE);
      }
```

```
else if (spos(ItemName, "Graphics Device Options") > 0)
  {
    ChoiceVal =  (int) xv_get(item, PANEL_VALUE);
    switch (ChoiceVal)
      {
         case 0:
           graphdevice = HPGL;
           break;
         case 1:
           graphdevice = VGACOLOR;
           break;
         case 2:
           graphdevice = SUNVIDEO;
           break;
         case 3:
           graphdevice = POSTSCRIPT;
           break;
      }
  }
else if (spos(ItemName, "Line Style") > 0)
  {
    ChoiceVal =  (int) xv_get(item, PANEL_VALUE);
    switch (ChoiceVal)
      {
         case 0:
         case 1:
         case 2:
         case 3:
           plinestyle = ChoiceVal + 1;
           break;
      }
  }
else if (spos(ItemName, "Grid Type") > 0)
  {
    ChoiceVal =  (int) xv_get(item, PANEL_VALUE);
    switch (ChoiceVal)
      {
         case 0:
         case 1:
```

continues

201

Listing 7.2. continued

```
            case 2:
            case 3:
            case 4:
              gridtype = ChoiceVal;
              break;
          }
        }

      return XV_OK;

}/* end of PolySelect */


/*+====================================================================
== int PolyWrite: Write polygon parameter file...              ==
== Author: Scientific Concepts, Inc.                           ==
== Copyright (c) 1990-1993. All rights reserved worldwide.      ==
======================================================================*/
int PolyWrite()
{

      int          errc         ;/* error code                    */
      int          Quiet        ;/* mode of plot control read funct*/

      Quiet=1;
      errc = PutPlotSpec(" ", POLYCTL,Quiet);
      if (errc != 0)

      return XV_OK;


}/* end of PolyWrite */


/*+====================================================================
== void PolyQuit: Destroy frame and exit menu...               ==
== Author: Scientific Concepts, Inc.                           ==
== Copyright (c) 1990-1993. All rights reserved worldwide.      ==
======================================================================*/
```

```
void PolyQuit()
{
      xv_destroy_safe(PolyFrame);

}/* end of PolyQuit */
```

Analysis of POLYMENU.C

The first step in structuring the program is to include the XView header files that contain the attributes and object definitions. The list included here is by no means complete, but it is sufficient for the POLYMENU.C program:

```
#include <xview/xview.h>
#include <xview/frame.h>
#include <xview/panel.h>
#include <xview/notice.h>
#include <xview/cms.h>
#include <xview/tty.h>
#include <xview/font.h>
```

Next, you define global handles for the XView objects and data items or attributes used to build the menu structure:

```
Frame         PolyFrame        ;/* base frame for polygon menu    */
Panel         PolyPanel        ;/* base panel for polygon menu    */

Panel_item    PolygonName      ;/* Name of polygon to draw        */
Panel_item    PolyFile         ;/* Poly data base file            */
Panel_item    PolyPrim         ;/* Poly plot primitive file name  */
Panel_item    PolyGraphDevice  ;/* Poly graphics device           */
Panel_item    PolyFileOutput   ;/* Poly protocol output option    */
Panel_item    PolyForeColor    ;/* Poly foreground color          */
Panel_item    PolyBackColor    ;/* Poly background color          */
Panel_item    PolyGrid         ;/* Poly grid selection option     */
Panel_item    PolyLineStyle    ;/* Poly line style                */
```

The Frame and Panel data types are used to set up the menu box within which the buttons, scrollbars, and data entry blanks are placed. They initialize a titled frame in the following code fragment:

```
PolyFrame = (Frame)xv_create(NULL, FRAME,
        FRAME_NO_CONFIRM, TRUE,
        FRAME_INHERIT_COLORS, TRUE,
        FRAME_LABEL, "POLYMENU - Polygon Menu Test Program",
        NULL);

PolyPanel = (Panel) xv_create(PolyFrame, PANEL, NULL);
```

In the next fragment, you use the xv_create function to register several dialog box elements consistent with your parameter file requirements:

```
PolyFile  = xv_create(PolyPanel, PANEL_TEXT,
        PANEL_NEXT_ROW, -1,
        PANEL_LABEL_STRING, "Parameter File Name",
        PANEL_VALUE,            POLYCTL,
        PANEL_VALUE_DISPLAY_LENGTH, 50,
        PANEL_VALUE_X,          200,
        PANEL_NOTIFY_PROC,   PolySelect,
        NULL);


        .
        .
        .


PolyFileOutput = xv_create(PolyPanel, PANEL_CHOICE,
        PANEL_LABEL_STRING,  "Output To File?",
        PANEL_NEXT_ROW,      20,
        PANEL_VALUE,         filesnap,
        PANEL_VALUE_X,       200,
        PANEL_CHOICE_STRINGS,"NO",
                             "YES",
                             NULL,
        PANEL_NOTIFY_PROC,   PolySelect,
        NULL);


        .
        .
        .


PolyForeColor = xv_create(PolyPanel, PANEL_LIST,
        PANEL_LABEL_STRING,  "Foreground",
        PANEL_NEXT_ROW,      20,
        PANEL_VALUE_X,       200,
```

```
        PANEL_NOTIFY_PROC,    PolySelect,
        PANEL_LIST_STRINGS,   "BLACK","CYAN",  "GREEN","BROWN","YELLOW",
                              "LIGHTRED","RED","MAGENTA","WHITE",
                              "DARKGRAY","LIGHTBLUE","LIGHTGREEN",
                              "LIGHTCYAN","GREEN","LIGHTMAGENTA","BLUE",
                              "BRIGHTWHITE",
                              NULL,
        NULL);
        .
        .
        .


(void) xv_create(PolyPanel, PANEL_BUTTON,
        PANEL_LABEL_STRING,   "Exit Polygon Menu System",
        PANEL_NOTIFY_PROC,    PolyQuit,
        NULL);
```

In this fragment, you create four different panel objects:

```
PANEL_TEXT
```

```
PANEL_CHOICE
```

```
PANEL_LIST
```

```
PANEL_BUTTON
```

Each object has a different set of possible attributes with common attributes for placement such as PANEL_NEXT_ROW and PANEL_VALUE_X. Initial values are set by the attribute PANEL_VALUE.

The most important attribute for the object is telling the window manager or notifier which routine to signal when a button has been pushed or a character string entered. This is done by the attribute PANEL_NOTIFY_PROC.

The next code fragment identifies where procedural programming ends and event programming begins:

```
window_fit(PolyFrame);
xv_main_loop(PolyFrame);
```

In this case, the call to xv_main_loop surrenders control to the X Window manager program to process events registered by the previous code fragments. Once any of the specified events occurs, the XView toolkit invokes the specified function, and processing of the event is now up to the user.

You define three possible classes of events in POLYMENU.C by defining the following three functions:

```
void PolyQuit();

int PolyWrite();

int PolySelect();
```

As indicated by the names of the functions, you may quit (leave the menu), change an option, or write a new parameter file reflecting the menu changes.

The function PolyQuit is attached to the button labeled Exit Polygon Menu System. When the button is pressed, the function is activated, destroying the menu panel and returning control to the operating system.

The function PolyWrite is attached to the button labeled Write Parameter File. When the button is pressed, the function is activated, which invokes the PutPlotSpec of the DIGL library to write out a new parameter file.

Unlike the simple button operations, the function PolySelect is attached to all other objects defined on the menu. You already know that there are several different types of objects, so how does the function know "who rang"?

The beginning of the PolySelect function contains declarations of formal parameters:

```
Panel_item item;
Event *event;
```

These two pieces of data are sufficient to allow a user-defined function to figure out who called and what to do—with the help of other functions of the XView library.

Consider the next code fragment from the body of PolySelect:

```
    .
    .
    .


strcpy(ItemName , (char *)xv_get(item, PANEL_LABEL_STRING));

if (spos(ItemName, "Plot Output File") > 0)
  {
    strcpy(plotprim , (char *)xv_get(item, PANEL_VALUE));
  }
```

```
   .
   .
   .
else if (spos(ItemName, "Foreground") > 0)
  {
    idx=0;
    ForeColIdx = -1;
    plotfor[0]='\0';
    while ((idx < MAXCOLORS) && (ForeColIdx < 0))
      {
        if (xv_get(PolyForeColor, PANEL_LIST_SELECTED, idx))
          {
            ForeColIdx = idx;
            strcpy(plotfor , xv_get(PolyForeColor,
              PANEL_LIST_STRING, ForeColIdx));
          }
        idx++;
      }

  }

   .
   .
   .


else if (spos(ItemName, "Line Style") > 0)
  {
    ChoiceVal =  (int) xv_get(item, PANEL_VALUE);
    switch (ChoiceVal)
      {
         case 0:
         case 1:
         case 2:
         case 3:
           plinestyle = ChoiceVal + 1;
           break;
      }
  }
else if (spos(ItemName, "Grid Type") > 0)
  {
    ChoiceVal =  (int) xv_get(item, PANEL_VALUE);
```

```
    switch (ChoiceVal)
      {
          case 0:
          case 1:
          case 2:
          case 3:
          case 4:
            gridtype = ChoiceVal;
            break;
      }
  }

return XV_OK;

  .
  .
  .
```

Use the call

```
(char *)xv_get(item, PANEL_LABEL_STRING)
```

to return the string name of the object. Based on the name, you use a nested if-then-else structure to make decisions based on the data type related to the object in question.

In the case of the PANEL_CHOICE object, an index representing the button pushed is either used as is or as an index to a string array of possible values, such as the color lists of the PANEL_LIST object. You use this information to modify select parameters of the DIGL graphics state as desired.

Summary

Chapter 6 presents ideas on window design from the ground up in a DOS environment. This chapter focuses on high-level window library interfaces. You can create a complete working menu utility built around the parameter file routines of the DIGL library and X Window routines of XView for UNIX systems.

It is my intention to give you a quick introduction to high-level X Windows programming. The subject is far too extensive for a complete tutorial in one chapter of any book. I recommend that those interested in pursuing this beyond the scope of this chapter consider reference books on the subject. A good source for detail on the design and use of the XView toolkit can be found in Dan Heller's book, *XView Programming Manual* (see Bibliography).

The next chapter presents a more exhaustive list of ways to modify and extend the DIGL concept by using the object-oriented approach.

THE OBJECT-
ORIENTED
APPROACH

In Chapters 1 through 4 of this book, I discussed issues related to the design constraints and performance of a device-independent graphics library. I defined many graphics operations and described how various graphics devices are used to implement them. I discussed performance trade-offs. In Chapters 5 through 7, I discussed how the DIGL model is implemented and used to build two- and three-dimensional applications.

In this chapter, to help you to prepare for the future, I answer two interesting and important questions:

1. What is the scope of the modifications that can be made to the DIGL?

2. How can the DIGL model be extended to have a more object-oriented approach to development?

The next sections of this chapter deal with these issues in detail. This information serves as a rough outline of the order in which changes should be made.

The Scope of Modifications to the DIGL

When you attempt to modify the DIGL and the applications presented in this book, remember that you have access to 100 percent of the source code. You must consider where and when to modify the code. It depends on your individual expertise with such things as the C programming language, software library maintenance, graphics techniques, and various applications.

It is impossible for me to predict how every reader will fare in these areas. I can, however, anticipate the kinds of changes that most likely you will need to make. In this section, I suggest modifications that you can make. I discuss these modifications in order of least to most difficult and risky. The word *risk* is defined as the measure of the complexity and cost in debug and development time associated with a particular change. A high risk change involves much more time to implement.

Of course, use your own judgment to decide how you approach these tasks. Before you make any changes to a software package, it is best to read the design and user documentation first. In this case, read this entire book—including the appendixes.

Extending the Support Libraries

Extending the existing support libraries is a simple and low-risk task. It has no impact on how the DIGL already works, provided, of course, that the changes do not involve manipulating global data that are visible to the DIGL. You can add additional file and string operations to the corresponding support libraries without creating problems. Some of your applications might require these additional operations.

Modifying a DIGL Application

I provided a variety of DIGL applications (in addition to the library) as a test configuration for the library itself. The applications should also give you a template to use. For example, if you are interested in a specific type of linear plot different from the one presented in this book, start with most of what already exists in the linear plot for file access and graphics initialization. In most cases, this proves to be much easier than writing a completely new program from the beginning.

Adding or Porting Graphics Applications

When you adapt another graphics application for the DIGL, consider these questions:

- Is the application structured so that all required interactive support is processed before plotting?

- Does the existing DIGL package support the graphics primitives that the application requires?

- Does the application work properly in its present form?

Depending on the answers to these questions, you might want to restructure the application before you use the DIGL to implement it. If the new code is well structured and the graphics primitives that it requires are supported by the DIGL system, you will have little difficulty adding or porting the application.

Adding Graphics Macros

How difficult it is to add a macro depends on whether the macro uses existing primitives or requires new primitives.

If the macro uses existing primitives, you need only to add algorithmic code that supports the macro. If the macro is similar in form and structure to an existing one, you can simply copy that macro and modify it. However, if the macro requires one or more new primitives, it is best to identify and add the new primitives first. Then, add the algorithmic code.

Adding Graphics Primitives

Adding graphics primitives is a more difficult modification. This is because you are making changes in areas that are globally visible to the entire graphics library. However, if you follow a few basic guidelines, you can add graphics primitives without much trouble.

When you add graphics primitives, start with the DIGL graphics state discussed in Chapter 5, "A Design Prototype for the DIGL." The GRASTATE.H file contains constant parameters that represent the primitives known to the system. When you add new parameters, first make sure that at least one—and preferably all—of the graphics drivers in your configuration can implement the parameter. If the new primitive can be implemented, then:

1. Create a name for the primitive and add it to the graphics primitives section of the GRASTATE.H file. The order of the primitives in this file is not important. However, you might want to place it at the end so that later on you can identify changes easily.

2. Find the primitive in the PRINLIB.C file closest to the new primitive that you want to add. Modify it or create your own function. Add that to the PRIMLIB.C library file and to the PRIMLIB.H header file.

3. Pick the graphics driver that is the easiest to use as a test case for implementing the new primitive. Modify this driver by adding the new primitive case to the section where the if-then-else structure checks for each primitive operation.

4. Create an application—or modify an existing one—to execute the primitive function and verify its correctness.

5. Modify all the remaining graphics drivers that can support the new primitive. Repeat step 4.

Extending Parameter File Keywords

The parameter files used in the DIGL and the parameter file parsing routines are far from complete for initializing and implementing a full set of plotting features. As they are implemented on the DIGL disk, the parameter files contain only a few lines that relate to options such as the graphics device and the output destinations of graphics primitives. In a fully developed system, a considerable number of new primitives and plotting data might be added.

Here is an example of what a more developed parameter file might look like:

```
GRAPDEV    // VGACOLOR
VIEWPORT   // 0.00,100.00,0.00,100.00        ;PLOTTING AREA
OUTTOFIL   // FALSE                          ;PLOT TO FILE ?
XANDY      // FALSE                          ;EXPECT X,Y PAIRS ?
AUTOPEN    // TRUE                           ;VIDEO PEN ?
GRAPHCLEAR // FALSE                          ;CLEAR GRAPHICS ?
UNDERSURF  // FALSE                          ;SEE UNDER SURFACE ?
HIDDENON   // TRUE                           ;USE HIDDEN LINE REMOVAL ?
CROSSHATCH // FALSE                          ;USE PERSPECTIVE CROSSHATCH ?
NORMALIZE  // FALSE                          ;NORMALIZE AMPLITUDE ?
HEADEROFF  // FALSE                          ;SKIP MAIN TITLES ?
ROTATE     // FALSE                          ;ROTATE 3D DATA ?
LOGUNIT    // 6                              ;LOGICAL UNIT NUMBER
DIRECT     //                                ;FILE DIRECTORY
DATAFI     // LINETEST.DAT                    ;USER DATA FILE
POLYFI     // TERMINAL.POG                    ;USER POLYGON FILE
PLOTFI     // LINEAR.PLT                      ;PLOT OUTPUT FILE
PLOTLINK   //                                ;NEXT CONTROL FILE NAME
CONSTYLE   //                                ;LINE TYPE PER CONTOUR COLOR
USERXMIN   // -180.000                       ;X AXIS MINIMUM RANGE
USERXMAX   //  180.000                       ;X AXIS MAXIMUM RANGE
USERYMIN   //  -10.000                       ;Y AXIS MINIMUM RANGE
USERYMAX   //   10.000                       ;Y AXIS MAXIMUM RANGE
USERZMIN   //    0.000                       ;Z AXIS MINIMUM RANGE
USERZMAX   //  160.000                       ;Z AXIS MAXIMUM RANGE
;
```

```
POINTSX     // 361                          ;# OF POINTS
POINTSY     // 30                           ;# OF POINTS
POINTSZ     // 70                           ;# OF POINTS
;
PERDEPTH    // 21.50                        ;PERSPECTIVE DEPTH PERCEPTION
AZIMUTH     // 0.00                         ;ISOMETRIC AZIMUTH ANGLE
ELEVATION   // 0.00                         ;ISOMETRIC ELEVATION ANGLE
POLYXF      // 1.00                         ;SYMBOL X AXIS SCALE FACTOR
POLYYF      // 1.00                         ;SYMBOL Y AXIS SCALE FACTOR
POLYAN      // 0.00                         ;SYMBOL ROTATION ANGLE
PLOTTOP     // 0.00                         ;OFFSET MAX PLOT HEIGHT
LEGLOCX     // 0.00                         ;LEGEND X AXIS LOCATION
LEGLOCY     // 0.00                         ;LEGEND Y AXIS LOCATION
LEGSIZX     // 1.50                         ;LEGEND X AXIS SIZE
LEGSIZY     // 1.50                         ;LEGEND Y AXIS SIZE
COMLOCX     // 0.00                         ;COMMENT X AXIS LOCATION
COMLOCY     // 0.00                         ;COMMENT Y AXIS LOCATION
COMSIZX     // 1.50                         ;COMMENT X AXIS SIZE
COMSIZY     // 1.50                         ;COMMENT Y AXIS SIZE
;
TITLE1      // MICROPLOTS
TITLE2      //
TITLE3      // Linear Plot Example
TITLE4      // (Sine Function - Bug In Data ??)
TITLE5      // ADVANCED COMPUTING CONCEPTS
XTITLE      // User Units
YTITLE      // Ampl
ZTITLE      //
;
LINPENS     // 5                            ;# LINEAR PLOT PENS
LOGPENS     // 5                            ;# LOG PLOT PENS
POLPENS     // 5                            ;# POLAR PLOT PENS
CONPENS     // 5                            ;# CONT/PIXEL PLOT PENS
ISOPENS     // 5                            ;# ISOMETRIC PLOT PENS
;
GRIDTYPE    // 2                            ;GRID SELECTION
BARWIDTH    // 0.90                         ;BAR CHART BAR WIDTH (%)
CONTIVAL    // 60.00                        ;CONTOUR INTERVAL
;
XMAJOR      // 6                            ;X MAJOR TICS
XMINOR      // 3                            ;X MINOR TICS
YMAJOR      // 5                            ;Y MAJOR TICS
```

```
YMINOR      // 5                       ;Y MINOR TICS
ZMAJOR      // 0                       ;Z MAJOR TICS
ZMINOR      // 0                       ;Z MINOR TICS
;
XSIGFID     // 2                       ;X SIGNIFICANT DIGITS
YSIGFID     // 2                       ;Y SIGNIFICANT DIGITS
ZSIGFID     // 0                       ;Z SIGNIFICANT DIGITS
LINESTYLE   // 1                       ;LINE TYPE SETTING
FILLTYPE    // 1                       ;POLYGON FILL SETTING
;
BAKCOL      // BLACK                   ;VIDEO BACKGROUND COLOR
FORCOL      // CYAN                    ;PLOT LABELING COLOR
COMSTR      //                        ;COMMENT LABEL STRING
BARLABS     //                        
;
;
SYMBCON     // TRUE                    ;CONNECT DOTS ?
GLOGX       // FALSE                   ;LOG OF X GRID ?
GLOGY       // FALSE                   ;LOG OF Y GRID ?
PLOGX       // FALSE                   ;LOG OF X BEFORE PLOT ?
PLOGY       // FALSE                   ;LOG OF Y BEFORE PLOT ?
ZOOM        // FALSE                   ;ZOOM IN ON DATA ?
OVERLAY     // FALSE                   ;PLOT OVERLAY STATUS
;
DATAXMIN    //  -2.000                 ;X AXIS MINIMUM RANGE
DATAXMAX    //   2.000                 ;X AXIS MAXIMUM RANGE
DATAYMIN    //   0.000                 ;Y AXIS MINIMUM RANGE
DATAYMAX    //  20.000                 ;Y AXIS MAXIMUM RANGE
DATAZMIN    // -20.000                 ;Z AXIS MINIMUM RANGE
DATAZMAX    //  20.000                 ;Z AXIS MAXIMUM RANGE
XOFFSET     //   0.000                 ;X AXIS DATA OFFSET
YOFFSET     //   0.000                 ;Y AXIS DATA OFFSET
ZOFFSET     //   0.000                 ;Z AXIS DATA OFFSET
```

Parameter file keyword additions are required either when an existing primitive is not supported in the parameter file parsing routines, or when a new primitive that is not supported by the parsing routines is required. If an existing primitive is not supported, add the new parsing code to the keyword parse routines located in the PARAMLIB.C library file. If a new primitive is required, first add the new primitive to the system; then add the new parsing code.

Modifying or Adding Device Drivers

If you use a video system other than UNIX on a Sun workstation or DOS with Microsoft C, you need to write your own graphics driver. How complex this is depends on how well you understand the graphics driver that you want to add and the compiler that you are using. In general, modifying or adding device drivers is similar to modifying or adding graphics primitives:

1. Decide on a name for the driver and add it to the GRASTATE.H graphics state file.

2. Find a graphics driver whose structure and performance are similar to the one that you want to add. For example, to add a driver for Tektronix video, a similar video driver is DOS video that uses the Microsoft compiler. On the other hand, to add a pen plotter other than HPGL, the HPGL driver is the best place to start.

> The PostScript and HPGL drivers are in the DRIVRLIB.C file. The Microsoft C drivers are in the MSCVILIB.C file. The UNIX X11 drivers are in the SUNVILIB.C file.

3. Each driver is referenced in three stages during the DIGL graphics process—initialization, primitive execution, and termination. These stages are controlled by the following routines from DRIVRLIB.C. Add code that corresponds to the new driver to the existing case structure.

```
devinit()          ;/* initializes graphics device    */
gracur()           ;/* graphics conversion primitives */
devend()           ;/* ends current graphics mode     */
```

4. Modify the routines in the PARAMLIB.C file—such as initdevice—so that they recognize the parameter name of the new driver.

5. Modify a parameter file so that it specifies the new driver. Test it with an existing graphics application.

Improving the Efficiency of the DIGL

Many routines in the DIGL can be modified to improve their efficiency. A good place to start is with polygon operations and structures in the POLYLIB.C and POLYLIB.H files. Notice that the DIGL does not use dynamic memory allocation anywhere, and that many data arrays and structures are static and globally visible. The initial design of DIGL emphasized readability over efficiency. Browse through the libraries one at a time; you will find many places where algorithms can be implemented more efficiently.

The DIGL and Object-Oriented Development

In this section, I discuss the issues that pertain to object-oriented analysis. *Object-oriented* is a term that surprisingly few programmers really understand. It is not easy to explain how to apply object-oriented concepts to well-established applications, such as graphics. Object-oriented is far too broad a topic to cover completely in this section. However, I will define a few terms and discuss them in relation to the DIGL model in its present form.

Object-Oriented Analysis of the DIGL

Before I discuss applying object-oriented techniques to the DIGL, here are some terms for you to keep in mind:

Object-oriented   A style of programming that is not procedural. Object-oriented programming relies most heavily on inheritance and data encapsulation.

Procedural   A style of programming in which implementation is sequential. Information is passed and acted on as a series of sequential steps.

Class   A class corresponds to a data type or class of objects, such as binary trees or a box (in terms of graphics).

Objects   Objects are dynamic in nature. They can be created and destroyed readily during the execution of a program.

219

Inheritance A language mechanism by which a new class of objects is defined as an extension of a previously existing class.

Information hiding The interface to a program or package specification is separated from the details of its implementation. For example, a stack might consist of an array of items and counters that represent the items currently in (pushed) and the items currently out (popped). To use the stack, the user does not need to know the name of the array or where the array is. With information hiding, all the user needs is an interface that represents the data items to be pushed and popped.

Object-Oriented Implementation

How can you use object-oriented analysis to improve the DIGL? The DIGL consists of two central mechanisms for organizing and controlling graphics operations. These mechanisms are:

■ The representation of data types that relate to the various stages of graphics operations—that is, the DIGL graphics state

■ The implementation of various low- and high-level graphics operations to produce a graphics image

To represent these two mechanisms more naturally, consider graphics operations as classes of objects instead of collections of unrelated macro operations. Figure 8.1 shows how the macro-oriented form of the library looks when you attempt to add a new figure, the wagon.

The figure represents the procedural form of the DIGL macro library. As Figure 8.1 illustrates, there are mechanisms—in the form of functions—to draw circles, lines, and boxes. However, many of the existing macros exist as disjoint operations even though they share classes of operations. The box macro is a form of line. The polygon macro is a collection of line, circle, and all the other macros. If you want to draw a new complex shape—such as the wagon on the right side of the figure—you need to write a new routine that makes calls to the box and circle macro operations. Code must be added and interfaced to various functions to obtain this result.

With an object-oriented approach, however, the wagon is simply an extension of the box and circle macros. Instead of using the procedural approach that I just discussed, you define a class called figure. The figure class inherits the properties of the circle and box objects. Therefore, in the figure implementation, the subclasses draw themselves until the result is the wagon figure.

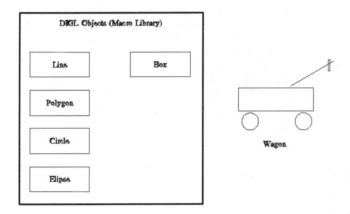

Figure 8.1. DIGL object-oriented analysis.

To use this object-oriented approach, you must add code. However, the amount of code that you must add is less than what you would have to add if you used a procedural approach, and you do not need to modify the code that already works. Applying an object-oriented approach to the whole DIGL significantly increases its image rendering capabilities, which can be adjusted dynamically or at runtime.

Summary

In this chapter, I discuss how you can approach changes to the DIGL. I pointed out how certain changes are more difficult than others. However, most things in the DIGL are there for a reason. Often, other options exist. What is most important, though, is that the DIGL works. A more efficient algorithm is not useful if nothing works after it is implemented. Be patient and careful. Pay particular attention to Appendix H, "When Things Go Wrong—Debugging Hints."

The DIGL is by no means a static system. Feel free to contact me and make suggestions for future improvements. I welcome all suggestions from readers on how to improve this software as much as possible.

You are now ready to tackle a wide variety of problems and graphics applications. Read the appendixes thoroughly to identify your configuration and to get additional pointers on how to use the source code in this book.

CHAPTER

9

ADVANCED
GRAPHICS
PLOTTING
TECHNIQUES

In Chapter 5, "A Design Prototype for the DIGL," I used the graphics tools of the DIGL software developed in this book to introduce you a few simple plotting algorithms. In this chapter, I examine some of the issues associated with more complicated plotting requirements.

Business presentations and scientific applications are two major classes of graphics plotting programs. With business presentation graphics, plots such as pie charts and bar graphs in two and three dimensions are quite common. With scientific programming, you want to represent data taken from scientific calculations or data acquisitions in two and three dimensions. In this chapter, I concentrate on a few two- and three-dimensional plot algorithms that are more suited to scientific applications.

In this chapter, I discuss many technical problems and design decisions. The DIGL software utilities provide useful solutions. All the applications discussed in this chapter are part of the DIGL source files on the disk supplied with this book.

General Plotting Issues

Before you can examine the plotting algorithms, you need to make a few decisions about design, specifically the range of features and limitations.

Data Representation

As with the applications discussed earlier in the book, the data input for all plots is in ASCII format, in which one or more whitespace characters separate values. The format is general-purpose. Decimal points and exponential formats are optional. In addition, all the data and parameter files used in these plotting algorithms permit comments that start with a semicolon.

Parameter Input

In Chapter 5, I based the application input on the DIGL parameter file and used prompts as part of the application process. In this chapter, I go further by enabling users to enter data from the command line and to use additional general-purpose parameter files.

All of the parameter routines used in these applications share a common format and structure. You might decide to make a plotting application library and combine some of these features. The parameter files for these examples ;use the .def file extension instead of .ctl.

Labels and Fonts

This version of the DIGL does not include an internal font or stroke table. To label the plots, you have two options:

- Import the plot into a word processing or drawing program and annotate it.

- Use the hooks already in the DIGL and add your own fonts or stroke tables. Stroke tables are treated like any other polygon that uses the transformations provided in the library.

2-D Linear Plots

Two-dimensional linear plots are the most basic requirement of any plotting package. However, the limitations built in to the plotting algorithm vary substantially. For this implementation of the DIGL, my three goals are

- A linear plot parameter file that specifies the data file, the user window limits, the grid type, the graphics parameter file, and the tick marks for the grid

- Comments in the linear parameter file

- An infinite number of plotting points

The DIGL provides support library functions in the FILELIB.C file that satisfy my first two goals. These libraries are described in Appendix A, "DIGL Support Libraries." The getstringtoken(), getinttoken(), and getrealtoken() functions in FILELIB.C enable an application to remove and format individual parameters from a file. These functions ignore comments while they parse tokens.

Here is an example of the parameter file that I use for the linear plot:

```
;                       2-D Plot Definitions
;

vga                     ;graphics parameter file name
cheby.dat               ;data file name
1                       ;grid type

8 4 6 3                 ;xmajor xminor ymajor yminor (tic marks)
0 360 -40 0             ;xmin xmax ymin ymax
```

This parameter file differs from the DIGL parameter files discussed earlier in two important ways:

■ It does not use a keyword or a delimiter to indicate the type of value. It interprets values based on the order in which they appear in the file.

■ It enables you to group arbitrarily any number of related values on a single line. This improves readability.

Each plot that I introduce in this chapter has slightly different parameter requirements.

As for my third goal—to plot an infinite number of points—I have to compromise. The linear plot that I develop reads the data file in segments as opposed to reading in all the other data at one time. Because a data file may be larger than the memory available for the linear plot, the segments are small data arrays representing a few (512) data points at a time. This segment is contained in a loop that enables the plotting to continue up to its maximum size. I can use a long integer as a loop counter and 512 data points—that is, 2×256 pairs—as the arbitrary length of the segment. Therefore, this linear plot handles up to the maximum size of a long integer—more than 2 billion points!

Global Data Structures

The linear plot is named LINEPLOT.C on the DIGL application disk. The beginning of LINEPLOT.C names the global variables:

```
/*================ Data Structures and Definitions ================*/

#define        MAXSEGMENT  512 /* maximum plot segment length    */
#define        NOEVEN        0  /* no isotropic grid in window     */


/*=========================== Macros ============================*/


/*========================Global Variables========================*/

        static int  PlotPoints          ;/* number of points to plot  */
        static int  Gridtype            ;/* rectangular grid selection */
        static int  XMajor              ;/* tics on x major axis      */
```

```
static int   XMinor              ;/* tics on x minor axis      */
static int   YMajor              ;/* tics on y major axis      */
static int   YMinor              ;/* tics on y minor axis      */

static char DefFileName[80]      ;/* plot definition file name */
static char DataFileName[80]     ;/* plot data file name       */
static char ParamFile[80]        ;/* DIGL parameter file name  */

FILE         *DataFile           ;/* data file handle          */

static long int TotalPoints      ;/* total of points plotted   */
static long int TotalPairs       ;/* total of x,y pairs plotted */

static double Wxmin              ;/* window x minimum          */
static double Wxmax              ;/* window x maximum          */
static double Wymin              ;/* window y minimum          */
static double Wymax              ;/* window y maximum          */
static double DataPoints[MAXSEGMENT] ;/* data point values     */
```

Compare the variable names to the names of the parameters in the parameter file. The names of the parameters were chosen to correspond to the variable names in the program.

Here is the pseudocode for a linear plot based on the design parameters discussed so far:

1 *Begin LinePlot(pfile : char[])*

2 *Read linear parameter file <pfile>*
3 *Set global values based on <pfile> contents*
4 *Initialize DIGL graphics state*
5 *Set viewport and user window*

6 *While not at end of data file*
7 *Read next data segment*
8 *While not at end of data segment*
9 *Plot data pair*
10 *End While*
11 *End while*

12 *Terminate graphics state*

13 *End LinePlot*

In LINEPLOT.C, line 2 of the pseudocode is represented by the following code from the `GetLinearPlotDef()` function:

```
DefFileHandle = fileopen(DefFileName, "asc");
if (DefFileHandle != NULL)
  {
    status = getstringtoken(DefFileHandle, ParamFile);
    status = getstringtoken(DefFileHandle, DataFileName);
    status = getinttoken(DefFileHandle, &Gridtype);

    status = getinttoken(DefFileHandle, &XMajor);
    status = getinttoken(DefFileHandle, &XMinor);
    status = getinttoken(DefFileHandle, &YMajor);
    status = getinttoken(DefFileHandle, &YMinor);

    status = getrealtoken(DefFileHandle, &Wxmin);
    status = getrealtoken(DefFileHandle, &Wxmax);
    status = getrealtoken(DefFileHandle, &Wymin);
    status = getrealtoken(DefFileHandle, &Wymax);


/*+++++++++++++++++++++++++++++++++++++++++++++++++++++++++++++++++++++++++
++ Do 'a little' error checking here...                                  ++
+++++++++++++++++++++++++++++++++++++++++++++++++++++++++++++++++++++++++*/

    if ((status) &&
        (Wxmin < Wxmax) && (Wymin < Wymax) &&
        (XMinor <= XMajor) && (YMinor <= YMajor)) Errc=0;

    fileclose(DefFileHandle);
  }
```

The filename of the linear parameter file is used to open the file. The parameters are parsed and formatted to match the global variables that the linear plot requires. Error checking is done at the end to ensure that the maximum and minimum values for ticks and windows make sense—in other words, max > min.

Lines 6 through 11 of the pseudocode are the core of the plotting routine. They are implemented in LINEPLOT.C by the following code from the `PlotLinearData()` function:

```
PlotPoints = ReadData(DataFileHandle, DataPoints,
  (int) (MAXSEGMENT-1));

if (PlotPoints >= 0)
  {
```

```
TotalPoints=0;
idx=0;
while (PlotPoints >= 0)
  {
    if (TotalPoints == 0)
      move(DataPoints[idx], DataPoints[idx+1]);
    else
      draw(DataPoints[idx], DataPoints[idx+1]);

    TotalPoints = TotalPoints + 2;
    idx = idx + 2;

    if (idx >= PlotPoints)
      {
        PlotPoints = ReadData(DataFileHandle, DataPoints,
          (int) (MAXSEGMENT-1));
        idx=0;
      }
  }
}
```

As this code indicates, the data are plotted by means of the DIGL draw command, which plots continuous line segments until the entire file is plotted. Figure 9.1 is an example of the output from the linear plot program that uses the linear parameter file.

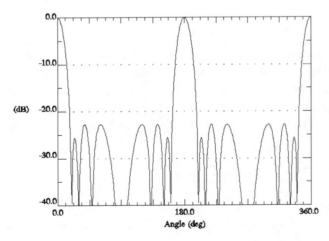

Figure 9.1. Example of a linear plot.

2-D Scatter Plots

Instead of plotting the data as continuous curves, you can plot each data point individually without line segments connecting the points. This type of plot is often referred to as a *scatter plot*. This implementation uses the DIGL polygon operations to plot the data points with symbols from the polygon library. The basic form of the linear plot algorithm that defines the plot parameter file remains the same except for a few additions. My design goals are the same as for the linear plot, but I also want to enable the user to specify:

■ The name of the polygon symbol used

■ The size and the angle of rotation of the polygon symbol used

Here is an example of the parameter file that I use for the polygon plot:

```
;               2-D Plot Definitions
;

vga             ;graphics parameter file name
curve.dat       ;data file name
gavel           ;polygon file name
8.5             ;polygon size in percent (0-100)
33.0            ;polygon angle of rotation
0               ;grid type

8 4 6 3         ;xmajor xminor ymajor yminor (tic marks)
0 15 -5 1       ;xmin xmax ymin ymax
```

In this example, the parameters indicate that the gavel.pog polygon data file is used to plot the curve.dat data file. The polygon is rotated by 33 degrees and scaled to 8.5 percent of the current viewport. The polygon plotting routine inherits all the other features of the linear plot. The polygon plot routine is named POLYPLOT.C on the DIGL applications disk.

Global Data Structures

The beginning of POLYPLOT.C looks almost identical to the linear plot except for the additional global variables that are needed for polygon manipulation.

```
/*=============== Data Structures and Definitions ================*/

#define        MAXSEGMENT  512 /* maximum plot segment length    */
#define        NOEVEN       0  /* no isotropic grid in window    */


/*============================ Macros ============================*/


/*========================Global Variables========================*/

        static int  PlotPoints         ;/* number of points to plot  */
        static int  Gridtype           ;/* rectangular grid selection */
        static int  XMajor             ;/* tics on x major axis      */
        static int  XMinor             ;/* tics on x minor axis      */
        static int  YMajor             ;/* tics on y major axis      */
        static int  YMinor             ;/* tics on y minor axis      */

        static char DefFileName[80]    ;/* plot definition file name */
        static char DataFileName[80]   ;/* plot data file name       */
        static char PolygonFileName[80];/* polygon file name         */
        static char ParamFile[80]      ;/* DIGL parameter file name  */

        FILE        *DataFile          ;/* data file handle          */

        static long int TotalPoints    ;/* total of points plotted   */
        static long int TotalPairs     ;/* total of x,y pairs plotted */

        static double Wxmin            ;/* window x minimum          */
        static double Wxmax            ;/* window x maximum          */
        static double Wymin            ;/* window y minimum          */
        static double Wymax            ;/* window y maximum          */
        static double PolyAngle        ;/* polygon rotation angle    */
        static double PolySize         ;/* polygon size (0-100%)     */
        static double DataPoints[MAXSEGMENT] ;/* data point values    */

        TWODMATRIX  PolyFig            ;/* polygon data structure    */
        TWODMATRIX  PolyTemp           ;/* polygon temporary         */
```

Compare the variables to the polygon plot parameter file; the variables and descriptions are consistent.

To deal with polygon manipulations, the pseudocode for the polygon plot includes a few additions. Based on the design parameters that I have discussed so far, the pseudocode is

1   *Begin* `PolyPlot(pfile : char[])`

2   *Read linear parameter file* `<pfile>`
3   *Set global values based on* `<pfile>` *contents*
4   *Get and scale the polygon based on parameters*
5   *Initialize DIGL graphics state*
6   *Set viewport and user window*

7   *While not at end of data file*
8   *Read next data segment*
9   *While not at end of data segment*
10   *Move to x,y data point location*
11   *Draw polygon*
12   *End While*
13   *End While*

14   *Terminate graphics state*

15 *End* `PolyPlot`

In POLYPLOT.C, line 4 of the pseudocode is represented by the following code from the `GetScalePolygon()` function:

```
/*++++++++++++++++++++++++++++++++++++++++++++++++++++++++++++++++++++++++++++++
++ Get polygon file and scale based on definitions...                        ++
++++++++++++++++++++++++++++++++++++++++++++++++++++++++++++++++++++++++++++++*/

    Errc=getpoly(PolyName,&PolyFig, &PolyVect);

    if (Errc == 0)
      {
        framepoly(&PolyFig, &Pxmin, &Pxmax, &Pymin, &Pymax);
        XSfact = fabs(PolySize/100.0*(Wxmax-Wxmin)/(Pxmax-Pxmin));
        YSfact = fabs(PolySize/100.0*(Wymax-Wymin)/(Pymax-Pymin));
        matrixscale(&PolyFig, &PolyTemp, XSfact, YSfact);
        matrixrotate(&PolyTemp, &PolyFig, PolyAngle);
      }
```

The getpoly DIGL function uses the filename of the polygon to retrieve it. Once a polygon is retrieved, the framepoly DIGL function calculates the size of the smallest rectangle that encloses it. The frame size and the scale and window limits are used to scale and rotate the polygon. After the final transformation matrix is obtained, the frame size is used in the body of the plotting algorithm to plot the polygon.

Lines 7 through 13 of the pseudocode are the core of the plotting routine. They are implemented in POLYPLOT.C by the following code from the PlotPolygonData() function:

```
PlotPoints = ReadData(DataFileHandle, DataPoints,
  (int) (MAXSEGMENT-1));

if (PlotPoints >= 0)
  {
    TotalPoints=0;
    idx=0;
    while (PlotPoints >= 0)
      {
        move(DataPoints[idx], DataPoints[idx+1]);
        if (TotalPoints != 0) drawipoly(&PolyFig);

        TotalPoints = TotalPoints + 2;
        idx = idx + 2;

        if (idx >= PlotPoints)
          {
            PlotPoints = ReadData(DataFileHandle, DataPoints,
              (int) (MAXSEGMENT-1));
            idx=0;
          }
      }
  }
```

As this code indicates, the data are plotted by means of polygons drawn with the drawipoly() function. Figure 9.2 is an example of the output from the polygon plot program that uses the polygon parameter file.

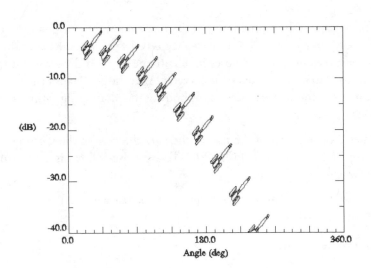

Figure 9.2. Example of a polygon plot.

3-D Perspective Plots

Perspective plotting involves projecting data from three dimensions onto a two-dimensional surface. It requires transformations that are beyond the scope of this book. However, to give you some idea of how the code for the 3-D plot works, I will briefly explain the basic techniques of perspective plotting.

Usually, three-dimensional data represents multiple copies of two-dimensional data that are based on a third, varying parameter. The z dimension varies as a function of x and y—or, in this case, row and column. Unlike the 2-D model, the 3-D model does not contain actual samples of x and y in the data file. Some applications require x and y data that is not evenly spaced. For the sake of simplicity, assume that the data are evenly spaced.

A true perspective plot involves projecting the data at some θ and φ, which I call `azimuth` and `elevation`. You can specify an `azimuth` angle to rotate the data around the x-axis. You can also specify an `elevation` angle to tilt the data around the y-axis.

In this implementation, these features are incorporated into the basic form of the perspective plot algorithm. The variables are initialized to values that are defined in the plot parameter file. I have five goals for the design of the perspective plot:

- To enable the user to specify an azimuth rotation angle in degrees.

- To enable the user to specify an elevation rotation angle in degrees.

- To enable the user to specify the viewing transformation parameters.

- To implement hidden line removal.

- To enable the user to turn hidden line removal on or off.

My third goal requires flexible parameters that represent the variables that control the projection of the 3-D data into the view volume. These parameters include:

- The viewing distance

- The view point—that is, the location of viewer's eye

- The screen size—that is, the plotting surface

- The scale factor—an arbitrary constant

In the parameter files supplied, these values have been optimized for best viewing at multiple angles. You can change them. However, unless you want to spend a significant amount of time experimenting, I suggest that you leave them alone.

My fifth goal gives rise to the name for the plotting program—MESHPLOT.C. If you turn hidden line removal off, the plot has the appearance of wire mesh in which all the lines in the foreground and the background are visible.

Here is an example of the parameter file that I use for the perspective plot:

```
;               3-D Plot Definitions
;

vga             ;graphics parameter file name
hat.dat         ;data file name

45.0            ;/* azimuth angle in degrees            */
33.0            ;/* elevation angle in degrees          */
91              ;/* number of x points (number of rows) */
```

```
91              ;/* number of y points (points per row)    */
0.0             ;/* z-axis user minimum value              */
1.0             ;/* z-axis user maximum value              */

420.0           ;/* viewing distance                       */
22.0            ;/* view point                             */
2.0             ;/* screen size                            */
1.4             ;/* scale factor                           */
1               ;/* hidden line off/above/above below      */
```

In this example, the parameters indicate that the HAT.DAT data are plotted at an azimuth angle of 45 degrees and an elevation angle of 33 degrees. All the other features of the perspective plot are inherited from the 2-D plotting routines. The perspective plot routine is named MESHPLOT.C on the DIGL applications disk.

Global Data Structures

The beginning of MESHPLOT.C is similar to the 2-D plots except that it adds global variables that are needed for perspective plotting:

```
/*================ Data Structures and Definitions ================*/


/*=========================== Macros ============================*/

#define XMAXRANGE      10.0     /* maximum x scaled volume range   */
#define XMINRANGE     -10.0     /* minimum x scaled volume range   */
#define YMAXRANGE      10.0     /* maximum x scaled volume range   */
#define YMINRANGE     -10.0     /* minimum x scaled volume range   */
#define ZMAXHEIGHT     10.0     /* maximum z scaled volume height  */
#define ZMINHEIGHT      0.0     /* minimum z scaled volume height  */
#define GRIDSIZE        600     /* maximum size of volume window   */
#define MAXSEGMENT      512     /* maximum plot segment length     */


/*=======================Global Variables=========================*/

        static double Azimuth     ;/* azimuth angle in degrees     */
        static double Elevation   ;/* elevation angle in degrees   */
        static double ViewDist    ;/* viewing distance             */
        static double ViewPoint   ;/* view point                   */
```

```
static double VolScreen     ;/* screen size                  */
static double ScaleFact      ;/* scale factor                 */
static double XUserMin=0.0 ;/* x axis user minimum value    */
static double XUserMax       ;/* x axis user maximum value    */
static double YUserMin=0.0 ;/* y axis user minimum value    */
static double YUserMax       ;/* y axis user maximum value    */
static double ZUserMin       ;/* z axis user minimum value    */
static double ZUserMax       ;/* z axis user maximum value    */

static double CosElRad       ;/* cosine of elevation in radians */
static double SinElRad       ;/* sine of elevation in radians   */
static double CosAzRad       ;/* cosine of azimuth in radians   */
static double SinAzRad       ;/* sine of azimuth in radians     */

static double DataPoints[MAXSEGMENT] ;/* data point values    */
static double YminVisible[GRIDSIZE] ;/* grid hidden line lower*/
static double YmaxVisible[GRIDSIZE] ;/* grid hidden line upper*/

static int    NewLine        ;/* x indicates start of line    */
static int    Hidden         ;/* hidden line removal starts   */
static int    RowPoints      ;/* number of points per row     */
static int    NumRows        ;/* number of rows in file       */

static char   DefFileName[80] ;/* plot definition file name   */
static char   DataFileName[80] ;/* plot data file name        */

static char   ParamFile[80] ;/* mesh plot parameter file name */

FILE          *DataFile         ;/* data file handle          */
```

The pseudocode for the mesh plot includes steps that are required for the transformations:

1   *Begin* MeshPlot(pfile : char[])

2   *Read linear parameter file* <pfile>
3   *Set global values based on* <pfile> *contents*
4   *Initialize DIGL graphics state*
5   *Set viewport and user window*

6   *While not at end of data file*
7   *Read next data segment*

237

9	*While not at end of data segment*
8	*Scale 3-D* x,y,z *point into view volume*
9	*Convert 3-D* x,y,z *point to 2-D* x,y *point*
10	*Plot point according to hidden line requirements*
11	*End While*
12	*End While*
13	*Terminate graphics state*

14 *End MeshPlot*

Lines 6 through 12 are the core of the plotting routine. They are implemented in MESHPLOT.C. by the following code from the PlotMeshData() function:

```
PlotPoints = ReadData(DataFileHandle, DataPoints,
  (int) (MAXSEGMENT-1));


NumPoints= (int) YUserMax - 1;
for (Xtemp=XUserMax; Xtemp > XUserMin; Xtemp=Xtemp-1.0)
  {
    NewLine=1;
    count=0;
    PointsRead = ReadData(DataFileHandle, DataPoints, NumPoints);
    for (Ytemp=YUserMin; Ytemp < YUserMax; Ytemp=Ytemp+1.0)
      {
        Xval=Xtemp;
        Yval=Ytemp;
        Zval= DataPoints[count];

        PointScale(&Xval, XUserMin, XUserMax, XMINRANGE, XMAXRANGE);
        PointScale(&Yval, YUserMin, YUserMax, YMINRANGE, YMAXRANGE);
        PointScale(&Zval, ZUserMin, ZUserMax, ZMINHEIGHT, ZMAXHEIGHT);

        Conv3d2d(&Xpoint, &Ypoint, Xval, Yval, Zval);

        PlotMeshPoint(Xpoint, Ypoint);

        count++;
      }
  }
```

As this code indicates, the data are plotted after the mathematical transformations contained in the Conv3d2d() routine are performed. Figure B.3 is an example of MESHPLOT.C without hidden line removal applied; Figure B.4 shows MESHPLOT.C with hidden line removal applied.

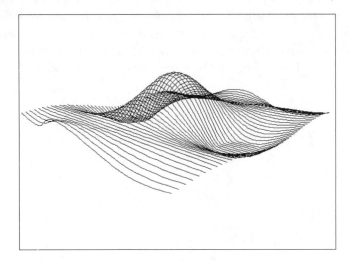

Figure 9.3. Perspective plot—hidden line removal not applied.

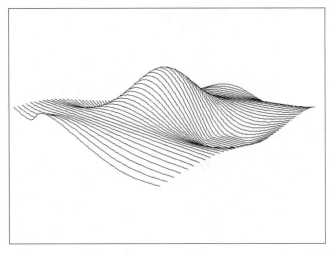

Figure 9.4. Perspective plot—hidden line removal applied.

Summary

In this chapter, I presented more examples of two- and three-dimensional applications that use practical scientific data. You can experiment with the applications by changing the parameter files or creating new ones. You can consolidate many of the functions in these applications to form another plotting library. You can also port your own applications into the DIGL system. Please read the appendixes thoroughly. You should be able to extend these libraries and applications with surprisingly little effort.

APPENDIX

A

DIGL SUPPORT
LIBRARIES

This appendix contains information on support functions mentioned throughout this book. The support libraries cover the DIGL graphics functions. They also cover three additional areas:

■ *String functions:* Functions that represent various numeric-to-string conversions and string formatting operations.

■ *File operations:* File retrieval operations that are shared among graphics applications, such as data retrieval and ASCII-to-numeric conversions.

■ *Miscellaneous:* General-purpose functions, such as message output and formatting.

If you are proficient in the C programming language, these library functions might appear redundant—for example, `stringint` (string to integer) versus `atoi`, which is built in to C. However, many of the C built-in functions are not easy to remember without constantly checking reference documentation. This is because of the lack of consistency in the number and types of formal parameters from function to function.

This appendix discusses each of these libraries. Appendix B, "DIGL Function Reference," contains information on the functions of each library file.

STRNGLIB.C—String Functions

This library contains many string conversion and formatting operations that can be used with any application. The STRNGLIB.H file contains the function prototypes that resolve forward referencing when these functions are called from other modules.

scrunch

Name

scrunch() removes all blanks from a string.

Synopsis

```
void scrunch(s)
char *s;
```

Description

This function performs whitespace string trimming operations. All whitespace characters are removed from the string represented by the formal parameter.

Diagnostics

The formal string argument is returned as NULL if the only characters found are whitespace characters.

This function assumes that the string is NULL-terminated.

See Also

```
strlen()
```

parse

Name

parse() parses a string into two substrings.

Synopsis

```
void parse(pstr, subst1, subst2, token)

char pstr[];
char subst1[];
char subst2[];
char token[];
```

Description

This function parses, or separates, a string into two subcomponents around a delimiter string that is contained in the original string.

Diagnostics

The original string is left unchanged after the parsing operation.

If parsing delimiter is not part of the original string, both substrings are left unchanged. The substrings must be declared large enough to contain the result of the parsing operation.

See Also

```
spos()
strlen()
```

Esleft

Name

sleft() shifts a string supplied by the user one position to the left.

Synopsis

```
void sleft(s)
char *s;
```

Description

This function moves all the characters in a string supplied by the user one position to the left. The new position is filled with a space character.

Diagnostics

The string character array supplied is increased in length by one for each operation.

This function assumes that the string is declared large enough for this operation and that it is NULL-terminated.

See Also

```
sright()
strim()
```

sright

Name

sright() shifts a string supplied by the user one position to the right.

Synopsis

```
void sright(s)
char *s;
```

Description

This function moves all the characters in a string supplied by the user one position to the right. The new position is filled with a space character.

Diagnostics

The string character array supplied is increased in length by one for each operation.

This function assumes that the string is declared large enough for this operation and that it is NULL-terminated.

See Also

```
sleft()
strim()
```

sjoin

Name

sjoin() appends, or concatenates, two strings.

Synopsis

```
void sjoin(s1, s2)
char *s1;
char *s2;
```

Description

This function joins two strings by appending the second string to the end of the first string.

Diagnostics

This function assumes that both strings are NULL-terminated.

The storage allocation for the first string must be large enough to contain all the elements of both strings.

See Also

    strlen()

intstring

Name

    intstring() converts an ASCII string to an integer.

Synopsis

```
void intstring(ival, pstr)
int *ival;
char *pstr;
```

Description

This function converts an ASCII string to an integer. It is similar to the atof function that is built into C. However, this routine ignores bad input, such as non-numeric characters in the input string.

Diagnostics

The formal parameter that represents the string can contain blanks or non-numeric characters. Every occurrence of such characters is ignored.

> When bad character input is converted, the result is always numeric and in the range of integers. Bad character input usually returns a zero value.

See Also

    realstring()

realstring

Name

    realstring() converts a double-precision real number to a string.

Synopsis

```
void realstring(rval, pstr, places)
double *rval;
char *pstr;
int places;
```

Description

This function converts a double-precision real number (`double`) to a string whose precision the user specifies. Precision is specified in terms of the number of decimal places required. This function supports automatic exponentiation.

Diagnostics

There is a difference between precision and accuracy. Using double-precision numbers ensures precision within 16 decimal places, instead of six places for single-precision real numbers (`float`).

The string supplied should be long enough to contain the number of characters that the specified decimal places require.

See Also

```
pow()
strcpy()
strlen()
spos()
sjoin()
sprintf()
```

stringint

Name

`stringint()` converts a string to an integer.

Synopsis

```
void stringint(pstr, ival)
char *pstr;
int *ival;
```

Description

This function converts a string to an integer.

Diagnostics

If the string contains a decimal point, value is rounded up or down to the nearest integer. The value is restricted to the range of a two-byte integer value.

> The string can contain characters that are not numerals. However, characters of this type are ignored.

See Also

```
scrunch()
```

stringreal

Name

stringreal() converts a string to a double-precision real number.

Synopsis

```
void stringreal(pstr, rval)
char *pstr;
double *rval;
```

Description

This function converts a string to a double-precision real number. The string can contain exponential notation.

Diagnostics

The string input to the function can contain non-numeric digits. If it does, the conversion stops with the first occurrence of an unacceptable character.

The value that the string represents must be within the range of acceptable values for a double-precision real number.

See Also

```
scrunch()
atof()
```

slen

Name

slen() returns the length of the string.

Synopsis

```
int slen(pstr)
char pstr[];
```

Description

This function returns the length of the string, which is determined by counting all of the characters in the character array. Unlike the C built-in strlen, trailing spaces are not counted.

Diagnostics

This function works in option base 1.

In calculating the length, this function ignores space characters from the end. However, other whitespace characters, such as \r or \n, are counted.

See Also

```
strlen()
```

spos

Name

spos() finds the position of the first occurrence of a substring in a string supplied by the user.

Synopsis

```
int spos(st1, st2)
char st1[];
char st2[];
```

Description

This function finds the first occurrence of a substring in a string supplied by the user. The number returned is in option base 1—1 represents the first character, known as element 0, in the character string array.

Diagnostics

The formal arguments are not modified.

If the substring is not found, a negative value is returned.

See Also

```
strlen()
```

strim

Name

`strim()` trims leading and trailing blanks from a string.

Synopsis

```
void strim(s)
char *s;
```

Description

This function trims leading and trailing blanks from a string.

Diagnostics

This function assumes that a single-character array is used.

The string must be NULL-terminated.

See Also

```
lstrim()
rstrim()
```

lstrim

Name

lstrim() trims leading blanks from a string.

Synopsis

```
void lstrim(s)
char *s;
```

Description

This function trims leading blanks from a string.

Diagnostics

This function assumes that a single-character array is used.

The string must be NULL-terminated.

See Also

```
strlen()
rstrim()
```

rstrim

Name

rstrim() trims trailing blanks from a string.

Synopsis

```
void lstrim(s)
char *s;
```

Description

This function trims trailing blanks from a string.

Diagnostics

>   This function assumes that a single-character array is used.

>   The string must be NULL-terminated.

See Also

```
strlen()
lstrim()
```

FILELIB.C—File Operations

This library contains many operations for file access, data conversion, and formatting. They can be used with any application. The FILELIB.H file contains the function prototypes that resolve forward referencing when these functions are called from other modules.

ReadData

Name

>   ReadData() reads a data segment from a data file until it reaches the end of the file.

Synopsis

```
int ReadData(DataFile, DataPoints, NumPoints)
FILE *DataFile;
double DataPoints[];
int NumPoints;
```

Description

>   This function reads an ASCII data file and parses the tokens into real numbers (type float). The values are placed into the array specified by the formal argument DataPoints. The function returns either the number of values read or the number of remaining data points in the file—whichever one is smaller.

Diagnostics

> This function assumes that the file is open and available for read access.

> The size of the array must be consistent with the number of values requested to be read.

See Also

```
getrealtoken()
```

getrealtoken

Name

> `getrealtoken()` reads the next token from a file and converts it to a real number.

Synopsis

```
int getrealtoken(sfile, rval)
FILE *sfile;
double *rval;
```

Description

> This function reads the next token from a data file and converts it to a real number. A token is an sequence of ASCII characters that are separated by one or more whitespace characters. If the data file is at the end, 0 indicates failure.

Diagnostics

> This function assumes that the file is open and available for read access.

> This function converts the next token in the data file that is not whitespace to a real number. The file contents and structure must be consistent with this operation.

```
getstringtoken()
stringreal()
```

getinttoken

Name

getinttoken() reads the next token from a file and converts it to an integer.

Synopsis

```
int getinttoken(sfile, ival)
FILE *sfile;
double *ival;
```

Description

This function reads the next token from a data file and converts it to an integer. A token is a sequence of ASCII characters that are separated by one or more whitespace characters. If the data file is at the end, 0 indicates failure.

Diagnostics

This function assumes that the file is open and available for read access.

This function converts the next token in the data file that is not white-space to an integer. The file contents and structure must be consistent with this operation.

See Also

```
getstringtoken()
stringreal()
```

getstringtoken

Name

getstringtoken() reads the next token from a file.

Synopsis

```
int getstringtoken(sfile, stoken)
FILE *sfile;
char stoken[];
```

Description

This function reads the next token from a data file. A token is a sequence of ASCII characters that are separated by one or more whitespace characters. If the data file is at the end, 0 indicates failure.

Diagnostics

This function assumes that the file is open and available for read access.

> This function assumes that the next non-whitespace token in the data file is the required token. The file contents and structure must be consistent with this operation.

See Also

```
fgetc()
isspace()
```

fileappend

Name

`fileappend()` opens a file and adds to it—if it exists—for read-write.

Synopsis

```
FILE *fileappend(fname, mode)
char fname[];
char mode[];
```

Description

This function opens a file for read/write operations if it already exists. This function is used to add information to the end of a file.

Diagnostics

This function uses mode flags to indicate the type of file—for example, `bin` for binary and `asc` for ASCII.

To avoid creating a new file inadvertently, make sure that the file exists before you issue an `append` command.

See Also

`fopen()`

fileread

Name

`fileread()` reads a sequence of bytes from a file to an array.

Synopsis

```
int fileread(fp, lbuf, nbytes)
FILE *fp;
char lbuf[];
int nbytes;
```

Description

This function reads a line from a file into a specified array. The actual number of bytes that are returned is either the amount requested or the number of remaining characters in the file—whichever is smaller.

Diagnostics

A pointer to the character buffer is used as the buffer location to store the number of bytes specified.

Space in the pointer buffer must be sufficient to contain the number of bytes requested.

See Also

    getc()

filereadasc

Name

filereadasc() reads a buffer line from the file (ASCII text).

Synopsis

```
int filereadasc(fp, lbuf, nbytes)
FILE *fp;
char lbuf[];
int nbytes;
```

Description

This function reads a line from a file into a specified array. The actual number of bytes that are returned is either the amount requested or the number of remaining characters in the file—whichever is smaller.

Diagnostics

The pointer to the character buffer is used as the buffer location to store the number of bytes specified.

Space in the pointer buffer must be sufficient to contain the number of bytes requested.

See Also

    getc()

fileopen

Name

fileopen() opens a file for read if it exists.

```
FILE *fileopen(fname, mode)
char fname[];
char mode[];
```

Description

This function opens a file for read if it exists. The pointer to the file handle is returned if the file is opened successfully. If the file open operaton is unsuccessful, a NULL value for the file pointer is returned to indicate failure.

Diagnostics

The formal parameters are left unchanged.

> The mode character flag must be consistent with the required method of access—for example, `bin` for binary and `asc` for ASCII.

See Also

```
fopen()
fileclose()
```

filecreate

Name

`filecreate()` creates a new file and opens it for read-write access.

Synopsis

```
FILE *filecreate(fname, mode)
char fname[];
char mode[];
```

Description

This function creates a new file and opens it for read-write access. If the file already exists or if an error is encountered, a NULL file handle is returned.

Diagnostics

The formal parameters are left unchanged.

The mode character flag must be consistent with the required method of access—for example, bin for binary and asc for ASCII.

See Also

```
fileexist()
fopen()
```

filewrite

Name

filewrite() writes a buffer of data to a specified file.

Synopsis

```
int filewrite(fp, lbuf, nbytes)
FILE *fp;
char lbuf[];
```

Description

This function writes a buffer of data that is specified on input to a specified file.

Diagnostics

The formal parameters are left unchanged.

This function assumes that the file handle points to an file already opened for write access.

See Also

```
fwite()
```

filedelete

Name

filedelete() deletes an existing file.

Synopsis

```
int filedelete(fname)
char fname[];
```

Description

This function deletes a file specified by the ASCII string on input.

Diagnostics

The formal parameters are left unchanged.

The file path and the filename that are issued must be consistent with the naming conventions of the operating system that you are using.

See Also

```
remove()
```

fileclose

Name

`fileclose()` closes a file.

Synopsis

```
int fileclose(fp)
FILE *fp;
```

Description

This function closes a file that is currently open for read or write access.

Diagnostics

The formal parameters are left unchanged.

This function assumes that the file handle points to an file already opened for write access.

See Also

```
fileopen()
fopen()
```

fileexist

Name

fileexist() indicates whether a file already exists.

Synopsis

```
int fileexist(fname)
char fname[];
```

Description

This function checks whether a file, specified by a formal parameter, exists.

Diagnostics

The formal parameters are left unchanged.

> The file path and the filename that are issued must be consistent with the
> naming conventions of the operating system that you are using.

See Also

```
fileclose()
fileopen()
```

MISCLIB.C—
Miscellaneous Functions

This library contains general-purpose functions that are used for scaling and message control operations. They can be used with any application. The MISCLIB.H file contains the function prototypes that resolve forward referencing when these functions are called from other modules.

PointScale

Name

PointScale() scales a value.

Synopsis

```
void PointScale(Value, ValueMin, ValueMax, ScaleMin, ScaleMax)
double *Value;
        double ValueMin;
        double ValueMax;
        double ScaleMin;
        double ScaleMax;
```

Description

This function takes an arbitrary value in user units and scales it to the new reference frame. ScaleMin and ScaleMax indicate the new scale limits.

Diagnostics

The only value that is changed is the returned scale value.

The values supplied must be consistent with the minimum and maximum range for double-precision numbers.

See Also

scale()

BoxMessage

Name

BoxMessage writes a message that is formatted in box form.

Synopsis

```
void BoxMessage(String)
char String[];
```

Description

This function writes a message that is formatted in box form by using string that is centered within an 80-column window.

Diagnostics

Formal parameters are left unchanged.

If the string that is supplied contains newline characters, the message is split into multiple lines as required.

See Also

```
MaxMsgSize()
memset()
StringCenter()
BoxLine(stemp, BoxWidth);
```

MaxMsgSize

Name

MaxMsgSize finds the maximum size, or width, required for a message.

Synopsis

```
int MaxMsgSize(String)
char String[];
```

Description

This function finds the maximum size, or width, required for a message.

Diagnostics

The formal parameters are left unchanged.

This function assumes 80 columns as the width for formatting operations. Substrings are determined by the occurrence of \n or \r characters.

BoxLine

Name

BoxLine outputs one line of a box message.

Synopsis

```
void BoxLine(String, BoxWidth)
char String[];
int BoxWidth;
```

Description

This function outputs one line of a message to the standard output device.

Diagnostics

The formal parameters are left unchanged.

The character string must be NULL-terminated.

See Also

```
sright()
StringCenter()
slen()
```

StringCenter

Name

StringCenter centers characters in string.

Synopsis

```
void StringCenter(String, Size)
char String[];
int Size;
```

Description

This function centers characters in string by appending leading spaces as the string length requires.

Diagnostics

Centering based on the space character. Other whitespace characters are not ignored.

The string must be NULL-terminated. The storage allocation for the string must be consistent with the specified string length.

See Also

```
slen()
```

DIGL FUNCTION REFERENCE

This appendix contains information on support functions mentioned throughout this book. The DIGL can be built with three different configurations:

■ Generic or ANSI C on platforms other than UNIX or DOS with
Microsoft C

■ UNIX on a Sun workstation or compatible system (Option 1)

■ DOS with Microsoft C (Option 2)

Appendix G, "Configuring the DIGL for Your Environment," provides extensive detail on these configurations. The tables in this appendix list all the functions that are contained in each library. The functions are classified by the type of
C configuration that they require or that they can support. *Yes* indicates that the
function is compatibile with the configuration.

Table B.1. DRIVRLIB.C—graphics driver library.

Function	Description	Generic C	Sun UNIX (Option 1)	DOS with Microsoft C (Option 2)
devend	Ends the current graphics mode	Yes	Yes	Yes
devinit	Initializes a graphics device	Yes	Yes	Yes
gracur	Graphics conversion primitive	Yes	Yes	Yes
graphout	Outputs final graphics primitives	Yes	Yes	Yes
hpplot_drv	HPGL driver	Yes	Yes	Yes
post_drv	PostScript driver	Yes	Yes	Yes

Table B.2. FILELIB.C—file library.

Function	Description	Generic C	Sun UNIX (Option 1)	DOS with Microsoft C (Option 2)
fileappend	Adds to or creates a file for read-write	Yes	Yes	Yes
filecreate	Creates a nonexisting file for read-write	Yes	Yes	Yes
fileclose	Closes the current file stream	Yes	Yes	Yes
filedelete	Deletes a file	Yes	Yes	Yes
fileexist	Checks whether a file exists	Yes	Yes	Yes
fileopen	Opens a file for read-write	Yes	Yes	Yes
filereadasc	Reads a file in ASCII mode	Yes	Yes	Yes
fileread	Reads the number of bytes	Yes	Yes	Yes
filewrite	Writes the number of bytes	Yes	Yes	Yes
getrealtoken	Gets a real token from a file	Yes	Yes	Yes
getinttoken	Gets an integer token from a file	Yes	Yes	Yes
getstringtoken	Gets a string token from a file	Yes	Yes	Yes
ReadData	Reads an array of float data	Yes	Yes	Yes

Table B.3. MACROLIB.C—graphics macro library.

Function	Description	Generic C	Sun UNIX (Option 1)	DOS with Microsoft C (Option 2)
arc	Macro for drawing an arc	Yes	Yes	Yes
box	Macro for drawing a box	Yes	Yes	Yes
circle	Macro for drawing a circle	Yes	Yes	Yes
ellipse	Macro for drawing an ellipse	Yes	Yes	Yes
polargrid	Macro for a polar plot grid	Yes	Yes	Yes
rectgrid	Macro for a rectangular plot grid	Yes	Yes	Yes

Table B.4. MISCLIB.C—library of miscellaneous functions.

Function	Description	Generic C	Sun UNIX (Option 1)	DOS with Microsoft C (Option 2)
BoxLine	Writes a single line into a box	Yes	Yes	Yes
BoxMessage	Writes a message into a box	Yes	Yes	Yes
MaxMsgSize	Finds the total length of a message	Yes	Yes	Yes
PointScale	Scales a point to a new minimum/ maximum	Yes	Yes	Yes
StringCenter	Centers a string on an 80-column line	Yes	Yes	Yes

Table B.5. PARAMLIB.C—parameter file library.

Function	Description	Generic C	Sun UNIX (Option 1)	DOS with Microsoft C (Option 2)
init_plotcom	Default initialization of a graphics state	Yes	Yes	Yes
get_plotspec	Reads a plot control file	Yes	Yes	Yes
GraphicsEnd	Ends graphics operations	Yes	Yes	Yes
GraphInit	Reads and initializes a parameter file	Yes	Yes	Yes
initdevice	Initializes a graphics device	Yes	Yes	Yes
keyword	Keyword parser	Yes	Yes	Yes
ocomm	Outputs a comment to a parameter file	Yes	Yes	Yes
oreal	Outputs a number to a parameter file	Yes	Yes	Yes
ostring	Outputs a string to a parameter file	Yes	Yes	Yes
olog	Outputs logical to a parameter file	Yes	Yes	Yes
PutPlotSpec	Writes a plot control file	Yes	Yes	Yes

Table B.6. POLYLIB.C—graphics polygon library.

Function	Description	Generic C	Sun UNIX (Option 1)	DOS with Microsoft C (Option 2)
atoipoly	Converts from absolute to incremental	Yes	Yes	Yes
centerpoly	Centers the current polygon	Yes	Yes	Yes
drawapoly	Draws the current polygon in absolute	Yes	Yes	Yes
drawipoly	Draws the current polygon in incremental	Yes	Yes	Yes
getpoly	Reads polygon data file into a matrix	Yes	Yes	Yes
framepoly	Finds the minimum /maximum extents of a polygon	Yes	Yes	Yes
matrixrotate	2-D matrix rotation	Yes	Yes	Yes
matrix-translate	2-D matrix translate	Yes	Yes	Yes
matrixscale	2-D matrix scale	Yes	Yes	Yes
matrixshear	2-D matrix shear	Yes	Yes	Yes
matrixreflect	2-D matrix reflection	Yes	Yes	Yes
transformmul2D	General-purpose matrix multiply	Yes	Yes	Yes

Table B.7. PRIMLIB.C—graphics primitives library.

Function	Description	Generic C	Sun UNIX (Option 1)	DOS with Microsoft C (Option 2)
backcolor	Sets the background color	Yes	Yes	Yes
dig_beep	Sounds bell	Yes	Yes	Yes
draw	Draws a vector to a new x,y position	Yes	Yes	Yes
forecolor	Sets the foreground color	Yes	Yes	Yes
filltype	Sets a fill pattern	Yes	Yes	Yes
frame	Draws a frame around the viewport	Yes	Yes	Yes
gclear	Clears the graphics screen or device	Yes	Yes	Yes
ginit	Initializes a graphics device	Yes	Yes	Yes
idraw	Incremental draw to xval,yval	Yes	Yes	Yes
imove	Incremental move to xval,yval	Yes	Yes	Yes
laborigin	Defines the label origin	Yes	Yes	Yes
labsize	Sets the label size	Yes	Yes	Yes
labtext	Label with a supplied string	Yes	Yes	Yes
linetype	Sets the line type—dots, dashes, and so on	Yes	Yes	Yes
linewidth	Sets the line width	Yes	Yes	Yes

continues

Table B.7. continued

Function	Description	Generic C	Sun UNIX (Option 1)	DOS with Microsoft C (Option 2)
move	Moves a vector to xval, yval	Yes	Yes	Yes
pen	Selects a pen number	Yes	Yes	Yes
pencolor	Selects a pen color	Yes	Yes	Yes
rectfill	Fills a rectangular area	Yes	Yes	Yes
scale	Converts from user units to device units	Yes	Yes	Yes
show	Sets up isotropic units	Yes	Yes	Yes
viewport	Defines percent of usable area	Yes	Yes	Yes
window	Defines a display in user units	Yes	Yes	Yes

Table B.8. STRNGLIB.C—string library.

Function	Description	Generic C	Sun UNIX (Option 1)	DOS with Microsoft C (Option 2)
intstring	Converts an integer to a string	Yes	Yes	Yes
lstrim	Trims leading blanks from a string	Yes	Yes	Yes
parse	Breaks a string to parts on token	Yes	Yes	Yes

Function	Description	Generic C	Sun UNIX (Option 1)	DOS with Microsoft C (Option 2)
scrunch	Removes all blanks from a string	Yes	Yes	Yes
sjoin	Appends one string to another	Yes	Yes	Yes
sleft	Shifts a string one place to the left	Yes	Yes	Yes
slen	Returns the length of a user string (does not count spaces at the end)	Yes	Yes	Yes
spos	Finds the first occurrence of substring	Yes	Yes	Yes
sright	Shifts a string one place to the right	Yes	Yes	Yes
strim	Trims leading and trailing blanks from a string	Yes	Yes	Yes
stringint	Converts a string to an integer	Yes	Yes	Yes
stringreal	Converts a string to a double-precision real number	Yes	Yes	Yes
realstring	Coverts a real number to a string	Yes	Yes	Yes
rstrim	Trims trailing blanks from a string	Yes	Yes	Yes

Table B.9. SUNVILIB.C—Sun/X11 video graphics driver library.

Function	Description	Generic C	Sun UNIX (Option 1)	DOS with Microsoft C (Option 2)
AllocNamedColor	Allocates a color value to a name	No	Yes	No
ConnectToServer	Connects to X11 server	No	Yes	No
CreateGContext	Creates a graphics context	No	Yes	No
DIGLCloseXWindow	Waits for an event and closes window	No	Yes	No
DIGLInitXWindow	Connects to a server and opens window	No	Yes	No
OpenXWindow	Opens an X11 window	No	Yes	No
SetUpVisual	Sets up an X11 visual	No	Yes	No
SetUpColormap	Sets up and creates color map	No	Yes	No
X11video_drv	Sun X Window video driver	No	Yes	No
X11videoinit	Initializes an X11 graphics driver	No	Yes	No

Table B.10. MSCVILIB.C—Microsoft C PC video graphics driver library.

Function	Description	Generic C	Sun UNIX (Option 1)	DOS with Microsoft C (Option 2)
dosvideo_drv	DOS video CGA-VGA driver	No	No	Yes
dosvideoinit	Initializes a DOS graphics driver	No	No	Yes
ResetVideo	Clears video back to default	No	No	Yes

Table B.11. MSCWILIB.C—Microsoft C PC pop-up window library.

Function	Description	Generic C	Sun UNIX (Option 1)	DOS with Microsoft C (Option 2)
GetSegAddrress	Gets a segment address for ptr	No	No	Yes
GetVideoPage	Gets the number of the current video page	No	No	Yes
MemCopy	Copies a section from page to page	No	No	Yes
PageDown	Sets a video plane to the previous page	No	No	Yes
PageUp	Sets a video plane to the next page	No	No	Yes
PopTable	Displays a table by means of pop-up control	No	No	Yes

continues

Table B.11. continued

Function	Description	Generic C	Sun UNIX (Option 1)	DOS with Microsoft C (Option 2)
SetVideoPage	Sets the number of the current video page	No	No	Yes
WriteString	Writes a string directly to memory	No	No	Yes

C

DOS Video Drivers

This appendix contains information specific to Microsoft C compilers. Much of the information pertains to the available graphics adapters and to the methods of implementing drivers for them. Regardless of what compiler you use, you will find information that is important for modifying the source code.

This appendix discusses the methods for implementing the DOS video driver by using Microsoft C. Chapter 8, "The Object-Oriented Approach," discusses ways of enhancing this method.

Do not attempt to implement *any* of the SVGA modes shown in Table 8.1 until you make sure that your software checks whether your monitor can support that graphics mode. You can damage your display monitor if you are not extremely careful. The author and the publisher of this book assume no responsibility for damage to video monitors or to any peripherals caused by use of this software *as is* or in modified form. Consult your owner's manual for additional cautions and for suggestions on how to avoid possible damage to your configuration.

DOS Graphics Adapter Support

Chapter 3, "The Graphics Application Environment," discusses DOS graphics adapters. Table C.1 identifies differences among the resolutions of various graphics adapters. In this DIGL implementation, the highest graphics adapter resolution implemented is the standard 16-color VGA mode with a resolution of 640x480 pixels. Table C.1 shows the SVGA modes that are not implemented.

Table C.1. PC SVGA graphics modes not supported by the DIGL.

Display Mode	Resolution x,y	Number of Colors
SVGA	640x400	256
SVGA	640x480	256
SVGA	800x600	16
SVGA	800x600	256

Display Mode	Resolution x,y	Number of Colors
SVGA	1024x768	16
SVGA	1024x768	256
SVGA	1280x1024	16
SVGA	1280x1024	256

DOS Graphics Adapter Implementation

Appendix G, "Configuring the DIGL for Your Environment," discusses the DOS video support library—Option 2 of DIGL options available for extended video driver support. In the MSC_DOS subdirectory of Option 2 is a file named MSCVILIB.C, which contains the Microsoft C video driver for DOS graphics adapters. It is compatible with Microsoft Versions 5.1 and 7.0 of C.

MSCVILIB.C

The MSCVILIB.C file contains the video driver initialization procedure and the graphics primitive algorithms. The corresponding file MSCVILIB.H contains the function prototypes that resolve forward referencing as these functions are called from other modules. Each function is described in this section.

dosvideo_drv

Name

dosvideo_drv(primitive) implements a primitive selected by the user application.

Synopsis

```
void dosvideo_drv(primitive)
int primitive;
```

Description

This function decodes each graphics primitive into a series of calls to the Microsoft C graphics library.

Diagnostics

The formal argument (primitive) is not modified.

Not all graphics primitives are supported by this driver. In addition, code exists in this function that supports future modes such as labeling and RGB color mixing. This mode is a real-time bit-mapped operation; you cannot output it to a disk.

See Also

```
dosvideoinit()
```

dosvideoinit

Name

`dosvideoinit()` initializes any CGA to VGA graphics adapters.

Synopsis

```
int dosvideoinit()
```

Description

This function initializes one of the graphics adapter modes—CGA to VGA—by using constants and library calls to the Microsoft C graphics library.

Diagnostics

An error code is returned if the selected graphics adapter mode cannot be set.

This routine does not check whether the monitor in use supports the graphics mode that is selected. This is not a problem in the CGA to VGA modes if the mode is not supported by the hardware. In the SVGA mode, damage to the monitor can result.

See Also

    dosvideo_drv(primitive)

ResetVideo

Name

    ResetVideo() resets the video display.

Synopsis

    void ResetVideo()

Description

This function returns the video monitor to what its state was before the current graphics adapter was selected. A pause is implemented; the video state is not restored until there is keyboard input from the user.

Diagnostics

No formal arguments are required for this operation.

This routine ensures a smooth transition between the graphics and text modes. If the graphics application software does not call this function—because of errors or bugs in the code—the display might be left in graphics mode. You can correct this by using the DOS mode command at the DOS prompt. Consult your DOS reference manual if you are unfamiliar with this command.

See Also

    GraphInit()

283

Analysis

Many graphics modes are available from CGA to VGA. The MSCVILIB.C file, though, contains only a few functions, which support all of the graphics modes. Although the modes contain resolutions of varying capabilities, once a mode is activated, the Microsoft graphics library uses the same calls to perform various graphics operations.

In the dosvideoinit routine, an if-then-else structure is used to implement the various graphics adapters. The following code is an excerpt from that routine, showing the if-then-else structure for each graphics adapter.

```
.
.
.
if (devtype==CGACOLOR)
  {
    grid_mapx[1]=0.0;
    grid_mapx[2]=319.0;
    grid_mapy[1]=0.0;
    grid_mapy[2]=199.0;

    absol_mapx[1]=0.0;
    absol_mapx[2]=319.0;
    absol_mapy[1]=0.0;
    absol_mapy[2]=199.0;
    if (hardinit) dummy=_setvideomode(_MRES4COLOR);
    devtype=DOSVIDEO;

    maxpens=4;
    origin[1]=0.0;
    origin[2]=199.0;

    iso_factx=.9650;
    iso_facty=1.0;
  }
else if (devtype==CGABW)
  {
    grid_mapx[1]=0.0;
    grid_mapx[2]=639.0;
    grid_mapy[1]=0.0;
    grid_mapy[2]=199.0;
```

```
      absol_mapx[1]=0.0;
      absol_mapx[2]=639.0;
      absol_mapy[1]=0.0;
      absol_mapy[2]=199.0;
      if (hardinit) dummy=_setvideomode(_HRESBW);
      devtype=DOSVIDEO;

      origin[1]=0.0;
      origin[2]=199.0;

      iso_factx=.4760;
      iso_facty=1.0;
   }
else if (devtype==EGACOLOR)
   {
      grid_mapx[1]=0.0;
      grid_mapx[2]=639.0;
      grid_mapy[1]=0.0;
      grid_mapy[2]=349.0;

      absol_mapx[1]=0.0;
      absol_mapx[2]=639.0;
      absol_mapy[1]=0.0;
      absol_mapy[2]=349.0;

      if (hardinit) dummy=_setvideomode(_ERESCOLOR);
      devtype=DOSVIDEO;

      maxpens=16;
      origin[1]=0.0;
      origin[2]=349.0;

      iso_factx=.760;
      iso_facty=1.0;
   }
else if (devtype==HERCULES)
   {
      grid_mapx[1]=0.0;
      grid_mapx[2]=719.0 ;
      grid_mapy[1]=0.0;
      grid_mapy[2]=347.0;
```

```
         absol_mapx[1]=0.0;
         absol_mapx[2]=719.0;
         absol_mapy[1]=0.0;
         absol_mapy[2]=347.0;

         if (hardinit) dummy=_setvideomode(_HERCMONO);
         devtype=DOSVIDEO;

         maxpens=1;
         origin[1]=0.0;
         origin[2]=347.0;

         iso_factx=.760;
         iso_facty=1.0;
      }
   else if (devtype==EGABW)
     {
         grid_mapx[1]=0.0;
         grid_mapx[2]=639.0;
         grid_mapy[1]=0.0;
         grid_mapy[2]=349.0;

         absol_mapx[1]=0.0;
         absol_mapx[2]=639.0;
         absol_mapy[1]=0.0;
         absol_mapy[2]=349.0;
         if (hardinit) dummy=_setvideomode(_ERESNOCOLOR);
         devtype=DOSVIDEO;

         maxpens=1;
         origin[1]=0.0;
         origin[2]=349.0;

         iso_factx=.760;
         iso_facty=1.0;
      }
   else if (devtype==VGACOLOR)
     {
         grid_mapx[1]=0.0;
         grid_mapx[2]=639.0;
         grid_mapy[1]=0.0;
         grid_mapy[2]=479.0;
```

```
      absol_mapx[1]=0.0;
      absol_mapx[2]=639.0;
      absol_mapy[1]=0.0;
      absol_mapy[2]=479.0;
      if (hardinit) dummy=_setvideomode(_VRES16COLOR);
      devtype=DOSVIDEO;

      maxpens=16;
      origin[1]=0.0;
      origin[2]=479.0;

      iso_factx=.9650;
      iso_facty=1.0;
  }
else if (devtype==VGABW)
  {
      grid_mapx[1]=0.0;
      grid_mapx[2]=639.0;
      grid_mapy[1]=0.0;
      grid_mapy[2]=479.0;

      absol_mapx[1]=0.0;
      absol_mapx[2]=639.0;
      absol_mapy[1]=0.0;
      absol_mapy[2]=479.0;
      if (hardinit) dummy=_setvideomode(_VRES2COLOR);
      devtype=DOSVIDEO;

      maxpens=1;
      origin[1]=0.0;
      origin[2]=479.0;

      iso_factx=.9650;
      iso_facty=1.0;
  }
```

Each adapter mode has a different constant for the aspect ratio—used for drawing circles, for example. The origin (0,0) for the Microsoft C graphics system is the upper-left corner. To avoid inverted drawings, the origin is remapped—origin[1] represents *x*, and origin[2] represents *y*—to convert it to a coordinate system that is consistent with the DIGL. Once the user-selected graphics adapter is initialized, the parameter DOSVIDEO represents all adapters and prevents duplication of code in the driver routine dosvideo_drv.

Examples of DOS Video Driver Display Resolutions

Figure C.1 and Figure C.2 represent the output from the GLOBES.C application from Chapter 5, "A Design Prototype for DIGL." They illustrate the differences in resolution between the CGA and VGA modes. In Figure C.1, the graphics adapter used is a CGA with a resolution of 320x200 pixels.

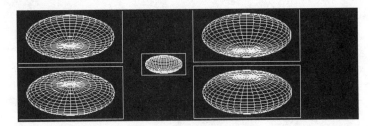

Figure C.1. The output from the GLOBES.C program—CGA mode.

In Figure C.2, the graphics adapter used is a VGA with a resolution of 640x480 pixels. Both figures represent the same algorithm. The differences in their appearances indicate how important high-resolution modes are.

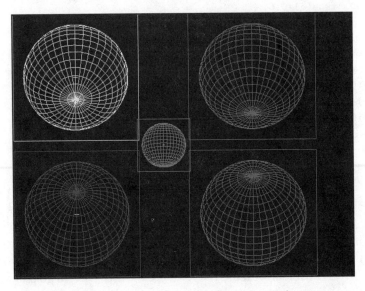

Figure C.2. The output from the GLOBES.C program—VGA mode.

D

UNIX X11
VIDEO DRIVERS

This appendix contains information specific to the X Window X11 (Xlib) driver library. However, a significant portion of the information pertains to the graphics adapters available and methods of implementing drivers for them. The X11 video driver library supplied as part of DIGL under Option 1 (see Appendix G, "Configuring DIGL for Your Environment") has been tested on color and monochrome Sun Sparcstations. There are numerous UNIX X11 configurations other then Sun Sparcstations that should be compatible with this implementation, but you may have to make slight modifications to this video driver package in those cases.

X11 Video Graphics Support

A brief introduction into X Windows and high-level interfacing through the XView model is presented in Chapter 7, "High-Resolution Graphics Windows." Because of the need to have more direct control over the X Window drawing and event-handling process of X Windows, the X11 video driver for X Windows interfaces at a much lower level. This increases the level of complexity, but modifications for the DIGL X Window video driver library should be very straightforward for experienced X11 programmers. If you are not experienced in low-level X11 interfacing, this appendix is not sufficient to train you. The information presented here is in reference form and must be supplemented with additional X Window programmer reference material.

There are some differences in procedural versus event-based programming. The DIGL graphics application model is procedural; that is, the graphics application initializes the graphics state first and then the graphics device. Once the graphics device is initialized, the drawing takes place on the graphics surface, followed by an optional interactive request for display termination.

In simple video adapters such as MS-DOS video, this procedure amounts to initializing the graphics screen, drawing, and clearing to text mode on completion. Unfortunately, in X Window graphics, things are not that simple.

There are many X Window functions and objects to assist you in performing the myriad of steps in creating and drawing on a graphics surface. The trick is finding out what the steps are and using the right information and data types to control the process. Here are the basic steps taken in the DIGL X11 graphics library to initialize a display:

1. *Connect to an X server.* Find a network server and request a connection to open a display. This process is complicated. It involves returning environment variables used to provide information about the display. A successful connection returns information such as X version, screen name, and display height and width.

2. *Set up the visual.* After step 1, a connection is established, but there is still more to be done prior to opening up a window for graphics. This step involves getting visual information to be used later in setting up color map definitions.

3. *Store the X display name and provide window manager hints.* Xlib programming requires that your application make some effort to cooperate with the window manager. This involves conforming to an X11 interface style.

4. *Set up the color map.* Remember, our DIGL model uses 16 standard colors as defined somewhat arbitrarily to match the IBM PC. If color is available, Xlib has hundreds of predefined color mixes to choose from. In this case, you map the 16 predefined DIGL colors into the closest match in the Xlib color scheme. In the case of monochrome, map all 16 colors to black-and-white pixels.

5. *Create a graphics context.* Steps 1-4 are needed just to get you to the point where you can think about graphics operations in the window. The graphics context is a data structure that defines parameters of a drawable surface. In this case you must set foreground and background pixels and transfer information about display root and window names.

6. *Raise the window.* You still do not have an open window to draw in. In this step, you finally open (raise) the window for your first graphics drawing operations.

At this point, there are still several design issues to think about. Steps 1-6 create and open a window that can be closed and reopened at any time until it is destroyed. This can be done gracefully by the window manager process. Remember also that this display may be covered up at any time by other applications running on the same server—either locally or via remote operations.

If the display is closed, it is turned into an icon and all graphics information must be redrawn by the application. Redraw operations may also be necessary if the display is covered and uncovered.

> The sample DIGL applications do not perform automatic redraw
> operations on window close and reopen operations. Hooks are in the
> library for extending the event handling process. If you would like to
> perform these operations, you must modify the applications accordingly.

X11 Video Driver Library Implementation

Appendix G discusses the Sun Sparcstation video support library as Option 1 of
two options available for extended video driver support available with DIGL. The
file in the Option 1 subdirectory (SUN_UNIX) named SUNVILIB.C contains
the UNIX X11 (Xlib) video driver for X Window systems.

SUNVILIB.C

The video driver initialization and graphics-primitive algorithms are contained in
Listing D.1. The corresponding file SUNVILIB.H contains global variables, structures, constants, and function prototypes needed to resolve forward referencing
as these funcions are called from other modules.

Listing D.1. SUNVILIB.C.

```
/*=================================================================
== SUN/X11 Video Graphics driver library function header and      ==
== prototypes                                                     ==
== Author: Scientific Concepts, Inc.                              ==
== Copyright (c) 1990-1993. All rights reserved worldwide.        ==
=================================================================*/


#include <X11/Xlib.h>
#include <X11/Xutil.h>
```

```
/*================ Data Structures and Definitions ================*/

#define          BORDERWIDTH   15
#define          WINDOWNAME    "DIGL LIBRARY"
#define          APPLNAME      "DIGL APPLICATION"
#define          MAXX11COLORS 16



/*=========================== Macros ============================*/

     typedef struct x11colnode_st
       {
         unsigned long value;
         char name[MAXX11COLORS];
       } X11COLNODE;



/*===================== Global Variables=========================*/

     Display      *display      ;/* X11 pointer to disp structure  */

     Window        rootwindow   ;/* X11 root window               */
     Window        userwindow   ;/* X11 graphics application window*/

     XWMHints      WinManHints  ;/* Window manager hints          */
     XClassHint    class_hints  ;/* Window class hints            */
     XSizeHints    sizehints    ;/* Window size hints             */
     Colormap      XColormap    ;/* X11 color map properties      */

     static Visual *XVisual = CopyFromParent; /* X11 visual       */

     XEvent        event        ;/* X11 event data                */

     GC            GraphContext ;/* X11 graphics context          */

     static int    ColorSupport=0;  /* indicates multi-color video */
     static int    WinScreen          ;/* X1 screen id code        */
     static int    WinDepth           ;/* X1 screen depth code     */
```

continues

293

Listing D.1. continued

```
static int      WinXLoc = 10        ;/* x location of window    */
static int      WinYLoc = 10        ;/* y location of window    */
static int      WinWidth = 500      ;/* window width in pixels  */
static int      WinHeight = 500     ;/* window height in pixels */

enum  XCOLORS {
                BLACK, BLUE, GREEN, CYAN, RED, MAGENTA, BROWN,
                WHITE, DARKSLATEGRAY, LIGHTBLUE, LIGHTGREEN,
                LIGHTCYAN, LIGHTRED, LIGHTMAGENTA, YELLOW, SNOW
              };

static X11COLNODE   X11Map[MAXX11COLORS]=
                        {
                            0, "BLACK" ,
                            0, "BLUE",
                            0, "GREEN" ,
                            0, "CYAN" ,
                            0, "RED" ,
                            0, "MAGENTA" ,
                            0, "BROWN" ,
                            0, "WHITE" ,
                            0, "DARKSLATEGRAY" ,
                            0, "LIGHTBLUE" ,
                            0, "LIGHTGREEN" ,
                            0, "LIGHTCYAN" ,
                            0, "LIGHTRED" ,
                            0, "LIGHTMAGENTA" ,
                            0, "YELLOW" ,
                            0, "SNOW"
                        };


/*====================== Function Prototypes ======================*/

int DIGLInitXWindow()           ;/* connect to server and open win */
int DIGLCloseXWindow()          ;/* wait for event and close       */
Display *ConnectToServer()      ;/* connect to X11 server          */
```

```
GC CreateGContext()             ;/* create a graphics context    */
Window OpenXWindow()            ;/* open a window                 */
void SetXHints()                ;/* setup window manager hints    */

int SetUpVisual();
int SetUpColormap();
unsigned long AllocNamedColor();


void X11video_drv()             ;/* sun X window video driver     */
int X11videoinit()              ;/* initialize X11 graphics driv. */
```

Most of the variables in the global variable section of the file pertain to pointer handles used to identify certain data structures when making calls to Xlib. The location and size of the graphics window opened is arbitrarily set to an x, y location of 10,10 and a width and height of 500. This is accomplished using the global variable assignments:

```
static int    WinXLoc = 10
static int    WinYLoc = 10
static int    WinWidth = 500
static int    WinHeight = 500
```

These can be readily changed to suit your individual preferences. However, if you adjust the window size, you may need to change the aspect ratio variable. The following sections describe each library function.

X11video_drv

Name

X11video_drv(primitive) decodes and dispatches specific X Window graphics commands and parameters to the selected output device.

Synopsis

```
void X11video_drv(primitive)
int primitive;
```

Description

> Once an X Window is opened with the proper graphics context established, this routine decodes the graphics primitives supported and dispatches the appropriate calls to the Xlib library.

Diagnostics

> The formal string argument (primitive) is not modified.

> All graphics primitives may not be supported by this driver. In addition, code exists in this function to support future modes such as labeling and RGB color mixing. This mode is considered a real-time bit-mapped operation and cannot be output to disk.

See Also

> X11videoinit()

X11videoinit

Name

> X11videoinit() initializes the X Window graphics context and opens the window for later graphics-primitive output.

Synopsis

> int X11videoinit()

Description

> This function maps DIGL specific parameters into an existing X Window, setting colors, aspect ratios, and origin controls.

Diagnostics

> No formal parameters are required. However, the connection to the server is required prior to any graphics operations.

If no valid X server connection is made, all of the remaining steps of the X Window initialization process are aborted.

See Also

X11video_drv()

DIGLInitXWindow

Name

DIGLInitXWindow() connects to the X server and initializes and opens X_Window.

Synopsis

int DIGLInitXWindow()

Description

This function initializes the X Window graphics context and opens the window for later graphics-nprimitive output. This involves connecting to the server, setting the color map, creating a graphics context, and waiting for an exposure event to open the window.

Diagnostics

No formal parameters are required. However, the connection to the server is required prior to any graphics operations.

If your X11 environment does not provide proper color map information, the DIGL color map defaults to monochrome. This is indicated by a warning message issued through the terminal or shell to the window from where the graphics application was initiated.

See Also

```
ConnectToServer()
SetUpVisual()
OpenXWindow()
XMapRaised()
XFlush()
XNextEvent()
```

DIGLCloseXWindow

Name

DIGLCloseXWindow() waits for the exposure event and kills (removes) the
X window.

Synopsis

```
int DIGLCloseXWindow()
```

Description

This function waits for an event as specified via the event variable and the
call to XNextEvent, using the display handle. When the event is of type
Expose and the count matches the number of events allowed, the display is
removed via the XCloseDisplay function of Xlib.

Diagnostics

No formal parameters are required. However, the event handling
mechanism may not be optimal for your requirements.

Exposure events may occur when the window is moved, opened, or closed
by the user using the mouse on the window border. This routine and the
graphics application have to be modified to allow redraw operations after
a window is closed and reopened.

See Also

```
XNextEvent()
XCloseDisplay()
```

SetXHints

Name

SetXHints() provides some hints for the window manager.

Synopsis

```
void SetXHints(display, userwindow)
Display *display;
Window userwindow;
```

Description

This function provides hints such as window width, height, and x,y location. Use of the X11 sizehints structure is required.

Diagnostics

Formal parameters are not modified.

> Some type of window manager hint process is required in all X Window applications—this routine sets up the minimum. You may want to add additional hint parameters more pertinent to your environment.

See Also

```
XSetWMNormalHints()
XSetClassHint()
XSetWMHints()
```

ConnectToServer

Name

ConnectToServer() connects to the X server and prints statistics if successful.

Synopsis

```
Display *ConnectToServer(display_name, Screen, rootwindow)
char display_name[];
int *Screen;
Window *rootwindow;
```

Description

This function connects to the server by opening an X display and getting information such as version numbers and display names from the X server.

Diagnostics

This routine must return valid information from the server relating to display name and screen data types via formal parameters supplied.

Invalid server connections abort the remainder of the X11 initialization process.

See Also

```
XOpenDisplay()
DefaultScreen()
RootWindow()
ServerVendor()
VendorRelease()
DisplayWidth()
DisplayHeight()
```

CreateGContext

Name

CreateGContext() creates a graphics context on an X Window via an X server.

Synopsis

```
GC CreateGContext(display, drawable, forecolor, backcolor)
Display *display;
Drawable drawable;
unsigned long forecolor;
unsigned long backcolor;
```

Description

This function creates a drawable graphics context. Predefined foreground and background colors and line width are set for the X display.

Diagnostics

Formal parameters are not modified.

The mapped colors for foreground and background must be correctly preassigned to produce a displayable image.

See Also

```
XCreateGC()
```

OpenXWindow

Name

OpenXWindow() opens a window at the X server.

Synopsis

```
Window OpenXWindow(display, parent, bordercolor, backcolor,
event_mask)
Display *display;
Window parent;
unsigned long bordercolor;
unsigned long backcolor;
unsigned long event_mask;
```

Description

This function opens a window at the X server using predefined parameters for border width, even masks, and visual attributes.

Diagnostics

Formal parameters are not modified.

When setting X attributes, be sure that they are consistent with the allowable range of values.

See Also

    XCreateWindow()

SetUpVisual

Name

SetUpVisual() finds the pseudocolor visual for the current X display.

Synopsis

```
int SetUpVisual(visual, depth)
Visual **visual;
int *depth;
```

Description

This function finds and sets up pseudovisual information to be used in determining the color capability of the display.

Diagnostics

Visual information structure data is returned as part of the formal parameter structure.

This function is critical to determining color map and display depth. DIGL assumes a minimal configuration using default visual information if possible. Custom color visuals are beyond the scope of this version of DIGL.

See Also

```
DefaultVisual()
DefaultDepth()
XGetVisualInfo()
XFree()
```

SetUpColormap

Name

SetUpColormap() creates an X color map based on the screen and visual information returned prior to calling this function.

Synopsis

```
int SetUpColormap(visual, colormap)
Visual *visual;
Colormap *colormap;
```

Description

This function creates an X color map based on the screen and default visual information returned prior to calling this function. If a successful color map is not returned, monochrome is assumed.

Diagnostics

Color map information is returned as part of the formal parameter list if successfully created.

If your X11 environment does not properly respond to the color map creation commands, the DIGL color map is reset to monochrome.

See Also

```
DefaultVisual()
DefaultColormap()
XCreateColormap()
XSetWindowColormap()
```

AllocNamedColor

Name

AllocNamedColor() allocates a color cell based on color names.

Synopsis

```
unsigned long AllocNamedColor(colorname, default_color)
char colorname[];
unsigned long default_color;
```

Description

This function allocates color map entries in global data structure to match the color names supplied as part of the 16 colors of DIGL. If an exact color match cannot be found, an attempt is made to use a hardware color approximation.

Diagnostics

The formal parameter match color either is set to the specified index of the X11 color table match or reset to a default color such as black if a match is not found.

> Check the X11 color table include file for a list of names defined for color values. Compare those with those in the DIGL color table for the best match.

See Also

```
XAllocNamedColor()
```

X11 Video Driver Analysis

In the routine X11video_drv, an if-then-else structure is used to implement the various graphics-primitive options. The following code excerpt from that routine illustrates how this is done:

```
.
.
.
if (primitive==GINI)
  {;}
else if (primitive==BELL)
  {;}
```

```
else if (primitive==GDRA)
  {
    startx = (int)(lscaledx+.5);
    starty = (int)(lscaledy+.5);
    endx = (int)(cscaledx+.5);
    endy = (int)(cscaledy+.5);
    XDrawLine(display, userwindow, GraphContext,
      startx, starty, endx, endy);
  }
else if (primitive==GCLR)
  {;}
else if (primitive==LINE)
  {;}
else if (primitive==FTYP)
  {;}
else if (primitive==REFL)
  {;}
else if (primitive==BKCO)
  {
    strcpy(pramstring,prams[PONE].sval);
    stringint(pramstring, &i);
    i = ((i >= 0) && (i <= MAXX11COLORS)) ? i : 1;
    XSetBackground(display, GraphContext, X11Map[i].value);
  }
else if (primitive==FOCO)
  {
    strcpy(pramstring,prams[PONE].sval);
    stringint(pramstring, &i);
    i = ((i >= 0) && (i <= MAXX11COLORS)) ? i : 1;
    XSetForeground(display, GraphContext, X11Map[i].value);
  }
else if (primitive==GPEN)
  {
    strcpy(pramstring,prams[PONE].sval);
    stringint(pramstring, &i);
    i = ((i >= 0) && (i <= MAXX11COLORS)) ? i : 1;
    XSetForeground(display, GraphContext, X11Map[i].value);
  }
```

.

.

.

Note that only a few of the graphics primitives are needed to perform most of the graphics operations of DIGL required by the graphics applications supplied.

UNIX X11 Video Driver Display

When the X11 display is first opened, information about version numbers and window information is returned to the shell or terminal window. Once the exposure events criteria is met or the user closes the window, the X display is closed and control is returned to the shell or root window.

THE DOS COMPILER AND OPERATING SYSTEM

This appendix summarizes the impact that the DOS operating system and compiler have on how you implement some or all of the DIGL software. Regardless of the compiler you are using, there are a few hints and suggestions worth noting that should make your development time as short as possible. The information presented here provides one method out of many that can be used to build the DIGL system. If you have other systems or conventions you are familiar with, please feel free to use them.

The last section of this chapter examines several compiler options, using Microsoft C as the featured compiler. Although many of the options discussed may differ from compiler to compiler, the central theme remains the same.

Appendix G, "Configuring DIGL for Your Environment," provides information on DIGL file locations and options specific to your configuration.

DOS Options

In this section, some of the DOS limitations are presented, with information as to how they might have an impact on your use of this software on the DIGL disk.

Memory and Addressing

When discussing limitations of DOS, the first issue that many programmers bring up is the limitation of program and data size. Those with larger and more sophisticated operating systems are used to the concepts of virtual memory, where the operating system finds space for your program and data even if it has to use disk space to do it. Unfortunately, the PC world began with 16-bit address limits—which probably seemed like a lot at the time. Over the last few years, large applications with large data and address requirements have exposed the serious flaws in the addressing schemes of the initial PC architecture.

The Intel 8086 microprocessor has a segmented memory architecture with a total address space of 1M. Unfortunately, it can be addressed only in 64K chunks. There are four main 64K segments that are organized as code, data, stack, and extra. This dreaded 64K limitation on segments has caused an incredible amount of confusion, frustration, and expense to many programmers over the years.

Loading your PC with several megabytes of memory does not guarantee that most or all of it is usable by your program without some nightmarish memory management requirement. Memory management options eventually filter down to you through switch and compiler options that you must manage on behalf of your program at compile time. To accomplish this, you must have some knowledge of memory models.

Memory Models

The most popular DOS C compilers offer up to six different memory models. Table E.1 summarizes the memory models available and the limitations on code and data size.

Table E.1. Memory model summary.

Model	*Code*	*Data*
Tiny	<64K	<64K
Small	64K	64K
Medium	No limit	64K
Compact	64K	No limit
Large	No limit	No limit
Huge	No limit	No limit

For the Compact and Large memory models, the data can be any size. However, *no single data item* can be larger than 64K.

As indicated in the table, your choice of memory model makes an impact on the size and total amount of data you can define in your application. In addition, some compilers place additional restrictions on the size of an individual array declaration. Considering the size of an application such as DIGL, the large and huge memory models are the only practical choices.

You may be tempted to insert compiler directives for individual control of the size of data pointers. If you do, you will quickly find yourself with a nonportable and difficult-to-maintain mess. Other than an occasional `#ifdef`, do not use compiler directives in any code that you expect someone else to maintain.

Memory Protection

Memory protection can be provided by the operating system or hardware or some combination of both. Languages using pointers such as C often allow your program to inadvertently bypass these protection mechanisms and force you to reboot your computer.

Automated Processing

Like most operating systems, DOS provides a mechanism for supplying input to programs automatically instead of typing at the command prompt every time. The DOS batch file system is not nearly as sophisticated as those found on more mature operating systems such as UNIX, but it does provide for variable string substitution and nesting of multiple batch files, which is a minimum requirement for automated program development.

This process is useful for controlling various phases of the program development cycle, such as compiling and linking. For a large software system such as DIGL, where there may be in excess of 50 different files to control, the DOS batch processing capability is quite useful. Some compilers substitute their own flavor of batch command processing in the form of make files.

Building DIGL

For DOS, the DIGL disk provides some batch files that are based on compiler and linker commands for the Microsoft compiler (Versions 5.1 through 7.0). If you are using this compiler, you may not have to make any changes unless you are using different options, such as different names for library files. If you are using a different compiler such as Borland C/C++, you may still want to read these sections for suggestions on how to modify the files for your configuration. If you are using integrated development environments such as Microsoft C's Programmer's Workbench, make sure you are aware of how to build user libraries.

Installing and Checking Your Compiler

After you have copied the DIGL files to your directory of choice, the first step in building DIGL is to make sure that the compiler you are using is properly installed and all environment variables are set accordingly. The set command can be used to display the status of environment variables. In the case of Microsoft C, this command produces output similar to the following:

```
COMSPEC=C:\COMMAND.COM
TZ=EST5EDT
NFSDRIVE=D
PROMPT=Enter 'EXIT' to return to WordPerfect$_$p$g$e[44m
PATH=D:\PCC\BIN;D:\PCC\BINB;D:\PCC\EXE;D:\PCC;C:\;C:\MOUSE;C:\DOS;D:\UTILS;
D:\NFS;D:\WP51;C:\WINDOWS
LIB=D:\PCC\LIB;
INCLUDE=D:\PCC\INCLUDE;
INIT=D:\PCC\SOURCE\ME=INI:
```

In this example, the Microsoft C compiler is installed in the directory PCC on drive D. The environment variables LIB, INCLUDE, and INIT are also consistent with this location. For other DOS compilers, a different set of environment variables may be required.

Library Organization and Control

Before compiling any of the DIGL application examples, you must build the DIGL library. The DIGL library files discussed throughout the book and in Appendix A, "DIGL Support Libraries," all end in LIB.C. Table E.2 summarizes the DIGL files for library support needed for Generic C (any ANSI C compiler) on DOS and for Microsoft C (Option 2).

Table E.2. DIGL library files for DOS and Microsoft C.

Filename	Description	Generic C	Microsoft C (Option 2)
DRIVRLIB.C	Graphics drivers	Yes	Yes
FILELIB.C	File support	Yes	Yes
MACROLIB.C	Graphics macros	Yes	Yes
MISCLIB.C	Miscellaneous functions	Yes	Yes
PARAMLIB.C	Parameter processing	Yes	Yes
POLYLIB.C	Polygon transformations	Yes	Yes
PRIMLIB.C	Graphics primitives	Yes	Yes
STRNGLIB.C	String support	Yes	Yes
MSCVILIB.C	Microsoft C video drivers	No	Yes
MSCWILIB.C	Microsoft C pop-up windows	No	Yes

As indicated in the table, the library files MSCVILIB.C and MSWVILIB.C are specific to Microsoft C. The other files should be compatible with any ANSI C compiler.

For example, using Microsoft C to create a batch file named LIBBUILD in order to build a library file named DIGLLIBL, you can use the following two lines:

```
CL /c /AL %1.C
@IF NOT ERRORLEVEL 1 LIB DIGLLIBL -+ %1;
```

The first line performs a Microsoft C compile on the source file specified after typing the name of the batch file. /c instructs the Microsoft C compiler to perform a compile only. /AL selects the large memory model. %1.C appends the characters .C to the file specified by the first parameter on the command line used to invoke the batch file.

For example, to add the DIGL file DRIVRLIB.C to the library at the DOS prompt, you can use

```
LIBBUILD  DRIVRLIB
```

For a compiler other than Microsoft C or to add additional compile options, the first line must be changed accordingly.

The second line adds the compiled module to the library (DIGLLIBL). The first part of the line (@IF NOT ERRORLEVEL 1) checks to abort the library process if any errors were detected as a result of the first line. -+ instructs the librarian to first remove the file from the library, if it already exists, before adding it. %1 identifies the name of the library module as specified on the command line.

For a library manager other than LIB of Microsoft C or to add additional library options, the second line must be changed accordingly.

This batch file (or something equivalent) must be run on all files pertinent to your configuration, as indicated in Table E.2.

Building DIGL Applications

Once you have successfully built all the DIGL library support files, you can build the applications. Once again, using Microsoft C, you could create a batch file named APPMAKE to make an executable based on a DIGL library file named DIGLLIBL. The file could contain the following two lines:

```
CL /c /AL %1.C
@IF NOT ERRORLEVEL 1 link %1  /STACK:12000,%1,,DIGLLIBL+GRAPHICS;
```

The first line performs a Microsoft C compile on the source file specified after typing the name of the batch file. The actions performed are identical to those in the previous batch file discussion.

The second line links the compiled module with the libraries (DIGLLIBL+GRAPHICS) needed to build the executable. The first part of the line (@IF NOT ERRORLEVEL 1) checks to abort the library process if any errors were detected as a result of the first line. /STACK:12000 instructs the linker to use a stack size of 12,000 bytes. This number is somewhat arbitrary. You could try the default and increase the number if needed. The first occurrence of %1 identifies the name of the program module as specified on the command line. The second occurrence uses the same root name as the name of the executable. `, ,DIGLLIBL+GRAPHICS` skips the optional map file and specifies the library files to be used for the final phase of building the executable (.EXE) file.

For a linker other than LINK of Microsoft C or to add additional linker options, the second line must be changed accordingly.

This batch file (or something equivalent) must be run to build all application files pertinent to your configuration, as indicated in Table E.2.

THE UNIX COMPILER AND OPERATING SYSTEM

This appendix discusses the UNIX operating system and compiler and their impact on how you implement some or all of the DIGL software. For UNIX configurations, the DIGL has been tested primarily on the Sun Sparcstation, both monochrome and color. The UNIX-specific portions of the DIGL are used for high-level interface with the X Windows menu development libraries in Chapter 7, "High-Resolution Graphics Windows." The video driver for graphics operations is based on lower-level interfaces into the X11 library. Appendix D, "UNIX X11 Video Drivers," provides information on the X11 interface library of functions. Appendix G, "Configuring the DIGL for Your Environment," provides information on DIGL file locations and options that are specific to your configuration.

The development options discussed in this appendix are based on the standard UNIX C compiler cc, as opposed to the ANSI gcc option. If you are just learning the UNIX operating system, or if this is your first attempt at large-scale development with user-created libraries, you should familiarize yourself with the basic script programming features of the UNIX shell that you are using. The various UNIX shells, such as csh and ksh, differ considerably. This appendix does not provide sufficient detail for new UNIX programmers; it must be supplemented with specific UNIX reference material.

Regardless of your level of UNIX experience, the hints and suggestions provided in this appendix should make your development time as short as possible. The information presented here provides one method out of many that you can use to build the DIGL system. If you are familiar with other systems or conventions, feel free to use them.

UNIX Options

In this section, some of the UNIX tools and utilities are presented, with information as to how they might have an impact on your use of the software supplied with the DIGL disk.

Memory Protection

Memory protection is much more strictly enforced in multitasking environments such as UNIX. If you are a DOS programmer, you are used to a programming environment that is less restrictive when writing to reserved memory locations.

Memory is provided by the operating system or the hardware—or by both. Languages that use pointers—for example, C—often enable your program inadvertently to bypass this protection mechanism. For UNIX environments, the result is a `segmentation fault` or a `bus error` error message. Both mean that the operating system aborted your program because it attempted to write beyond the assigned address boundaries. If you make changes to DIGL that are not consistent with its design scheme, you will probably encounter one of these errors.

UNIX Debugging Tools

Other than `printf`, the debugger utility (`dbx`) is your best option for serious debugging efforts when you make major changes. `dbx` is a utility for source-level debugging and execution of programs written in Sun C, C++, FORTRAN, Pascal, Modula-2, and ANSI C. Unfortunately, `dbx` is a complex tool that takes a considerable amount of time and patience to learn—this is true for many UNIX tools. To avoid hours of frustration when you debug major changes to the DIGL

1. Thoroughly read Chapter 8, "The Object-Oriented Approach."

2. Unless—and until—you are thoroughly familiar with the design theory behind the DIGL, make changes in small, incremental steps.

Automated Processing

UNIX provides several mechanisms that enable you to supply input to programs automatically instead of typing at the command prompt every time. The script and make file options permit variable string substitution and nesting of multiple script files—the minimum requirement for automated program development.

Automated processing is very useful for controlling various phases of program development, such as compiling and linking. In a large software system such as the DIGL, where there might be more than 50 different files to control, UNIX script file processing is very useful.

Building the DIGL

The DIGL has been ported routinely between DOS and UNIX for testing purposes. The result is a software system that should compile in the UNIX environment without warnings or errors. For UNIX systems, the DIGL disk provides script files that are based on compiler and linker commands that use the cc compiler and the ar utility for creating library archives. For a quick review of these utilities, examine the UNIX online man manual.

Library Organization and Control

Before you compile any of the DIGL application examples, you must build the DIGL. The DIGL library files discussed throughout this book and in Appendix A, "DIGL Support Libraries," all end with LIB.C. Table F.1 summarizes the DIGL files for library support that are needed for generic C—that is, any ANSI C compiler—and UNIX Sun C files (Option 1).

Table F.1. DIGL library files for generic C and UNIX Sun C.

Filename	Description	Generic C	Sun C (Option 1)
DRIVRLIB.C	Graphics drivers	Yes	Yes
FILELIB.C	File support	Yes	Yes
MACROLIB.C	Graphics macros	Yes	Yes
MISCLIB.C	Miscellaneous functions	Yes	Yes
PARAMLIB.C	Parameter processing	Yes	Yes
POLYLIB.C	Polygon transformations	Yes	Yes
PRIMLIB.C	Graphics primitives	Yes	Yes
STRNGLIB.C	String support	Yes	Yes
SUNVILIB.C	Sun Sparc C video drivers	No	Yes

As Table F.1 indicates, the library SUNVILIB.C file is specific to Sun Sparc C. It contains low-level calls to the X11 library.

Building a UNIX DIGL

There are two basic steps for creating a library file. The source file must be compiled, and the object file that is created must be added to the library. For example, performing these steps on the MISCLIB.C library file uses the following two lines of code:

```
cc -I. -c misclib.c
ar rv libdiglc.a misclib.o
```

The first line compiles the source file. The -I. option instructs the compiler to look for include files in the current directory (.) and in the standard include designations in the path. The -c option suppresses linking with ld(1) and produces an .o file for each source file. A single object file can be named explicitly with the -o option.

The second line adds the compiled module to the library (diglc) by means of the ar archiver utility. In the rv option, the r instructs the archiver utility to replace the named file in the archive. The v stands for verbose. Used with the r, d, m, or q option, the rv describes, file by file, the creation of a new archive file from the old archive and constituent files. The archiver appends lib in front of the library file diglc.

This process must be run on all the library files shown in Table F.1. The script files in the UNIX subdirectory automate this process.

Building DIGL Applications

Once you have successfully built all the DIGL library support files, you can build the applications. Two basic steps are required for each application file. To build the BOX.C application, these lines of code are used:

```
cc -I. -c box.c
cc box.o -lX11 -L. -ldiglc -lm -o box
```

The first line compiles on the BOX.C source file. The actions performed in the first code line are identical with those actions in the first code line for the previous batch file.

319

The second line links the compiled module with the UNIX X Windows library and the user-created DIGL library (X11 and diglc), which are needed to build the executable. In the second line, -1 identifies the library file to link with the object library. This option must follow the source file arguments. -L. adds <directory> to the list of directories that contain the object library routines for linking that use ld(1). The -o option names the output file. It must have the appropriate suffix for the type of file that the compilation will produce.

These operations (or something equivalent) must be used to build all application files pertinent to your configuration, as indicated by Table F.1.

CONFIGURING THE DIGL FOR YOUR ENVIRONMENT

The DIGL has been designed with filename conventions that make it easy for you to identify the file components of its layered structure. The DIGL has also been designed to enable you to include your application code or libraries regardless of what compiler or operating system you are using. However, your development environment determines what initial features and options of the DIGL you can use and the best installation procedure for the DIGL disk. Figure G.1 shows the layers of the DIGL and the compatibility options that are available for each configuration. This release of the DIGL has a generic kernel with two additional configuration options.

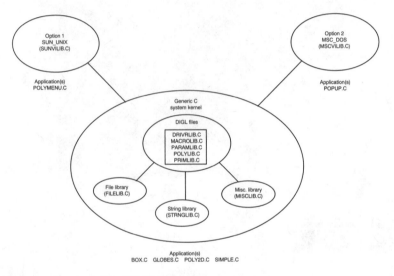

Figure G.1. An overview of the DIGL file structure.

The generic kernel is compatible with any ANSI C compiler. All the application and library files in this kernel reference only those header files and functions that are compatible across multiple C compilers and operating systems. Options 1 and 2—and any additional features you might add—also require the basic kernel. See Appendix A, "DIGL Support Libraries," for more information. In this appendix, I explain the installation requirements and provide suggestions for the generic kernel and the two additional library options.

Generic Kernel for C Compiler Environments

The generic C configuration is the basic foundation for the DIGL system. It represents about 80 percent of the code on the DIGL disk. Options 1 and 2 also require the files in this configuration. Using the generic kernel, you can compile all the application examples, except for ones that are specific to UNIX or DOS. Use Option 1 to compile UNIX-specific applications, and Option 2 to complile DOS-specific applications.

The built-in graphics drivers for this kernel are HPGL and PostScript. No video driver is included in the kernel. To use a video driver, you must either use Option 1 or 2, or develop your own. If you design your own video driver, you can use Option 1 or 2 as a template.

The applications and libraries that are exempt from this configuration are discussed in Chapters 7 and 8. They deal with low-level pop-up menus and high-level X Windows menus. Figure G.1 lists the filenames of these applications.

There are three instances when you must use the generic kernel without Option 1 or 2:

- When you use a C compiler other than Microsoft C for DOS
- When you use an operating system other than DOS or UNIX System V release 4.0 or later
- When your UNIX configuration does not offer access to X11 driver libraries

With the generic C option, any ANSI C compiler is compatible. All the files for the generic option are located at the highest level—that is, in the root directory—on the DIGL disk. Options 1 and 2 are located in subdirectories below this level.

To install the generic option, copy the files to the designated location for the DIGL. If you want to separate your application files from library files, move all the files that end with LIB.C to a specified destination for library files. You can do this in DOS with

```
copy ?????lib.c <dest>
```

where <dest> is the path for your library files.

In UNIX, you can use

```
mv *lib.c <dest>
```

where <dest> is the path for your library files.

> If you are using Option 1 or 2, skip to the instructions for conditional
> compilation of either Option 1 or Option 2 in later sections of this
> appendix.

The DIGL uses conditional compilation flags to include or exclude video driver code that is specific to the system or the compiler. You might need to modify the SYSHEAD.H file. To make conditional compilation compatible with this kernel, insert /* in front of the compiler directive #define. The effect is that you "comment out" the constants MICROSOFT_DOS and SUN_UNIX for the DOS with Microsoft C and UNIX video drivers located at the top of SYSHEAD.H. The following code is the beginning of the modified SYSHEAD.H file:

```
/
*+========================================================================
== DIGL system header file: * NOTE * There are two constants       ==
== defined to allow conditional compilation of video drivers       ==
== depending on the compiler and operating system you are using.    ==
== If you are unsure of how this works, please read "Appendix G:     ==
== Configuring DIGL for Your Environment" of the book "Computer     ==
== Graphics Environments" before you proceed...                    ==
==                                                                  ==
== Author: Scientific Concepts, Inc.                               ==
== Copyright (c) 1990-1993. All rights reserved worldwide.          ==
========================================================================*/

/*#define MICROSOFT_DOS    0        /* include video driver for dos   */
/*#define SUN_UNIX    0             /* include video driver for sun   */
 .
 .
 .
```

Even if this file has already been modified for this mode, you should double-check its contents before compilation.

Option 1—UNIX Sun Sparcstation or X11-Compatible

Use Option 1 in addition to the generic kernel when you are using a Sun Sparcstation or a UNIX configuration that gives you access to X11 driver libraries.

> Access to the XView library is required for only the application that illustrates high-level X Windows menu development—POLYMENU.C. If you are using another menu development system, you can remove the POLYMENU.C file.

Option 1 requires UNIX and X Windows library compatibility. In addition to features provided by the basic kernel, this option contains video driver libraries for low-level interface with the X11 X Windows library. This library is contained in the SUNVILIB.C file. Chapter 8, "The Object-Oriented Approach," has details on the menu application. Suggestions for using and compiling this library are provided in Appendix F, "The UNIX Compiler and Operating System."

To install Option 1, first install the generic kernel. Next, copy the files in the SUN_UNIX subdirectory to your destination of choice. (The files for Option 1 are located in the SUN_UNIX subdirectory on the DIGL disk.) The filename conventions for the library and application files are identical with those described in the section on the generic kernel.

The DIGL uses conditional compilation flags to include or exclude video driver code that is specific to the system or the compiler. You might need to modify the SYSHEAD.H file. To make the conditional compilation compatible with Option 1, insert /* in front of the compiler directive #define. The effect is that you "comment out" the constant MICROSOFT_DOS for DOS with Microsoft C. Then, remove the comment characters preceding the compiler directive for the constant SUN_UNIX for UNIX video drivers, which is located at the top of SYSHEAD.H.

The following code is the beginning of the modified SYSHEAD.H file. It illustrates the correct modification for Option 1.

```
/
*+============================================================================
== DIGL system header file: * NOTE * There are two constants    ==
== defined to allow conditional compilation of video drivers    ==
== depending on the compiler and operating system you are using. ==
== If you are unsure of how this works, please read "Appendix G:  ==
== Configuring DIGL for Your Environment" of the book "Computer  ==
== Graphics Environments" before you proceed...                  ==
==                                                               ==
== Author: Scientific Concepts, Inc.                             ==
== Copyright (c) 1990-1993. All rights reserved worldwide.       ==
=============================================================================*/

/*#define MICROSOFT_DOS    0       /* include video driver for dos   */
#define SUN_UNIX    0               /* include video driver for sun   */
.
.
.
```

Even if you have already modified this file, you should double-check its contents before compilation.

Option 2—DOS Microsoft C Compiler Environments

Use Option 2 in addition to the generic kernel when you are using a DOS configuration and the Microsoft C compiler.

All DIGL library and application files have been thoroughly tested on Microsoft versions 5.1 and 7.0 of C. The chances are that any version released between 5.1 and 7.0 will work without any problems. However, you should always upgrade to the newest compiler versions.

Option 2 provides video drivers for the CGA and VGA video modes of DOS in the MSCVILIB.C library file. The MSCWILIB.C file contains the library used for developing low-level pop-up window prototypes, which were discussed in

Chapter 6, "A Design Prototype for Text-Based Pop-Up Windows." Appendix C, "DOS Video Drivers," provides additional suggestions.

To install Option 2, first install the generic kernel. Next, copy the files in the MSC_DOS subdirectory to your destination of choice. (The files for Option 2 are located in the MSC_DOS subdirectory on the DIGL disk.) The filename conventions for the library and application files are identical with those described in the section on the generic kernel.

The DIGL uses conditional compilation flags to include or exclude video driver code that is specific to the system or the compiler. You might need to modify the SYSHEAD.H file. To make the conditional compilation compatible with Option 2, insert /* in front of the compiler directive #define. The effect is that you "comment out" the constant SUN_UNIX for UNIX X11 video drivers. Then, remove the comment characters preceding the compiler directive for the constant MICROSOFT_DOS for DOS with Microsoft C, which is located at the top of SYSHEAD.H.

The following code is the beginning of the modified SYSHEAD.H file. It illustrates the correct modification for Option 2.

```
/
*+=============================================================================
== DIGL system header file: * NOTE * There are two constants        ==
== defined to allow conditional compilation of video drivers        ==
== depending on the compiler and operating system you are using.     ==
== If you are unsure of how this works, please read "Appendix G:     ==
== Configuring DIGL for Your Environment" of the book "Computer      ==
== Graphics Environments" before you proceed...                      ==
==                                                                   ==
== Author: Scientific Concepts, Inc.                                 ==
== Copyright (c) 1990-1993. All rights reserved worldwide.           ==
=============================================================================*/


#define MICROSOFT_DOS    0           /* include video driver for dos    */
/*#define SUN_UNIX     0           /* include video driver for sun    */
  .
  .
  .
```

Even if you have already modified this file, you should double-check its contents before compilation.

WHEN THINGS
GO WRONG—
DEBUGGING HINTS

There is a good chance that you're reading this appendix before you've read this book. You copied the disk files to your computer and compiled them, and you're wondering what went wrong.

This appendix provides hints and solutions for the common problems you might encounter. Because you can run the files on a variety of configurations, I have divided the information in this appendix into three main sections:

- General DIGL and application problems
- DOS-related problems
- UNIX-related problems

In each case, I pose a typical problem and suggest how you can solve it.

General DIGL and Application Problems

The following scenarios are presented to help you pinpoint your problem and find its solution.

The program runs, but no graphics appear on the screen.

The parameter file controls the output or destination devices in the test applications supplied with the DIGL. For example, if the output is routed to a file, the CRT is used primarily to display the status of the program instead of graphics. If no graphics appear on the screen, check the parameter file for parameters that define the plot device and the graphics device type. Make sure that they are consistent with the type of graphics device that you intend to use.

The POLY2D application program draws only a small portion of the selected polygon data file.

The polygon application library requires that polygon data not exceed the size limit imposed by the MAXPOLYSIZE parameter in the POLYLIB.H file. This size limit can be as small as 175 vectors for environments other than UNIX. If not all the polygon data file is drawn, select a smaller polygon.

The GLOBES application program outputs egg-shaped globes on the selected graphics device.

Usually, this means that the aspect ratio constant in the DIGL library is incorrect for the device that you selected. Unless you have added a new graphics driver, the constants should be correct for HPGL, PostScript, DOS with Microsoft C, and UNIX X11 device types. Check whether the graphics driver file for your specific device has lines that contain the following variable:

```
iso_factx=.9850;
```

You should be able to adjust the value of this constant up or down until the egg becomes a circle. This is a trial and error process in which a test program, such as SIMPLE.C, can be used to test the results of each change. For example, you can adjust this ratio, recompile the library, and relink the SIMPLE.C program to check the result.

The program does not access the data that you specified.

The directory path specification and the data filename must be consistent with valid DOS or UNIX path specifications. (DOS and UNIX path specifications differ slightly syntactically.) In addition, the data file must exist before the specific plot will continue. Make sure that the file exists both under the directory path specification and with the specific filename that you specify.

The plot comes up, and the screen goes blank.

You have tremendous flexibility in choosing the user color selections and the color map definitions. Even a selection with a blue foreground on a blue background, for example, is possible. Usually, a blank screen indicates that the colors chosen for the plotting and the labeling regions are the same. Check your parameter file to make certain that this is not the case. If this is not the problem, check the color map definitions in the specific graphics driver that you are using.

The word processor or other software does not properly reproduce the HPGL file that you created.

Not all HPGL devices and emulation software are created equal. This is primarily due to changes in HPGL device characteristics and the fact that most HPGL emulation software routines recognize only a small subset of HPGL protocol. Usually, this condition means that the DIGL software—or extensions to it—has implemented an HPGL code that is not recognized by the device that you are attempting to use. Check the programmer's reference manual for your HPGL device or software emulation program. Compare this with other software reference information to see what commands are not being converted.

The graphics program aborts after it displays syntax errors from the parameter file.

All parameters used by the parameter file library routines are syntax- and range-checked. Any errors that are found cause the graphics program to abort before the graphics device is initialized. If you edit the parameter file by means of a text editor—a good shortcut for experienced users—be careful to observe the syntax conventions described in Chapter 5, "A Design Prototype for DIGL." Check the PARAMLIB.C file for routines that are used to read and parse the parameter file.

The HPGL or PostScript file output process takes a long time to create a disk file.

The HPGL process requires that each vector pair be converted to ASCII representation. This representation can extend to as many as 24 bytes for each plot point. PostScript is even more complicated; it requires many characters for each plot point. Character conversion to absolute plotting vectors also requires a large number of ASCII characters for each plotted character. It takes time for some applications—such as large polygon files—to process and output a display entirely in HPGL or PostScript format. So, if you have large data files to be converted to HPGL or PostScript format, be patient.

The plot produces ASCII characters on the screen instead of a graphic image.

Both the HPGL and PostScript formats use plot protocols that are based on ASCII output. Unless you explicitly redirected the output to an I/O channel that supports a device that is compatible with either of these formats, output is usually to the CRT screen or to a data file. If you selected an HPGL or PostScript graphics device type and did not select the output to file option in the parameter file, the program simply displays the output protocol on the CRT. Select a video graphics device type, or select a file as output for the HPGL or PostScript graphics protocol.

When it imports a PostScript file created by the DIGL to a graphics program such as WordPerfect 5.1 or DrawPerfect, the file does not print properly, if at all.

The DIGL PostScript driver creates a PostScript file that is not encapsulated. Many of the software emulators that recognize PostScript require the encapsulated form to be used. You should use another format—such as HPGL—to import or modify the PostScript driver so that it creates its output in encapsulated form.

The plotter plots with an empty pen carousel, when HPGL output to a digital plotter is used.

The HPGL driver of the DIGL is based on an eight-pen carousel—as in the HP7550 or its equivalent. The pen select codes range from 1 to 8. If you use a plotter with fewer than eight pens, this might be the problem. Make sure that colors selected for your graphics application do not exceed the number of pens available with your device.

DOS-Related Problems

The following scenarios are presented to help you pinpoint your problem and find its solution.

The DOS prompt and the characters are left with strange colors after the program runs.

A major requirement of any graphics system is to set and reset the display from text to graphics modes. Normally, after a graphics program is completed, all the applications routines that are based on the DIGL return the display to the default conditions—that is, the conditions present when the program was run. In the unfortunate—and unlikely—event that a graphics routine fails to exit gracefully, the display state is undetermined.

Because the default video conditions are *memory resident,* the only way to restore a normal video mode is to run the DOS mode command from the DOS prompt or to reboot DOS. If you find that this becomes a frequent scenario, there are probably problems with the graphics driver you are using.

Memory resident conditions enable runtime storage of data for program or process variables while—and sometimes after—a program is executed. Runtime storage can be used for communicating between programs and for controlling the execution state of one or more programs.

Your compiler of choice says that it cannot find selected DIGL source files.

If you have copied all the files from the DIGL to your working area, this condition usually is an indication that the environment and path settings are not consistent with your compiler settings. There are specific values for the location of `environment` variables and `include` files. These values must be set before the compiler or the linker is called. For example, if you use Microsoft C, the output from the `set` command is

```
COMSPEC=C:\COMMAND.COM
PROMPT=$p$g
PATH=D:\PCC\BIN;D:\PCC\BINB;D:\PCC\EXE;D:\PCC;..\;C:\;
    C:\PCBETA\BIN;C:\MOUSE;C:\UTILS;D:\WP51;C:\DOS;
    C:\PCASM\BIN;
LIB=D:\PCC\LIB;C:\PCASM\LIB
INCLUDE=D:\PCC\INCLUDE;
INIT=D:\PCC\SOURCE\ME\INI;
```

Check your compiler configuration and setup requirements and where your DIGL source files are located. Read Appendix G, "Configuring the DIGL for Your Environment."

When you attempt to type a program to the screen, it prints as though there is no `end-of-line` sequence.

DOS and UNIX have different conventions for end-of-line (EOL) and end-of-file (EOF). When I developed the DIGL, I copied the source code back and forth from each environment for testing purposes. Possibly, your version uses the UNIX convention if you are on a PC, or the DOS convention if you are on UNIX.

In either case, this is not a serious problem. Simply read the source files into your favorite editor, and write them back again. As an alternative solution, many systems provide `DOS-TO-UNIX` and `UNIX-TO-DOS` filters.

Your DOS compiler produces errors that indicate that it is looking for UNIX files.

The SYSHEAD.H header file has all the `include` files that the DIGL requires for both DOS and UNIX versions. At the top of the file, the flags for DOS and UNIX must be commented in or commented out to match your configuration. Here is an example of SYSHEAD.H for a typical DOS configuration:

```
#define MICROSOFT_DOS    0          /* include video driver for dos   */
/*#define SUN_UNIX    0             /* include video driver for sun   */
```

Be sure to read Appendix G, "Configuring the DIGL for Your Environment."

Your compiler or linker generates syntax errors when it compiles the DIGL code.

If your compiler is configured properly and you have not modified the DIGL code, this condition should not occur under normal circumstances. The DIGL has been tested on a variety of PCs and UNIX workstations. It is always possible, however, that differences among compilers might create difficulty.

Read Appendix G, "Configuring the DIGL for Your Environment." If you still have compiler or linker errors and you have not modified the DIGL code, you can contact me for further suggestions on how to proceed. Likewise, if you solve this kind of problem, I would appreciate having a description of what the problem was and what you did to solve it. Please contact me at

Scientific Concepts, Inc.
Suite 11-295
1033 Franklin Road
Marietta, Georgia 30067

At runtime, your program aborts with an error such as stack overflow or segment size exceeded.

Usually, this condition indicates that the combination of data space and code space that your program requires exceeds the address limits imposed by the operating system or the computer's architecture.

The DOS batch files supplied with the DIGL use the large memory model. As the DIGL is configured—unless you have made additions—you should not have a problem with any application or library file. The only exception involves the size of the MAXPOLYSIZE parameter, which is found in the POLYLIB.H file on the DIGL disk. The following code fragment is from the file in the Data Structures and Definitions section near the top:

```
#ifdef SUN_UNIX
#define MAXPOLYSIZE     2500    /* maximum row size of polygons    */
#else
#define MAXPOLYSIZE     175     /* maximum row size of polygons    */
#endif
```

The conditional compile ifdef statements enable the size of MAXPOLYSIZE to be substantially larger under UNIX configurations. It is restricted to something substantially smaller in other configurations, such as DOS. If you attempt to change this number in order to manipulate larger polygons, runtime errors, such as stack overflows, might result. You can also switch to the huge memory model in order to eliminate the 64K data array limitation.

UNIX-Related Problems

The following scenarios are presented to help you pinpoint your problem and find its solution.

The UNIX compiler indicates errors such as missing #endif, *but the code looks fine when it is viewed through the text editor.*

DOS and UNIX have different conventions for end-of-line (EOL) and end-of-file (EOF). When I developed the DIGL, I copied the source code back and forth from each environment for testing purposes. Possibly, your version uses the UNIX convention if you are on a PC, or the DOS convention if you are on UNIX. The UNIX compiler might not recognize the proper EOF character sequence and, therefore, it misinterprets the start of the # line compiler directive.

In any case, this is not a serious problem. Simply read the source files into your favorite editor, and write them back again. As an alternative solution, many systems provide DOS-TO-UNIX and UNIX-TO-DOS filters.

Your UNIX compiler or linker generates errors that indicate that it cannot find files.

UNIX is especially picky about the location of files for the various phases of the compile, link, and library generation process. In most cases, simply modifying the PATH statement is not sufficient to resolve some of these conflicts. Read Appendix G, "Configuring the DIGL for Your Environment."

Your application code terminates with segmentation fault *or* bus error.

Generally, either of these problems indicates an error in the code where a read or write is done outside the protective umbrella of the operating system. If your compiler is configured properly and you have not modified the DIGL code, this condition should not occur under normal circumstances. The DIGL has been tested on a variety of PCs and UNIX workstations. It is impossible, however, to guarantee that the DIGL system is totally compatible with all versions of UNIX and C compilers; differences among compilers might create difficulty.

Read Appendix G, "Configuring the DIGL for Your Environment." If you still have compiler or linker errors and you have not modified the DIGL code, you can contact me for further suggestions on how to proceed. Likewise, if you solve this kind of problem, I would appreciate having a description of what the problem was and what you did to solve it.

GLOSSARY

This glossary includes definitions of acronyms, words, and expressions used in this book. These terms span a wide range of topics in the fields of computers and electronics. This is not, however, a *complete* glossary of all the terms used in the computer and electronics industry. A more complete glossary is the *American National Dictionary for Information Processing* (1977) by the Computer and Business Equipment Manufacturers Association.

μ   Symbol for micron (10^{-6}).

μs   Symbol for microsecond (10^{-6} second).

algorithm   A set of well-defined rules that forms all or part of the solution to a problem with a finite number of instructions.

alphanumeric   A subset of the ASCII character set that contains only upper- and lowercase letters, numbers, and punctuation marks.

ASCII   American National Standard Code for Information Interchange. A coded representation of the 7-bit coded character set that includes an eighth bit for parity. The entire ASCII character set includes graphics and control characters.

assembler language   A lower-level computer language in which instructions are closely coupled with the hardware and the CPU. Assembly instructions usually translate into one to four machine language (binary) instructions.

BASIC   Beginner's All-Purpose Symbolic Instruction Code.

baud rate   The data transfer rate in bits per second over a serial communications line.

BIOS   Basic Input/Output System. A set of controls that supports the operating system of the IBM Personal Computer. The controls deal with I/O for hardware and memory-mapped control of video and text planes.

bit   Binary digit.

bit-mapped   A term indicating that the pixel elements on the graphics plane are individually controlled.

bus   A method of signal transmission or power control by means of one or more wires or conductors.

byte   A sequence of eight bits that represents a single ASCII character, a value, or a unit (component) of a word.

compile   A process by which the high-level instructions of a programming language are translated, or converted, to lower-level instructions such as assembler or machine language.

contiguous   Adjacent.

control character   A sequence of nonprintable characters used to start or stop control operations. Control characters are represented in the ASCII character set by values in the range 0 to 31 (decimal) or 0 to 1F (hexadecimal).

CPU   Central Processing Unit.

CRT   Cathode Ray Tube. A tube used to project an electron stream onto a fluorescent screen. This produces luminous spots that can be located at any position on the screen.

cursor   *1.* In computer graphics, a visible marker, such as crosshairs, that represents the location of the start or end of an operation.   *2.* In text operations, a rectangular block or an underline that indicates the location of the next character to be output.

DIGL   Device Independent Graphics Library.

dot matrix   A rectangular arrangement of dots that are individually addressable.

driver   A software function called from a higher-level program that performs a series of low-level operations at the I/O level. These operations are performed by means of mechanisms such as BIOS or other routines supplied with the I/O library.

EIA   Electronic Industries Association.

foreground   The character, dots turned on, or image produced on a video screen.

function   A self-contained set of instructions used to perform all or part of an algorithm. Functions contain an optional formal argument list and may return a value to the caller.

G   Symbol for gigabyte (10^{10} bytes).

GKS   Graphics Kernel System.

graphics protocol   A sequence of mnemonics that represents a set of predefined graphics operations.

handshake (*Xon/Xoff*)   A mechanism for interrupting the flow of characters between a computer and a peripheral.

Hz   Symbol for hertz. Cycles per second.

IEEE   Institute of Electrical and Electronics Engineers.

initialize   To set the values of variables or the starting point of a program to known, prescribed values at certain points (usually the beginning) of a computer program.

interface   A hardware or software mechanism that contains values and constraints used to control the transfer of information between two or more devices or program units.

I/O   Input/Output.

k   Symbol for thousand (10^3).

kHz   Symbol for kilohertz (10^3 hertz).

logical connection   A mechanism for interface between a program and I/O, usually in the form of an address mapping to I/O.

memory   Main storage unit(s).

MHz   Symbol for megahertz (10^6 hertz).

mnemonic   Symbolic abbreviations commonly used in computer instructions—for example, `sub` for `subtract`.

monitor   Synonym for CRT.

n   Symbol for nano (10^{-9}).

NULL   *1.* Representation of the ASCII value 0.   *2.* Representation of the constant 0.   *3.* Invalid or no value, as in the value of pointers in a computer language such as C before initialization.

operating system   Software that controls the execution of one or more programs by means of allocation of resources, program scheduling, I/O, and so on.

operator interface   The portion of a program that is dedicated to displaying and modifying information. This is accomplished by means of prompts with graphical displays of the devices to be controlled.

page   A unit of memory storage used for memory organization.

parallel transmission   Transmission of more than one bit at a time usually by means of a predefined bus architecture or hardwired interconnect scheme.

PC   Personal computer.

pixel   A single luminous dot on a CRT (from *pic*ture *el*ements).

primitive   A graphics operation, such as move or draw, that is performed at the device driver level.

prompt   A mechanism by which a program requests input from a user. Usually, a series of characters are output in the form of a question followed by a pause for user input—that is, an answer to the question.

pseudocode   A series of instructions written in ordinary language that represents an algorithm in conversational form. This representation is independent of a particular programming language.

RAM   Random-Access Memory.

raster   A pattern of horizontal lines that provides a rectangular pattern of coverage of a display.

RGB   Red Green Blue. A sequence of primary colors used to represent the color spectrum by combining some fraction of each color.

RISC   Reduced Instruction Set Computing.

ROM   Read-Only Memory.

routine   A unit of program instructions.

RS-232C   A standard for serial communications between a computer and one or more peripherals. This standard was developed by the EIA.

scale   A process that uses an integer or floating-point value to enlarge or reduce all or part of an image for display.

segment   A pointer to a paragraph boundary, usually smaller than a page. For the IBM PC, the segment points to one byte of a 16-byte unit.

semantics   The meaning conveyed by a series of characters or words that represent one or more instructions in a computer language. For example, a compiler might perform a semantic check on a second pass through source code.

SIGGRAPH   Special Interest Group on Graphics.

syntax   A series of characters or words that represents one or more instructions in a computer language.

TTL   Transistor Transistor Logic.

unformatted I/O   I/O sequences in which character sequences such as CR/LF or other carriage control characters are not output or input in order to terminate records.

vector operation   An operation on x,y-vectors in Cartesian space.

viewing transformation   A sequence of mathematical operations on objects, such as polygons, represented in matrix form. The operations may involve scaling, translation, rotation, or shearing in two or more dimensions.

viewport   The portion of the graphics area that is used to display a graphics image. Objects projected outside this region are clipped at the edges.

window   A visible portion of the viewport in which the units—user or real-world—are mapped by means of the viewing transformations.

B BIBLIOGRAPHY

Adobe Systems. *PostScript Language Tutorial and Cookbook.* Reading, Mass.: Addison-Wesley, 1985.

———. *PostScript Language Reference Manual.* Reading, Mass.: Addison-Wesley, 1985.

American Telephone and Telegraph Company. *Unix Programmer's Manual.* Edited by Steven V. Earhart. New York: Holt, Rinehart, and Winston, 1986.

Apple Computer Corporation. *Apple Technical Introduction to the Macintosh Family.* Reading, Mass.: Addison-Wesley, 1987.

Asente, Paul. *X Window Toolkit Programmer's Guide & Specification.* Englewood Cliffs, N.J.: Prentice Hall, 1990.

———. *X Window System ToolKit: The Complete Programmer's Guide & Specification.* Maynard, Mass.: Digital-Press, 1990.

Bach, M.J. *The Design of the UNIX Operating System.* Englewood Cliffs, N.J.: Prentice Hall, 1987.

Baecker, R., and B. Buxton. *Readings in Human-Computer Interaction.* Los Altos, Calif.: Morgan Kaufman, 1987.

Bolt, R.A. *The Human Interface: Where People and Computers Meet.* Belmont, Calif.: Lifetime Learning Press, 1984.

Bourne, S.R. "The UNIX Shell." *Bell System Technical Journal* 57, (July-August 1978).

———. *The UNIX System.* Reading, Mass.: Addison-Wesley, 1983.

Bradberry, John L. "Porting Fortran Programs from Minis to PCs." *Dr. Dobb's Journal,* September 1990.

———. "Designing Portable User Interfaces." *Dr. Dobb's Journal,* November 1992.

Bresenham, J.E. "Algorithm for Computer Control of a Digital Plotter." *IBM Systems Journal* 4, no. 1 (1965): 25-30.

Buhle, E. Loren. "Portability Issues in a Heterogeneous Computing Environment." *VAX Professional* 14 (May-June 1992): 7.

Card, S., T. Moran, and A. Newell. *The Psychology of Human Computer Interaction.* Hillsdale, N.J.: Lawrence Erlbaum Associates, 1983.

"Cross-Platform Tools Depict Keen Competitive Strategies." *PC Week,* 17 August 1992, S11(1).

Custer, Helen K. "Inside Windows NT: the Win32 Subsystem." *Windows-DOS Developer's Journal* 3 (August 1992): 5(7).

"DOS Applications Go UNIX." *MIDRANGE Systems,* 3 March 1992, p14(1).

Foley, James D., et al. *Computer Graphics—Principles and Practice.* Reading, Mass.: Addison-Wesley, 1990.

Graphics Standards Planning Committee. "Status Report of the Graphics Standards Planning Committee." *Computer Graphics* 13 (August 1979).

Heller, Dan. *XView Programming Manual.* O'Reilly & Associates, 1990.

Hewlett-Packard. *Interfacing and Programming Manual: HP7550A Graphics Plotter.* Palo Alto: Hewlett-Packard Press, 1986.

Institute of Electrical and Electronics Engineers. *IEEE Standard for Information Technology.* Std 1003.3-1991.

———. *Test Methods for Measuring Conformance to POSIX.* IEEE Standards. May 1991.

Kernighan, B.W., and D. Ritchie. *The C Programming Language.* Englewood Cliffs, N.J.: Prentice Hall, 1988.

Lewine, Don. *POSIX Programmer's Guide.* O'Reilly & Associates, 1991.

McCarron, S. *Developing Portable Applications for POSIX.* Englewood Cliffs, N.J.: Prentice Hall, 1990.

Microsoft Corporation. *Microsoft MS-DOS User's Reference and Microsoft MS-DOS Programmer's Reference.* Redmond, Wash.: Microsoft Press, 1989.

———. *Microsoft Operating System/2 Programmer's Reference.* Redmond, Wash.: Microsoft Press, 1989.

———. *Programming Techniques for MS-DOS and Windows Operating Systems: Microsoft C/C++ Version 7.0.* Redmond, Wash.: Microsoft Press, 1991.

Rochkind, Marc J. *Advanced C Programming for Displays.* Englewood Cliffs, N.J.: Prentice-Hall, 1988.

Seltzer, Larry J. "Microsoft Brings Back P-Code." *PC Week*, 11 May 1992, 61-2.

Sowerbutts, W.T.C. "A Surface-Plotting Program for Microcomputers." *Computer Aided Design* 15 (November 1983).

Swanke, John E. "The Realities of Portable Software." *Computer Language* 8 (November 1991): 57(6).

"The UNIX System." *The Bell System Technical Journal* 63 (October 1984).

Wheeler. *Open Systems Handbook.* New York: Bantam, 1992.

Wyatt, Allen L. *Using Assembly Language.* Carmel, Ind.: Que, 1987.

Zlotnick, Fred. *Practical Guide to the POSIX 1 Standard.* Benjamin-Cummings, 1991.

INDEX

G

H

M

Add to Your Sams Library Today with the Best Books for Programming, Operating Systems, and New Technologies

The easiest way to order is to pick up the phone and call

1-800-428-5331

between 9:00 a.m. and 5:00 p.m. EST.

For faster service please have your credit card available.

ISBN	Quantity	Description of Item	Unit Cost	Total Cost
0-672-30279-9		C++ Programming PowerPack	$24.95	
0-672-30309-4		Programming Sound for DOS and Windows (Book/Disk)	$39.95	
0-672-30287-X		Tom Swan's Code Secrets (Book/Disk)	$39.95	
0-672-30299-3		Uncharted Windows Programming (Book/Disk)	$34.95	
0-672-48470-6		Assembly Language: For Real Programmers Only (Book/Disk)	$44.95	
0-672-30230-6		Developing Online Help for Windows (Book/Disk)	$39.95	
0-672-30239-X		Windows Developer's Guide to Application Design (Book/Disk)	$34.95	
0-672-30315-9		The Magic of Image Processing (Book/Disk)	$39.95	
0-672-30295-0		Moving into Windows NT Programming (Book/Disk)	$39.95	
0-672-30274-8		Mastering Borland C++ (Book/Disk)	$39.95	
0-672-30248-9		FractalVision (Book/Disk)	$39.95	
0-672-30249-7		Multimedia Madness (Book/Disk-CD ROM)	$44.95	
0-672-30158-X		Advanced C++ (Book/Disk)	$39.95	
0-672-30168-7		Advanced C (Book/Disk)	$39.95	
0-672-30080-X		Moving from C to C++	$29.95	
0-672-27366-7		Memory Management for All of Us	$29.95	
0-672-30200-4		C++ Programming 101 (Book/Disk)	$29.95	
❏ 3 ½" Disk		Shipping and Handling: See information below.		
❏ 5 ¼" Disk		TOTAL		

Shipping and Handling: $4.00 for the first book, and $1.75 for each additional book. Floppy disk: add $1.75 for shipping and handling. If you need to have it NOW, we can ship product to you in 24 hours for an additional charge of approximately $18.00, and you will receive your item overnight or in two days. Overseas shipping and handling adds $2.00 per book and $8.00 for up to three disks. Prices subject to change. Call for availability and pricing information on latest editions.

11711 N. College Avenue, Suite 140, Carmel, Indiana 46032

1-800-428-5331 — Orders   1-800-835-3202 — FAX   1-800-858-7674 — Customer Service

Book ISBN 0-672-30305-1

What's on the Disk

The disk features the Device Independent Graphics Library (DIGL)—a complete graphics library with drivers, graphics primitives, and macros. DIGL is compatible with the following environments:

ANSI C compilers (DOS or UNIX)
DOS Microsoft C compiler
UNIX SUN Sparcstation or X11 compatible environments

The disk also includes the following:

- 2-D and 3-D graphics applications

- Source code for DIGL and the included applications

- Data files for use with the applications

- DOS batch files and UNIX script files

Installing the Floppy Disk

You'll need about 1M of free space on your hard drive to install the files from the floppy disk. To automatically copy all the files to your hard drive, follow these steps:

1. From a DOS prompt, change to the drive that contains the installation disk. For example, if the disk is in drive A:, type A: and press Enter.

2. Type INSTALL *drive* (where *drive* is the drive letter of your hard drive) and press Enter. For example, if your hard drive is drive C:, type INSTALL C: and press Enter.

This will install all the files to a directory named \CGE on your hard drive.

 Be sure to read the file README for more information about the different environments supported by DIGL and how to use the files. Your development environment will determine what initial features and options of DIGL you will be able to use.